PRESENTED TO:

_____

BY:

_____

ENTER HIS
GATES

ENTER HIS
GATES

A Daily Devotional

CHARLES STANLEY

OLIVER
NELSON™

THOMAS NELSON PUBLISHERS®
Nashville

A Division of Thomas Nelson, Inc.
www.ThomasNelson.com

Published in Nashville, Tennessee, by Thomas Nelson, Inc.

Library of Congress Cataloging-in-Publication Data

Stanley, Charles F.
  Enter His gates : a daily devotional / Charles Stanley.
      p.   cm.
  ISBN 0-7852-6580-5
  1. Christian life—Meditations. 2. Devotional calendars. I. Title.
  BV4811.S815   1998
  242'.2—dc21 983345

                                                                CIP

Printed in the United States of America

02 03 04 05 06 — 5 4 3 2 1

Introduction

In Bible times, city gates had tremendous importance in the natural world as well as significant spiritual meaning:

- Because of their central location, gates were spoken of as symbols of power and authority.

- Gates were the focus of enemy attack (Judg. 5:8; 1 Sam. 23:7; Ezek. 21:15, 22).

- People gathered there to hear the reading of God's Word (Neh. 8:1, 3), and both legal and judicial transactions occurred at the city gates (Zech. 8:16).

- In Israel, words from God's law were—and still are—inscribed on or above the gates of private homes (Deut. 6:9).

- To "possess the gates" was to possess the city (Gen. 24:60), and that is why God promised Abraham that his descendants would possess the gates of their enemies (Gen. 22:17).

- Gates were vital to the defense of cities in ancient Israel because they protected against enemy invasion. In the event of attack, the city gates were closed to shut out the enemy.

Exactly how many gates were in the city of Jerusalem is unknown because the number probably varied from century to century, but each gate of Jerusalem mentioned in the Bible has spiritual significance and is symbolic of a spiritual "gate" in our lives. If you fail to maintain your spiritual "gates," you, too, are open to attack by the enemy. That is why this devotional guide focuses on rebuilding your spiritual gates.

God has set before us twelve months of the coming year. These months are precious gateways to spiritual growth and development. Each month during this year, we will strengthen a different spiritual gate.

Are you ready to join me in this yearlong spiritual quest?

> *Go through,*
> *Go through the gates! (Isa. 62:10)*

January

THEME: The New Gate

REPRESENTING: New beginnings

Behold, I will do a new thing,
Now it shall spring forth;
Shall you not know it?
I will even make a road in the wilderness
And rivers in the desert. (Isa. 43:19)

The Life Before You

Therefore we also, since we are surrounded by so great a cloud of witnesses, let us lay aside every weight, and the sin which so easily ensnares us, and let us run with endurance the race that is set before us (Heb. 12:1).

❧ The new year will be full of surprises. As diligently as you may plan, tomorrow, next week, or next month is a puzzle to all but God. Your supreme purpose, then, for this year is to walk in harmony with His predetermined will by employing three essential disciplines:

1. *Lay aside every encumbrance and sin.* Willful sin or unproductive habits hinder your spiritual growth. By His grace ask Him to help you abandon these unnecessary weights.

2. *Concentrate on endurance.* Do not let disappointments or setbacks take you out of the race. Accept that they, too, are part of the course God has divinely planned.

3. *Focus on Jesus.* Turn away from all that distracts. Look by faith steadfastly to Him. Cast your burdens on Him. Seek His face daily through personal prayer and sustained intake of His Word.

A fixed focus of faith on Jesus Christ will lighten your load, equip you to handle the tough times, and guide you into His will for your life in this new year.

Confidence to Face the Future

Seek first the kingdom of God and His righteousness, and all these things shall be added to you (Matt. 6:33).

🐦 Who knows what the coming year may bring?

But herein lies our confidence—God knows. He is carefully, wisely, and deliberately orchestrating all things according to His schedule and eternal design. We can be secure because God is in full control of what the year brings forth. Our confidence is not in our abilities, but in His omniscience, omnipotence, and omnipresence. What seems perplexing and puzzling to us is perfectly rational and plain to our all-seeing, all-caring Father. Nothing catches Him by surprise. Nothing thwarts His purposes. Nothing foils His plan.

You may find yourself in hard times. But if you boast in God and endure and trust in Him, you can learn. You may encounter unanticipated changes, but your fears and anxieties can be dispelled as you rest in His providential direction and provision.

Do not worry about tomorrow. God is already there. He will guide you through the fog, lift you above the pain, and clarify your uncertainty. Be confident in Him.

God's Guide to Life

Behold, I will do a new thing,
Now it shall spring forth;
Shall you not know it?
I will even make a road in the wilderness
And rivers in the desert (Isa. 43:19).

❧ Have you ever felt that your life was a dry, barren desert? In today's passage of Isaiah, Israel felt spiritually and emotionally desolate. In their disobedience, they had wandered from God, and He had allowed them to go. When they came to their senses, they cried out in evidence of the burden they bore in their hearts. They were alone and needed a fresh touch from God.

The wonderful thing about God is that He is never at a distance. He is always beside us. Because faithfulness is a part of His nature, He cannot be unfaithful and still be God. That means when we are faithless, He is still faithful. And in the case of Israel, He proved true to His nature.

God always works in the present but looks to the future. Life at its best is not lived in the past—worrying over what happened or what once was. Instead, it is lived in the here and now, aware of one thing: God is a God of love, and He is always at work in your life to do something for your good and His glory.

Putting Off Procrastination

The hand of the diligent will rule,
But the lazy man will be put to forced labor (Prov. 12:24).

In *Gone with the Wind* Scarlett O'Hara repeatedly uttered this now celebrated line whenever faced with calamity: "I'll think about that tomorrow." How often do we—either intentionally or not—develop the same "tomorrow" outlook? We too easily find ways to put off until tomorrow what we can do today.

A sober look at procrastination's aftereffects, however, might help us realize its subtle dangers. Procrastination can cause us to miss out on God's best for our lives. When we fail to confront an issue or a situation, we fail to develop the godly, positive character God desires. By hesitating, we delay God's blessings. Prompt obedience always brings eventual blessings. When you procrastinate, you are dangerously close to disobedience—along with its consequences.

You can learn to face and deal with undesirable circumstances by trusting God to supply what you lack. He will give courage, wisdom, grace, mercy, power—whatever the need. As you confront your problems rather than avoid them, your faith is nurtured and stretched. Your confidence grows; your fears subside.

Let your motto be: "Do it now as the Lord directs and enables me." It will save a lot of heartache later.

The Key to Contentment

Godliness with contentment is great gain (1 Tim. 6:6).

❧ Secrets—whether a grandmother's special recipe or a company's unique product formula—are rarely revealed. In his letter to the Philippian church, the apostle Paul provided all who would read the Scriptures with the secret of contented living: "I can do all things through Christ who strengthens me."

The Greek word for contentment is translated "self-sufficiency" or "self-satisfaction." That may surprise you. At first glance, Paul appeared to say that the secret to contentment lay in his resilient self (Phil. 4:13).

But he was expressing this: "My self-sufficiency, my level of contentment, lies in the sufficiency of Christ to meet my every need. I can endure rain or shine, darkness or light, sorrow or joy, because through Him, I am equipped and sustained."

Paul's secret is yours. Despite circumstances, you can enjoy true contentment when you accept the truth that Christ is adequate for your every need—in good times and bad.

When Doors Are Closed

See, I have set before you an open door, and no one can shut it; for you have a little strength, have kept My word, and have not denied My name (Rev. 3:8).

❧ Your contract on your dream house just fell through. The promotion you were sure of fizzled at the last management meeting. The person you knew would become your spouse called off the relationship.

Slam. Slam. Slam. Doors you thought God had opened wide become curtains of steel. *What is God doing? What is He up to? Why is He placing me in this canyon?*

Despite your disappointment, remember this: God is sovereignly leading your steps in a path that will bring Him the ultimate glory and you the ultimate benefit as you abandon yourself to His care.

The next time your hopes are dashed and the doors of aspiration are slammed in your face, rely on the all-sufficient wisdom of God, who alone knows the end from the beginning.

Confronting Barriers

"The LORD is my portion," says my soul,
"Therefore I hope in Him!" (Lam. 3:24).

~❧ In her book *Grace Grows Best in Winter,* Margaret Clarkson writes that foreboding circumstances can be "God's hedges":

> For most of His children, God's hedges do not seemingly entail suffering, but only protection. For some, however, they mean unending pain and weakness, disappointment and sorrow, varying in degree to total imprisonment.
>
> Why this must be so, we may not know; sufficient for us to know that God Himself has hedged us in, and God's hedges are always hedges of protection and blessing.
>
> And God Himself, living there both with us and in us, longs to make of our thorny wall a thing of wonder to men and angels and demons—a thing that will one day bring forth holy blossom and fruit.

If God has entrusted you with a hedge of suffering, let Him teach you how to live within it so that His holy purpose and His life-giving fruit may be fully accomplished through you!

Giving New Life

He who has died has been freed from sin (Rom. 6:7).

❧ When the Holy Spirit imparts the gift of eternal life to you, far more has transpired than the mere possession of unending spiritual life. That is because the Holy Spirit brings to every Christian an entirely new quality of life that is divine, supernatural, and godlike.

Through the Holy Spirit, the born-again man or woman can enjoy a new way of living. Since the Holy Spirit allows you to share in the life of Christ, He opens up a radical new lifestyle that is conformed to God's commands and ways, not to culture.

You must remember that much of worldly behavior and methodology is based on wisdom that is flawed and tainted by sin. The Spirit of God reprograms your mind and transforms your attitude with His wisdom, dramatically altering your habits, rearranging your priorities, and establishing new standards.

At the same time, the Holy Spirit gives you a new power for living; the new lifestyle comes with the power to succeed. You are no longer limited to fighting your problems with your resources. You have God and the fullness of His Spirit to help you and deliver you.

What Is God Up To?

But as for you, you meant evil against me; but God meant it for good, in order to bring it about as it is this day, to save many people alive (Gen. 50:20).

❧ David was told that he was going to be king of Israel, but he spent most of the next ten years on the lam. Joseph had a dream in which he ruled over his brothers, but he spent the next thirteen years as a slave and a prisoner. Although you do know the outcome in both cases, you cannot foresee your own future. Yet you can trust God to operate on the same principles.

1. *God is in control.* Your life is not in a tailspin, controlled by fate or circumstance. An omniscient, sovereign God is ruling over everything. There are no accidents. He is never surprised.

2. *The God who is in control is working for your good and His glory.* He never promotes or fosters evil. He is always looking out for your best interests. The conflict comes because what He sees as working for your good is not what you desire. God uses adversity, dryness, temptation, and testing for your welfare.

3. *God will bless others through your wilderness.* He is working not only for your good but also for the benefit of all His people.

Covered by a New Covenant

Therefore, brethren, having boldness to enter the Holiest by the blood of Jesus, by a new and living way which He consecrated for us, through the veil, that is, His flesh (Heb. 10:19–20).

❧ The primary basis for the old covenant was the Mosaic Law. The sole basis for God's new arrangement in dealing with sinful human beings is the shed blood of Jesus Christ. The elements we reverently share at the Lord's Table are visual and tangible reminders that the forgiveness of God has been extended to us at a tremendous price: the spilled blood and bruised body of Jesus Christ. The blood and body of Jesus were the supreme sacrifice for sin, which was the only one that God, in His holy justice, could accept.

Since Jesus laid down His life for your sins, you now can receive God's new covenant of forgiveness. You can have peace with God because the blood of Jesus has cleansed you from all of your sin. The next time you hold the cup and bread in your hands, remember that all of God's grace, love, mercy, and hope is now yours because of Jesus' agony on the cross.

JANUARY 11

Setting Your Goals

Whether you eat or drink, or whatever you do, do all to the glory of God (1 Cor. 10:31).

❧ The Olympic Games are a masterpiece of athletes seeking to achieve enduring goals. Many accomplish their objectives, but some medal winners have been disqualified following their performances because of their illegal drug use. Their goals were reasonable, but their methods were tragically flawed—only reflecting the rationale that the end justifies the means.

That line of thinking runs against the scriptural grain in every way. God is just as interested in how you achieve a goal as He is in the goal itself.

First, you must establish the primary motivation that God desires you to use in setting your goals. The Westminster Catechism says, "Man's chief end is to glorify God and enjoy Him forever." Whatever your goal may be—financial, physical, spiritual, family— you must ask yourself this question: *Is my goal's supreme purpose to glorify God?*

Since that is the purpose for which you were created, it follows that your goals must reflect that basic purpose. Sift your goals through prayer, common sense, and biblical wisdom to see if your objective's chief purpose is to honor God.

God's Goals, God's Methods

Samuel said:
"Has the LORD as great delight in burnt offerings and
   sacrifices,
As in obeying the voice of the LORD?
Behold, to obey is better than sacrifice,
And to heed than the fat of rams" (1 Sam. 15:22).

❧ Saul wanted to be a good king who ruled fairly and followed the ways of God. However, his motives were not pure. God told him to completely destroy the Amalekites in battle. They had ruthlessly pursued Israel after the Exodus, killing the weak and disabled, and God never forgot the evil they committed against His people.

Saul complied with the Lord's command and headed into battle. However, once the dust settled, he decided to spare the Amalekite king, his strongest fighting men, and the best of his sheep and oxen. Saul tried in vain to convince Samuel that he had obeyed God by saving the best of the spoils as a sacrifice. But it was not obedience that motivated Saul; it was pride, and that cost him his throne.

Partial obedience is not obedience; it is disobedience, and there is never an excuse for it in the eyes of God. Whatever goal God has placed before you, He has a method in mind for you to follow in achieving it. Ask Him to give you His wisdom so that you may accomplish the goal perfectly, completely and—most important—obediently.

God's Goal for Your Life

We make it our aim, whether present or absent, to be well pleasing to Him (2 Cor. 5:9).

❧ Goals are a large part of business and personal agendas. We want to earn a degree in this field; we seek to finish a project by this date; we strive to create a certain amount of savings each year. These are all good tools to exercise faith. God wants us to plan, not to wander aimlessly about.

But life is unpredictable. An ill father prevents us from pursuing a degree; an unexpected assignment takes us away from our task; a major repair bill makes savings impossible. What do we do once our goals are capsized by circumstances? Have we failed? Should we cease planning?

Absolutely not. We must remember that our chief objective is clear—to be conformed to the image of Jesus Christ. God will use our plans and schemes, as topsy-turvy as they may seem, to reproduce Christ's divine character in us.

Set your goals, but remember your priority—to allow God to use both success and failure to conform you to the image of Christ.

Examine Your Methods

Having your conduct honorable among the Gentiles, that when they speak against you as evildoers, they may, by your good works which they observe, glorify God in the day of visitation (1 Peter 2:12).

❧ History records lamentable incidents, such as the Inquisition and the Crusades, that had seemingly spiritual goals but completely wrong methods. That's why, once the proper motivation for your goals for this year is established, it is essential that you assess the wisdom of your methods. Ask yourself these questions:

1. *Are my methods in keeping with the revealed will and principles of God as recorded in the Scriptures?* For instance, a goal of becoming the company president may be set with the proper motivation for leading the business overseas so that the markets abroad can be used as distribution points for gospel literature. However, accomplishing that goal by manipulating accounting records that falsely increase sales figures and thus mislead others is thoroughly condemned by the Scriptures.

2. *Are my methods in any way unjustly harming my fellow human beings?* If the individual described in the previous paragraph reaches his goal through slandering an employee who also seeks the same position, his methods are wrong.

Examine your methods by observing these standards. When you reach your goal, you can then be sure that God is honored.

Facing Life's Unknowns

He who calls you is faithful, who also will do it (1 Thess. 5:24).

❧ A delayed promotion, an unreached goal, a broken relationship—some of life's inexplicable turns. One way that God tests our faith is by allowing life's unknowns to invade our lives. Samuel anointed David as king over Israel. Yet nothing was mentioned about having to wait years before he sat on Israel's throne. Thanks to life's unknowns, David was forced to leave his family and friends and live like a common criminal on the run from a jealous and mentally impaired king.

At any point he could have proclaimed his frustration, but David went beyond bitterness and self-pity to claim the goodness of God. He realized God's ways were not the ways of people. All of life's unknowns are perfectly within God's sovereign control. If He has given you a promise, cling to it. He will do exactly what He has said He will do.

A Map for the Road Ahead

We also, since we are surrounded by so great a cloud of witnesses, let us lay aside every weight, and the sin which so easily ensnares us, and let us run with endurance the race that is set before us, looking unto Jesus, the author and finisher of our faith, who for the joy that was set before Him endured the cross, despising the shame, and has sat down at the right hand of the throne of God (Heb. 12:1–2).

❧ If most of us were to make topographical maps of our spiritual walks, they would probably look like a range of mountains jutting heavenward with many spiritual peaks and dropping just as sharply into spiritual valleys. That is because maintaining a consistent walk with Jesus Christ is one of the most difficult challenges we face.

Think for a moment. What is the primary culprit that disturbs your rest and confidence in God? Is it not reacting to your circumstances?

We are too dependent on the external things of life, which rise and fall like the stock market, to govern our relationship with God. That is not the way God designed it. As believers we have the unchanging, steady, indwelling presence of Jesus Christ. He can handle and solve anything.

The internal control of Christ will lead you into a daily, deliberate walk with God. Whatever happens you turn over to Him, asking Him to sustain, strengthen, and guide you. Such confidence and trust in Him stabilize your journey.

A Divinely Offered Opportunity

The LORD will guide you continually,
And satisfy your soul in drought,
And strengthen your bones;
You shall be like a watered garden,
And like a spring of water,
whose waters do not fail (Isa. 58:11).

❧ The company needs to know by Friday. Will you take the job in Wichita or not? The church wants an answer next week. Will you teach the Bible study this quarter or decline?

Decisions. Opportunities. Some of them come only once, and they demand a precise response. How do you know what to do?

When decisions are not so clear-cut, you still employ principles to seize the opportunities offered by God. You are to meditate in the Word constantly. His Word rolls back the darkness and doubt.

If you fail, if you make the wrong decision, God is still with you wherever you go. He uses even your botches to teach you. Above all, obey what you believe God has shown you. Even when you are wrong, you will still be all right.

Consider the Options

Jesus said to him, "I am the way, the truth, and the life. No one comes to the Father except through Me" (John 14:6).

❧ In his classic book *The Pilgrim's Progress,* John Bunyan told of the adventures of Christian on his spiritual journey as a believer in Christ. Christian knew that the straight and narrow path—the way of Jesus—was the only road to heaven, the Celestial City. But the path was often rough and rocky; trials and temptations surrounded him.

Discouraged, Christian looked away from the road at the soft grass of By-path Meadow and took what he thought was a shortcut, another way to God. Moments later, he was thrown into a dark dungeon as a prisoner of the Giant Despair. Christian got a hard look at the hopelessness of other options and learned where they led—away from Christ.

Understanding who Jesus is will keep you from false, tempting choices. When compared to Jesus, all other options pale. Nothing else will do. No other course brings true and lasting rewards. There are no substitutes, no bypass. His love and forgiveness are all-sufficient. He gives direction and purpose to your life. The way may be arduous at times, but it is the best route to a meaningful life.

Discovering God's Will

I delight to do Your will, O my God,
And Your law is within my heart (Ps. 40:8).

❧ Preparation is a major part of discovering the will of God. You want to know God's will, and you want to know it now. But have you been willing to make the sacrificial preparations to know and obey His plan? Are you ready to follow when God makes it clear what He desires? What you do today in terms of Bible study, prayer, meditation, fellowship, worship, and other scriptural exercises prepares you to do God's will. They sensitize your spirit, bend your heart to holiness, and equip you to hear and discern the voice of God as He speaks through the Scriptures, godly counsel, or the providential arrangement of circumstances.

If you want to know the will of God for the future, be disciplined for godliness today. When the time is right, your spiritual senses will be alert to the good and perfect will of the Father.

The Best Route

We walk by faith, not by sight (2 Cor. 5:7).

❧ If you pick up a road map, you can readily discern the best route to reach your destination. But while the map logically arranges the maze of highways so that you can stay on course, it does not provide a total picture of what the journey holds in store. Hills, curves, stoplights, restaurants, service stations, school zones, and other details of the trip can be discovered only as the trip unfolds.

Knowing God's will operates in a similar manner. God has a plan for your life, but the specifics you want so desperately are revealed only as you are committed to the journey of devotion and discipleship.

Solomon wrote in Proverbs that God will guide your steps and unveil His plan as you trust wholeheartedly in Him, refuse to rely solely on your limited wisdom, and obey Him consistently. As you do these things, combined with prayer and the study of Scripture, the details of His personal plan—a place of work, a marriage partner, a church to attend—will follow.

God wants you to know His will. Delight yourself in Him; put aside preconceived notions, and concentrate on trust, obedience, and a personal relationship with Christ. Wait on Him, and at the right time, the answer will come.

The Abiding Life

We who have believed do enter that rest, as He has said:
"So I swore in My wrath, 'They shall not enter My rest,'"
although the works were finished from the foundation of the
world (Heb. 4:3).

❧ Does an apple tree struggle to produce apples? Does a pear tree labor to make its sweet crop?

As simple as it may appear, the liberating principle for doing God's work God's way is learning to abide in Christ. Abiding in Christ means resting in the finished work of the Cross. The cry of Jesus at Calvary was, "It is finished!" He had accomplished the work of redemption, providing the way of victory over sin and Satan for all who place their faith in Him. Your toil or effort can add nothing to what Christ has done. Your task is to receive the complete sufficiency of Christ for every situation.

The abiding life is the restful life spoken of in Hebrews 4. It is the place of absolute trust and confidence in the person and work of Jesus Christ. Christ is all-sufficient. He will satisfy every need, fulfill every demand, and produce the abundant Christian life in you as you depend wholly on Him. He is able.

Begin Again with God

Your ears shall hear a word behind you, saying,
"This is the way, walk in it,"
Whenever you turn to the right hand
Or whenever you turn to the left (Isa. 30:21).

❧ Hiking the Appalachian Trail is one of North America's most exciting adventures. The trail offers breathtaking views, challenging terrain, and a chance to experience the peace and solitude of nature.

Since 1984, the Appalachian Trail Conference (ATC), a group of volunteers and fellow hikers, has maintained the trail. These people work all year to keep it free of debris and dangerous obstructions. However, the ATC is not responsible for unauthorized footpaths leading to or from the trail. If you want to enjoy the trail, ATC volunteers will tell you to practice safety and purchase official Appalachian Trail maps. Following unmarked trails can be disastrous.

A sad fact is that many of us do this very thing in life. We purchase fraudulent maps and take unmarked routes that lead us far from God's plan. Instead of reaping a reward of peace and safety, we stumble into dangerous ravines.

However, it's never too late to begin again with God. If you think you have taken the wrong trail, ask God to show you the way. Commit yourself to following His map from this point on, and He will lead you along a safe, sure path.

A New Beginning

For God so loved the world that He gave His only begotten Son, that whoever believes in Him should not perish but have everlasting life (John 3:16).

❧ She turned toward the window and stared out at the falling rain. The sound of the door closing behind her continued to echo through her mind. Gathering her courage and strength, she whispered, "I have made it on my own before, and I will do it again."

Her husband was gone, and the finality of his departure was agonizing. She was determined not to think about his leaving—perhaps in a few days, but not now.

However, thoughts of hopelessness immediately embattled her mind. *How would she live? Where would she go? How could she start over?* She prayed, "Dear God, I can't make it through this alone. If You are there, please come into my life and help me start over."

Most of the people who come to Jesus are searching for new beginnings. Each of us have a need only Christ can fill—love, acceptance, freedom from bondage, and eternal life.

Only the Son of God can take your brokenness and heartache and turn them into something of wonder and grace. You can trust Him to give you a new beginning, no matter what your circumstances may be.

A Second Chance

Jesus said to her, "Neither do I condemn you; go and sin no more"
(John 8:11).

❧ After the Pharisees departed, Jesus looked at the
woman caught in adultery, lying at His feet. That
was not the first time she had committed such an act,
but it was the first time she had appeared before
Jesus. There was no doubt in her mind that He was a
man of God. How exposed and embarrassed she
must have felt, that is, until the Savior revealed His
word of forgiveness and hope to her heart. Jesus did
not condemn the woman but instead challenged her
accusers to throw the first stone if one of them was
found to be without sin.

Perhaps there is something in your life you wish
you could erase. Just the thought of it brings feelings
of condemnation and sorrow. Adultery was an act
that the law declared punishable by stoning. Yet Jesus
set the woman free.

He gave her a second chance, and that is what He
gives you. If there is something you have done, know
that when you bring it to God in prayer seeking His
forgiveness, it is forgiven. God will never bring the
matter up again. His Son's death at Calvary was sufficient payment for all your sins. Only almighty God
can love you so much.

Forgiven

The free gift is not like the offense. For if by the one man's offense many died, much more the grace of God and the gift by the grace of the one Man, Jesus Christ, abounded to many (Rom. 5:15).

❧ We cannot earn God's grace. It is a gift He gives to all who come to Him. Lying at the Savior's feet, the woman caught in adultery probably thought her fate was sealed. The punishment for adultery was stoning.

Yet suddenly and unpredictably, Jesus offered her a second chance. Warren Wiersbe writes, "For Jesus to forgive this woman meant that He had to one day die for her sins. Forgiveness is free but it is not cheap."

Jesus was not soft on sin. "Nor is Christ's gracious forgiveness an excuse to sin," continues Wiersbe. "'Go and sin no more!' was our Lord's counsel . . . Certainly the experience of gracious forgiveness would motivate the penitent sinner to live a holy and obedient life to the glory of God." Grace is given so that we may know and accept what Jesus Christ did for us at Calvary.

Forgiven and blessed by His matchless grace are those who call Him Savior.

The Importance of Another Chance

God demonstrates His own love toward us, in that while we were still sinners, Christ died for us (Rom. 5:8).

❧ Each of us wants to know there is hope for a second chance when we fail to reach a goal, yield to sin, or fall short of what we've been instructed to do. Second chances are particularly important when sin is involved and feelings of guilt mount. How many of us have not longed for God's cleansing touch when convicted of wrongful actions?

W. E. Vine defines *sin* as "a missing of the mark." Sin always falls short of God's best for your life.

Even before you knew Christ, He knew you and loved you so much that He came to earth to give you a second chance at life: Jesus' life, death, and resurrection were God's supreme brush stroke of grace across the canvas of creation. He is the embodiment of all hope and grace. If you have accepted Him as your Savior, His life is alive within you, and His grace is sufficient to meet and remove every hint of sin's stain. Praise Him, for He is worthy of all your love and praise.

Hope for the Future

Why are you cast down, O my soul?
And why are you disquieted within me?
Hope in God, for I shall yet praise Him
For the help of His countenance (Ps. 42:5).

🕊 Hope brings an anticipation of blessing. To know hope, you must endure times of hopelessness. Hope represents an end to desperate longing—a need that begs to be satisfied and in the end is fulfilled. When hope burns within your heart, it cries out to be heard.

The psalmist wrote,

As the deer pants for the water brooks,
So my soul pants for Thee, O God . . .
My tears have been my food day and night,
While they say to me all day long,
    "Where is your God?" (Ps. 42:1–3 NASB).

What is your hope, your dream, the cry of your heart? Take a moment and go to Jesus with your deepest, most earnest pleas.

Realize that whatever is important to you is even more important to the Lord. Let Him be your Source of hope today.

God's Hand Is upon You

You have also given me the shield of Your salvation;
Your right hand has held me up,
Your gentleness has made me great (Ps. 18:35).

❧ The Bible contains many references to hands. Men shook or struck hands as a sign of commitment or pledge. In the United States and many other countries, people shake hands as a way of greeting. In the Bible, raised hands symbolize praise and thanksgiving (Ps. 63:4). The right hand, especially when used in connection with God, is a symbol of might and power (Ps. 44:3). The very touch of another's hand can communicate blessing and love.

The laying on of hands by the apostles in the New Testament separated men for God's service. It was a physical display of God's anointing (Acts 13:3). As children, we sang the song "He Has the Whole World in His Hands." This is the way God likes for us to view His awesome ability. Your entire life is kept safe in the palm of God's loving hand. There under His watch of safety are tremendous peace and security.

Continue in the Spirit

Are you so foolish? Having begun in the Spirit, are you now being made perfect by the flesh? (Gal. 3:3).

❧ The tackler could see it coming—a fullback carrying the football loosely at his side. A sudden turn and the tackler lunged after the ball. It popped loose and spiraled toward the ground.

He started to dive on the ball, but it bounded just high enough for him to pick it up and run. Breaking free from the other players, he started running down the football field as fast as he could run.

The crowd was shouting wildly as he crossed the goal line and pounded the ball proudly in the dirt. It was the first touchdown of his high school career—and perhaps his last—he had run into the wrong end zone.

We often have the right spiritual goal in mind but wind up in the wrong end zone. The Colossian believers had a sincere desire to serve God. However, they had become entangled in legalism and were imposing unrealistic demands on young believers. They had also begun judging actions of others (Colossians 2:16–23).

The moment you think you have it together enough to judge another person is the moment you run into the wrong end zone. Paul described legalism as bondage. Don't get caught up in it. Instead, "stand fast therefore in the liberty by which Christ has made [you] free" (Gal. 5:1).

Always Just Beginning

He has delivered us from the power of darkness and conveyed us into the kingdom of the Son of His love (Col. 1:13).

❧ Danny Buggs was an electrifying wide receiver in both the collegiate and the professional ranks. Playing for the University of West Virginia, the Washington Redskins, several World and Canadian Football League teams, and other National Football League teams, Buggs generated excitement and touchdowns galore.

But as with all athletes, Buggs's body soon wearied, and younger, sturdier men took his place. The story does not end there, however. Buggs received Christ as his Savior along the way and now works with youths from all walks of life, sharing Christ and His love with them. While his athletic exploits are finished, the gift of eternal life he received through Christ has only begun.

So it is with all believers. We here and now enjoy the benefits of eternal life. Christ, our Life, fills us with His purpose, joy, peace, power, and patience for life's daily struggles. We have a new, rich quality of life as heirs of God.

Death is but a doorway into the presence of God. Eternal life is yours forever, serving and living in the very presence of God. Eternal life means everything counts—here and hereafter. Nothing is meaningless; nothing is wasted; nothing is ever finished. You are always just beginning.

A Promising Beginning

So it was, when he had turned his back to go from Samuel, that God gave him another heart; and all those signs came to pass that day (1 Sam. 10:9).

≈ One of the most important elements in a race is a good start. In swift competition a poor start is tantamount to losing.

For believers, that start is the decision to trust Christ as Savior. Just as essential is the character building in the ensuing months and years. When the prophet Samuel identified Saul as king, it was obvious that Saul had begun his journey with admirable qualities. After Samuel anointed him king, Saul demonstrated his patience and humility by enduring the taunts of "certain worthless men" who mocked him (1 Sam. 10:27 NASB).

Perhaps your beginning hasn't been so favorable. Perhaps circumstances beyond your control have thwarted you at every turn. Perhaps you have never chosen to follow Christ. You can begin today. If you are not a believer, receive Jesus' offer of salvation by inviting Him in as your personal Savior.

If you do know Jesus but are continually frustrated, submit completely to His lordship, asking Him to take control of you and your circumstances. Trust Him to use even your problems for your welfare. He can do it if you turn to Him.

February

THEME: THE Water Gate

REPRESENTING: The Word of God

Jesus answered and said to her, "Whoever drinks of this water will thirst again, but whoever drinks of the water that I shall give him will never thirst." (John 4:13–14)

Begin Now!

Now in the morning, having risen a long while before daylight, He went out and departed to a solitary place; and there He prayed (Mark 1:35).

❧ Intimacy with Jesus Christ is one of the most important elements of the Christian life. It involves a lifelong journey filled with joy and immense pleasure. However, learning to love God takes time and a deep desire to get to know Him. Jesus made a point of being alone with the Father. He rose early to be alone in prayer.

Even as complicated as life is, there is still a place where you can find hope and the assurance of a greater love than anything this world has to offer. God's presence is the place. It is open to you anytime.

In being alone with Him, you discover a deeper wisdom that is fit to handle even the toughest situations. How do you start, especially if you have never scheduled regular time to be alone with God?

Begin this very minute. Close your eyes and sit for a moment without saying anything. Just focus your heart on God and the fact that He loves you more than anything else. Then pray and ask Him to give you a desire to get to know Him better. He will never turn you away.

A Fresh Encounter with God

He restores my soul;
He leads me in the paths of righteousness
For His name's sake (Ps. 23:3).

❧ Many times in the Psalms, David cried out to God to "restore," "revive," and "refresh" his soul. He uttered some pleas out of a sense of desperation. Others came out of his desire to know God more intimately. David was seeking a fresh encounter with God. You, too, often need times of renewed spiritual vitality.

Although fresh encounters with God cannot be programmed or scheduled, they seldom happen apart from a lifestyle of meditation on God's Word combined with honest prayer. God can break into your life explosively and suddenly or quietly and gradually. But when He does, you sense His presence anew. You are keenly aware of the Holy Spirit's active ministry within.

You walk with a new assurance of God's help. Your problems may stay, your circumstances may remain, but you know God is in control. You are focused on His adequacy, not your inadequacy.

There is no end to the seasons of fresh encounters you may have with God. You can never exhaust His fullness. Personal encounters with God will help you see your weaknesses and magnify the awesome reality of Christ's love for you. They can refresh the driest soul.

Spiritual Slippage

As you therefore have received Christ Jesus the Lord, so walk in Him, rooted and built up in Him and established in the faith, as you have been taught, abounding in it with thanksgiving (Col. 2:6–7).

❧ No-till farming has become a standard practice in the Midwest. To prevent the loss of fertile topsoil, crop stubble is left after harvest instead of plowed under, maximizing dirt and moisture retention.

Spiritual erosion can likewise be minimized and steady growth fostered as the Holy Spirit applies these time-tested principles to the soil of your soul:

A renewed concentration on the Word of God. You become firmly rooted in Christ as you implant the principles and power of God's Word in your mind and weave them into your behavior.

A heightened attention to worship and praise. The less awesome God becomes in your eyes, the easier it is to drift. Praise and adoration lead to an exalted view of God and restore your spiritual passion.

A revived focus on service to others. Ministering to the practical needs of others is a great stimulus for reversing spiritual erosion because it releases the power and love of God.

You can regain the joy, peace, and confidence you once had in your relationship with Christ. Apply at least one principle today, and watch God rebuild your life.

It Can Be Fixed

By grace you have been saved through faith, and that not of your-selves; it is the gift of God, not of works, lest anyone should boast (Eph. 2:8–9).

❧ Her mother worked for days making her a new school dress. Finally it was finished and ready to be worn. Giggling with excitement, she asked if she could wear it the next day. "Yes," was the answer, "but stay off the sliding board during playtime. You already have torn one dress. Let's keep this one nice."

However, playtime proved too tempting. Despite her mother's instruction, she climbed to the top of the slide and began a fast descent. It was then she heard a loud tearing noise. Later that evening, tears filled her mother's eyes as she studied the gaping hole. "It will take some effort, but I believe it can be fixed."

Even as a child, she was shocked at her mother's response. She expected punishment but received grace instead. While climbing into bed the next evening, she noticed the dress, mended and hanging in her closet. An attached note read: "Honey, I love you. Mom."

Maybe you have torn a gaping hole in the side of your life, and you think nothing can mend it. God can and will. He has already attached His note of love to your heart through the death of His Son.

Talking to God

The eyes of your understanding being enlightened; that you may know what is the hope of His calling, what are the riches of the glory of His inheritance in the saints (Eph. 1:18).

❧ Your progress in knowing and obeying God and realizing His blessing in every detail of your life hinges on receiving His wisdom and power. Prayer is the supernatural means by which Christ unveils His sovereign counsel and mind, giving you the direction and insight you need for yourself, your family, and your career.

Such treasures are discovered only through communion with God. They are not available to a prayerless person who is a walled fortress of mere intellect or good intentions.

Would you like the God of creation to show you great and mighty things? Is your life stuck in a rut, void of God's power and presence, lacking His loving, wise touch? If so, call on Him. Whether His answer is "yes," "no," or "wait," you can overcome your problem or reach your goal through His reply.

Praying with Authority

Therefore, brethren, having boldness to enter the Holiest by the blood of Jesus (Heb. 10:19).

❧ Your prayers may be weak and vague because you really doubt that God will come through. The writer of Hebrews, however, noted that your approach to God should be characterized by boldness. Here are three significant truths that can revolutionize your prayer life.

1. *You have complete freedom and access to a holy God through the blood of Christ.* You do not have to be afraid; you can confess to Him your problem sins. You can come to the throne of grace, to God the Father, who gives you not what you deserve but what His love bestows upon you through His Son.

2. *You come in agreement with God's Word.* If you pray according to the Scriptures, you can be sure that God will honor your prayers. You may not understand the specifics of how He will work, but He will fulfill His promises to you in the Bible.

3. *Focus and rest completely on the character of God.* Is He strong enough to handle your adversities? Is He wise enough to correct your problems? Is He loving enough to care for your hurts?

Your assurance is in His faithfulness, not yours. Your prayer life can become a cornerstone of confidence as you trust God for all things.

A Prayer Burden

We give thanks to the God and Father of our Lord Jesus Christ,
praying always for you (Col. 1:3).

❧ As you ask God to burden your heart with His
concerns, you may be surprised at His response. God
may bring to your mind an individual or a circumstance you never would have chosen.

Such a burden is usually one that forces you into
a new sense of dependence on God. You must know
that only the power of God can bring a solution.

You must be willing to persist in burden praying.
The burden that God places on your heart for an unsaved mate, a crumbling marriage, or a bitter friend
may last for years—even a lifetime.

Are you willing to pay the price for the burden
that God puts on your heart? Will you persevere until
God acts?

Devoted to Prayer

Continue earnestly in prayer, being vigilant in it with thanksgiving (Col. 4:2).

❧ Most of us are not likely to be devoted to someone or some objective unless we are convinced of its importance. It is not surprising then that Paul's appeal in today's passage—for the Christian to be devoted to prayer—is taken so casually. We must first be persuaded of the significance of prayer before we commit ourselves to it.

Prayer is an avenue through which the supernatural power of God is released into your circumstances. Do you have a need for God's power and provision in a relationship or endeavor? Prayer is a God-ordained method through which you can have access to His unlimited resources for your problems.

Prayer is the means by which you come to experience the loving will of God. When you pray, you confess your dependence on your sovereign, mighty God to accomplish His purposes in and through you; and His will is then done on earth as it is in heaven.

Your Greatest Privileges

I also, after I heard of your faith in the Lord Jesus and your love for all the saints, do not cease to give thanks for you, making mention of you in my prayers (Eph. 1:15–16).

🕊 Two compelling factors make prayer an exercise worth your wholehearted devotion.

Prayer is a means by which you come to know God. Is there anyone else you would rather know intimately than the living, eternal, awesome God?

When you pray, you come to know God in the most practical and personal way possible—His mind, His will, and His character. Knowing God can make a dull life exciting, a doubting life sure, a timid life bold, a wandering life purposeful.

Prayer is also a means by which you worship God. Have you ever thought about how you worship God? Certainly you can exalt Him through your lips and actions; but when you pray, you truly acknowledge Him as the Source and End of all. Prayer is an act of worship by which you confess your reverence and dependence on God.

Have you prayed today?

Solving Problems Through Prayer

O our God, will You not judge them? For we have no power against this great multitude that is coming against us; nor do we know what to do, but our eyes are upon You (2 Chron. 20:12).

🕊 Karl Marx, the Communist philosopher of the last century, sarcastically referred to religion as "the opium of the people." Christians obviously refute such tainted logic, but in practice we tend to treat prayer in a similar vein.

Prayer too often is seen as a last resort, a divine escape hatch if all else fails. We turn all the knobs, pull all the strings, exhaust all our resources—and then begrudgingly turn to prayer if what we do does not work.

Prayer is a divine management tool that can be availed, regardless of the nature of our predicament. But why don't we always view prayer as such? Pride. We do not want to admit our dependence on Christ. How blind we are; how twisted is our notion of prayer. God offers us His help, and we, in our human haughtiness, turn Him down.

God wants you to lean on Him. He longs to work on your behalf, to guide you and help you. Prayer is His divine provision. Should you ignore God's helping hand?

Praying to the Lord

When Jesus perceived that they were about to come and take Him by force to make Him king, He departed again to the mountain by Himself alone (John 6:15).

❧ Although Christ's disciples saw Him work many miracles during their three-year apprenticeship, the Bible records only one instance in which they asked their Master to explain His phenomenal power. "Lord, teach us to pray," they requested after observing Christ in a concentrated time of communion with the Father (Luke 11:1). They must have grasped that somehow prayer was the invisible source of Jesus' ministry and their success depended on understanding its secrets.

What followed was a pattern for all believers. At the heart of Christ's instructions was the pivotal phrase: "Thy kingdom come. / Thy will be done, / On earth as it is in heaven" (Matt. 6:10 NASB). That is the core of genuine prayer, seeking and submitting to the will of God in every circumstance.

Whatever your circumstance is today, let prayer steer you into His will.

The Ministry of Intercession

I know that this will turn out for my deliverance through your prayer and the supply of the Spirit of Jesus Christ (Phil. 1:19).

❧ Prayer for others is hard work; it does not come naturally; it can seem toilsome. But wouldn't you want someone else to labor in prayer on your behalf?

As an intercessor, you must persevere as you allow the Lord to pray through you His concerns for others. Prayers may be answered not within your urgent framework but according to God's timing. When you intercede for someone, keep praying until you see the need met.

When Epaphras prayed for the Colossian church, his purpose in intercession was that the Colossians "may stand perfect and fully assured in all the will of God" (Col. 4:12 NASB). The intercessor must make the will of God for others the chief pursuit.

Do you want to be used by God? Then pray for others and watch God work.

When Prayers Seem Not to Be Answered

He left them, went away again, and prayed the third time, saying the same words (Matt. 26:44).

❧ In the black-and-white 1950s, one of the most engaging shows on television was *Father Knows Best*. Despite the perils of raising a son and two daughters, the wise father always seemed to have a solution. In the realm of prayer, this principle is at work: our heavenly Father knows best.

When your petitions are mercifully granted—healing for a sick spouse, extra income for a pressing need, a promotion at work—you worship and thank God for His goodness.

When your requests are not granted—a sick mate does not improve, the financial need remains unmet, you are passed over for that promotion—you still worship and thank God for His goodness.

In the first instance that is easy. In the second that is extremely difficult, and you may think, *Why doesn't God come through? What is He trying to do to me? Doesn't He care?* Your view of God is fogged by the confusion over prayer's primary purpose. Prayer is trusting God to do what He knows is best for your life, not just in the short run but also in the long run. The character of God is the anchor for prayer. He loves you. He always works for your best. You can always trust Him.

Praying in the Will of God

Do not be unwise, but understand what the will of the Lord is (Eph. 5:17).

❧ Charles Finney was one of the foremost evangelists of the nineteenth century. The foundation of his ministry was persevering prayer. In his *Principles of Prayer,* Finney instructed the believer:

> There are three ways in which God's will is revealed to men for their guidance in prayer.
>
> 1. By *express promises or predictions in the Bible,* that He will give or do certain things.
>
> 2. *Sometimes God reveals His will by Providence.* When He makes it clear that such and such events are about to take place, it is as much a revelation as if He had written it in His Word.
>
> 3. *By His Spirit.* When God's people are at a loss (about) what to pray for, (but while also being) agreeable to His will, His Spirit often instructs them.
>
> When there is no particular revelation and Providence leaves it dark and we know not what to pray for as we ought, we are expressly told that the "Spirit also helpeth our infirmities" and "the Spirit itself makes intercession for us with groanings which cannot be uttered."

A Time to Stop Waiting

The LORD said to Joshua: "Get up! Why do you lie thus on your face?" (Josh. 7:10).

❧ The wise man Solomon wrote in Ecclesiastes 3:1: "There is an appointed time for everything" (NASB). Though not included in the list of appropriate seasons that followed, this principle rings just as true: "There is a time to wait—and a time to act."

When do you hover over a situation, and when do you launch out?

There are two conditions involved in determining the latter course. If you have done everything you know to discern God's leadership—praying diligently, gathering facts, searching the Word, obtaining good counsel, submitting totally to Jesus' lordship—and if a decision must be made now, then it is time to move forward.

If you want to please God sincerely, you must not worry about the consequences of your decisions. If it is the wrong decision, then He will forgive you and steer you rightly. But when a course must be charted, your confidence, faith, and courage are fully cast on the God who knows the future and has secured your relationship with Him.

Wait on God when you can, but act boldly in faith when you must, entrusting yourself to a faithful God.

A Time to Share

Let us therefore come boldly to the throne of grace, that we may obtain mercy and find grace to help in time of need (Heb. 4:16).

❧ In *The Believer's Guidebook*, Lawrence Richards writes this delightful synopsis on the privilege of coming before our loving Father in personal prayer:

> I've read many books on prayer. Too many of them approach prayer as if it were an obstacle course . . . prayer seems to become a tense, threatening chore.
>
> Our technique must be just right. God, the all-seeing Judge, gives points; and when we fail to clear the hurdles, He is quick to withhold the prize.
>
> What bothers me about such interpretations is that they're hardly honest to God. They distort the vision given in the Bible of a loving, welcoming God.
>
> To understand prayer, we simply need to look up at the character of God. We need to see the loving Father. We need to hear Him invite us to share every need and confess every sin.
>
> Prayer is nothing less than responding to the warm assurance of God's love and accepting His invitation to come to our Father and to share.

Praying for Others

I thank my God, making mention of you always in my prayers (Philem. 4).

❧ Prayer is a supernatural tool for developing genuine compassion and a burden for the needs of others. If we are honest, most of our time spent in prayer is for our personal requirements, sprinkled in with a pinch of worship and a neighborly request or two for others for good measure.

Laboring in prayer for the welfare of those mentioned does not come naturally, does it? That is why when you begin earnestly and systematically to intercede for others, you find a strange release from your selfish bent. Less time is spent on yourself, but you spend significantly more time praying for the needs of others.

In so doing, prayer becomes the spiritual scalpel that lifts off the stifling layers of self-preoccupation. You are freed to heed Jesus' great command: "Love one another, just as I have loved you" (John 15:12 NASB).

The Erosion of Your Life

Not lagging in diligence, fervent in spirit, serving the Lord (Rom. 12:11).

❧ Like water cutting a channel through rock, spiritual erosion happens slowly but surely. Such decline happens so subtly that you are often unaware of its deadly work. It often comes through these almost imperceptible means:

A gradual shift from devotion to performance. Christ commended the church at Ephesus for their ceaseless labor but admonished them for neglecting their "first love" (Rev. 2:4 NASB). Spiritual attrition is inevitable when your passion for Christ becomes secondary to your deeds.

A gradual change from commitment to convenience. Faithfulness in little things is the stuff disciples are made of. When your relationship with Christ is structured to fit into your tidy agenda, spiritual decline sets in. Christ demands your all—both in season and out of season. You will not move on to spiritual maturity if you keep making excuses for why you cannot press on to know God.

A gradual change from repentance to tolerance of sin. As your love for and commitment to Christ wanes, it becomes easier to condone your sins instead of repenting of them. Such sins then establish strongholds in your life and frustrate your growth.

The Power of Biblical Meditation

When He had sent the multitudes away, He went up on the mountain by Himself to pray. Now when evening came, He was alone there (Matt. 14:23).

❧ Once you decide to be alone with God, don't be surprised if you have difficulty finding the time. In the middle of a spiritual battle the enemy will do anything to distract you from praying, reading, and studying God's Word.

Because of this, you need to claim the armor of God each morning before you begin your quiet time or daily routine. The apostle Paul outlined the armor and its function in Ephesians 6. You can use his words as a framework for your prayers. Claiming the armor should never become a ritual. Instead, it is a way to remind yourself that God is with you each and every moment. Learning how to spend time alone with God opens doors of opportunity for spiritual growth.

Many times prayers may be one-way streets with you voicing your needs and never stopping to hear from the One who created you and loves you with His entire being. Getting to know God in a personal way is the most exciting part of life. The One who spoke all of creation into being waits for you!

The Requirements of Meditation

If then you were raised with Christ, seek those things which are above, where Christ is, sitting at the right hand of God. Set your mind on things above, not on things on the earth. For you died, and your life is hidden with Christ in God (Col. 3:1–3).

❧ In *Discipline: The Glad Surrender,* Elisabeth Elliot writes about the requirements of biblical meditation:

> We have been discussing making an offering of the body, which is an act of worship . . . offered by mind and heart. The next thing we are to do is to let our minds be remade and our whole nature transformed.
>
> We cannot do this by ourselves. It is the Holy Spirit who must do the work. But we must open our minds to that work, submit to His control, think on the things that matter rather than on the things that come to nothing in the end. Here again we see both the necessity of a sovereign God working in and through us and the responsibility of the disciple himself to adapt to what God wants to do . . .
>
> In times of prayer and meditation, do not try to think about nothing. "Set your mind," Paul says, not, "Empty your mind." Set it on Christ, not on earthly things. One phrase from God's Word can be taken and repeated quietly, asking that we may be given . . . the spiritual power of wisdom and vision, by which there comes the knowledge of Him.

The Rewards of Meditation

May my meditation be sweet to Him;
I will be glad in the LORD (Ps. 104:34).

❧ Meditation is a deficient discipline in most people because they fail to see future benefits. It is viewed in a strangely passive light, though it calls for active engagement of mind and spirit:

Meditation is the training ground for wisdom and insight. The progressive intake of Scripture, combined with sensitivity to the Holy Spirit, renews the mind, priming it for godly decisions in tough matters.

Meditation sifts the heart. Problem areas, sins that perhaps you didn't even know lurked within, are surfaced through the work of the Holy Spirit. This may be painful, but when it is accompanied by true repentance, you are liberated to live a holy, pure life.

Meditation accelerates obedience. God speaks quietly to your heart so that you can obey and reap the rewards.

Listen and let God cull the chaff. Wait patiently and obey His prompting. The rewards are bountiful.

Restoring Your Balance

Meditate on these things; give yourself entirely to them, that your progress may be evident to all (1 Tim. 4:15).

❧ In the clamor of home and job, relationships and tasks, losing your spiritual bearings is easy. Although it may be the last thing you think about, meditating on the Scriptures is God's way to restore balance to your hectic pace. Set aside a few hours in the evening or weekends, and find a quiet place. Take your Bible, a special book, and a notebook, and tell the Lord you are coming to find His guidance and help.

Make it your objective to listen to God. Be silent before Him. Read the Word slowly and carefully, letting His truth seep into your heart.

Give praise to Him. Sing familiar hymns. Thanksgiving stills the restless soul and focuses your attention on God's power instead of your circumstances. Seek God. He, not a new technique or method, is the answer.

Meditating upon the Scriptures will saturate your mind with His mind, helping you filter your circumstances through His wisdom. It will order your ways and thoughts, renew your vision, and refresh your soul.

Digesting God's Word

Let the words of my mouth and the meditation of my heart
Be acceptable in Your sight,
O LORD, my strength and my Redeemer (Ps. 19:14).

❧ During meditation slowly, steadily, and productively, the Word of God is distilled and digested. It is the process of patiently listening, hearing, and waiting upon God. However, meditation can be hindered for two significant reasons:

1. *Quiet time versus busy time.* You are harried and hurried. Your pace is fast, even on a slow day. But meditation requires time, still time where the voices of duty and responsibility are deliberately muted.

2. *Quality versus quantity.* Many Christians have a reading schedule that takes them from Genesis to Revelation in a year. This is a profitable exercise, but its benefits can be negated if the heart isn't set on digesting meaningful portions. Reading shorter passages of Scripture can facilitate biblical meditation, and often God will focus your attention on one verse.

Customize your schedule to find an appropriate quiet time that will allow you to maximize your investment.

Understanding Everything

Consider what I say, and may the Lord give you understanding in all things (2 Tim. 2:7).

❧ Have you ever encountered a tense situation and surprised yourself with an out-of-character reaction? One way to prevent such inconsistency is through the biblical practice of meditation. When you diligently and regularly cultivate a lifestyle of biblical meditation, you store a wealth of God's wisdom and God's truth.

Since the Source of the Scriptures is Jehovah God, you need His help to allow the Word of God to penetrate your heart: "Then He opened their minds to understand the Scriptures" (Luke 24:45 NASB). To fully comprehend God's perspective, you must ponder and weigh the content of His Scriptures, asking God to speak to your innermost being. The Lord will give you understanding in "everything" (2 Tim. 2:7 NASB).

Then when a crisis arrives, your inner person is ready for the unexpected. The words of your mouth and the deeds of your hands will flow from your heart, which has been nourished in and guarded by God, with wisdom from the Helper, the Holy Spirit, who "will teach you all things, and bring to your remembrance all that I said to you" (John 14:26 NASB).

When Faced with a Challenge

Only be strong and very courageous, that you may observe to do according to all the law which Moses My servant commanded you; do not turn from it to the right hand or to the left, that you may prosper wherever you go. This Book of the Law shall not depart from your mouth, but you shall meditate in it day and night, that you may observe to do according to all that is written in it. For then you will make your way prosperous, and then you will have good success (Josh. 1:7–8).

❧ The challenges of life come to us by many avenues. But with every challenge, God is preparing us for the future.

Joshua faced a life-changing challenge when chosen to lead the nation of Israel into the promised land. Years of training had seen Joshua grow into a finely tuned warrior. But he was accustomed to the feel of a javelin in his hand, not the rod of leadership.

God told Joshua on three separate occasions how to handle the challenge placed before him. Was God questioning Joshua's ability? No. He knew that with every challenge comes the possibility of falling to doubts and fears. Joshua enjoyed success in the midst of the challenge by recalling the words of God, binding them to his heart, and determining to walk in His ways. Begin your day with God's Word. He will lead you through every challenge just as He did Joshua.

The Purpose of Meditation

The word of God is living and powerful, and sharper than any two-edged sword, piercing even to the division of soul and spirit, and of joints and marrow, and is a discerner of the thoughts and intents of the heart (Heb. 4:12).

❧ In Oscar Wilde's classic novel *The Portrait of Dorian Gray,* the handsome character Dorian commissions a portrait of himself that will capture his good looks. He is so captivated by this picture that he makes a wish. He wants to stay young forever and let the picture grow old in his place.

Dorian gets his wish and then uses his youth and attractiveness to fulfill his desires. His motives are self-seeking, vain, and greedy in everything he does. As the years pass, Dorian periodically checks the picture in his back room.

Not only is the face in the picture growing old; it is becoming gnarled and vicious. Dorian is so ashamed that he covers the picture and refuses to let anyone look at it. The picture has become a horrifying portrait of his soul!

Dorian's picture was his "sin revealer," even as God's Word is the instrument of conviction in your life. When you meditate on Scripture and feel the tug of His Word on your heart, pay attention. God is urging you to confess your sin and experience the renewing power of forgiveness in Christ.

Drifting from Your Devotion

Jesus answered and said to her, "Martha, Martha, you are worried and troubled about many things. But one thing is needed, and Mary has chosen that good part, which will not be taken away from her" (Luke 10:41–42).

❧ A boat adrift on the high seas is in a dangerous state—vulnerable to uncertain changes in currents and winds. In a similar manner Christians who have drifted from a loyal, loving, intimate relationship with Jesus Christ are in danger of being swept into trivial pursuits. Christ saved us for Himself. He wants to draw us into His exciting fellowship and fit us into His plans.

Somehow on our journeys we lose sight of Him. We begin to operate on scattered feelings or changing circumstances. Before long, our love affair with the Master has cooled. Our passion is diminished by unfulfilled expectations, tiresome labor, and the general weariness of life.

The secret of the burning heart is a never-wavering focus on the person of the Lord Jesus Christ. Not Christian work. Not Christian growth.

Christ is all! Set your heart ablaze and your paths straight by narrowing your focus on Jesus—His attributes, His character, His care, His plans, His sufficiency for all of life.

Are You Off Course?

He who overcomes, I will make him a pillar in the temple of My God, and he shall go out no more. I will write on him the name of My God and the name of the city of My God, the New Jerusalem, which comes down out of heaven from My God. And I will write on him My new name (Rev. 3:12).

❧ A small sandbar off the coast of Tybee Island, Georgia, emerges during extremely low tides. Area natives love to venture out to it because it is a haven for sand dollars and small shells.

However, there is a trick in navigating the walk. The sandbar is located at the mouth of an inland river, and returning high tides can quickly overtake and strand inexperienced people. Beachcombers often start back to shore with a certain destination in view. But with little warning, ankle-deep water soon becomes knee deep and then chest deep. Before they know it, they are drifting off course into dangerous waters.

The same thing happens to people when they are entangled in matters that hinder their devotion to God. Those who fall prey to spiritual drifting never see it coming. They think, *I'm just a little off course. I can get back.* But before they know it, they have been swept away by an invading sin or temptation.

Make it your goal to stay on course with God. Ask Him to order your daily steps and keep your heart turned toward Him.

March

THEME: The Valley Gate

REPRESENTING: Suffering, testing, and trials

I consider that the sufferings of this present time are not worthy to be compared with the glory which shall be revealed in us. (Rom. 8:18)

Testing Your Spiritual Moorings

When you pass through the waters, I will be with you;
And through the rivers, they shall not overflow you.
When you walk through the fire, you shall not be burned,
Nor shall the flame scorch you (Isa. 43:2).

❧ Your spiritual moorings are tested severely when adversity's ill winds reach their zenith. In these times you must embrace these crucial truths:

You must remember God's past deliverances. God's prior working in your life can be obscured in the storm. But in a moment of deliberate concentration, you need to remind yourself that God has delivered you before and He can do it again.

You must stake your claim on God's promises. God cannot lie; His Word is certain. In adversity you can rely on the promises of Scripture to sustain you and uphold you (Num. 23:19).

You must count on God's unfailing love. God's lovingkindness—His gracious presence, power, and purpose—is constantly at work on your behalf. God will not fail you. What He has begun in your life, He will complete (Phil. 1:6).

Rely on these truths and your faith will stand firm until the storm subsides.

Why?

About the ninth hour Jesus cried out with a loud voice, saying, "Eli, Eli, lama sabachthani?" that is, "My God, My God, why have You forsaken Me?" (Matt. 27:46).

🕊 "Why?" That is the universal response to adversity.

"Why did our child die?"

"Why did our business fail?"

"Why did our son reject us?"

In *On Asking God Why*, Elisabeth Elliot describes the proper context for asking "why":

> I seek the lessons God wants to teach me, and that means I ask why. There are those who insist that it is a very bad thing to question God. To them, "why?" is a rude question.
>
> That depends, I believe, on whether it is an honest search, in faith, for His meaning, or whether it is a challenge of unbelief and rebellion.

You may ask, but ask rightly. For God is the Potter, and you are the clay.

Christ Is the Answer

I have heard of You by the hearing of the ear,
But now my eye sees You (Job 42:5).

❧ Occasionally a *why* in adversity is met with a swift response from God. But on most occasions, God does not directly give explanations for adversity. To advance in your adversity, you must not dwell or linger too long on *why* but shift your focus to *who*—the person of Jesus Christ.

R. C. Sproul, in *Surprised by Suffering,* spoke of Job's situation:

> Job cried out for God to answer his questions. He desperately wanted to know why he was called upon to endure so much suffering. Finally, God answered him out of the whirlwind. But the answer was not what Job expected.
>
> God refused to grant Job a detailed explanation of His reasons for the affliction. The secret counsel of God was not disclosed to Job.
>
> Ultimately, the only answer God gave to Job was a revelation of Himself. It was as if God said to him, "Job, I am your answer."

Real, solid growth can occur in difficult circumstances when you bow before God and entrust yourself and your problems to Him without demanding a solution.

How You Profit from Suffering

If we endure,
> *We shall also reign with Him.*
If we deny Him,
> *He also will deny us (2 Tim. 2:12).*

❧ If suffering is not desirable, does that also mean it cannot be profitable? Does the pain have no purpose or meaning? Since "God causes all things to work together for good" (Rom. 8:28 NASB), suffering must have some positive consequences. Consider these:

1. *It drives you deeper to the heart of God.* Your ultimate purpose should be not to achieve pleasure or happiness but to know Christ and become like Him. Real trouble facilitates that goal, driving you closer to Him.

2. *Suffering causes You to receive more of God's marvelous, merciful grace.* You think you are strong, but suffering reveals your weaknesses. That's when you discover the inexhaustible resources of God. He gives you all you need to endure. His strength replaces yours.

3. *You develop a base of reality and compassion with which you can minister to and love others.* A former or present cancer sufferer is the best one to help another cancer patient.

Suffering is never desirable. But your sovereign, loving God can make it profitable.

Overcoming the World

Indeed the hour is coming, yes, has now come, that you will be scattered, each to his own, and will leave Me alone. And yet I am not alone, because the Father is with Me (John 16:32).

꙳ When Jesus saw that His disciples truly understood who He was, He made a startling statement: Read what He said in John 16:32.

God's plan for redemption did not include lifting the disciples out of their immediate surroundings. The pain and stress of facing life as children of God would never deliver them from the earthly reality of trouble. Jesus made that clear when He said, "In this world you will have trouble" (John 16:33 NIV).

Soon after He said those words, the agony of the Cross was His to bear. How did He withstand such tribulation? Christ's life was anchored in the plan of the Father, not in the things of the world. Jesus was not worried about people and their false accusations, nor was He overwhelmed by trials or earthly tribulations. He had overcome the world.

What is His personal word to you when trials come without warning? "Take courage; I have overcome the world" (John 16:33 AMPLIFIED).

Called Alongside

For as the sufferings of Christ abound in us, so our consolation also abounds through Christ (2 Cor. 1:5).

❧ God stooped down from the heavens to rescue you from sin, and He continues to extend His hand to you each day to soothe your damaged emotions, your frayed nerves, your broken dreams, your heartaches.

"But He seems so distant, so remote, so detached at times," you say. Although you may feel this way, it is not the truth. God said that He will never fail you, forsake you, or leave you without support. (See Heb. 13:5.)

What a promise! And God certainly keeps His word. He performs this divine pledge through the person of the Holy Spirit. The Holy Spirit is God inside you. He is called the *Comforter,* meaning "one called alongside to help and aid."

When you are down, the Holy Spirit knows exactly how to encourage you. When you are grieving, the Holy Spirit knows the balance between shedding tears of grief and gently wiping them from your cheeks. He is at work to comfort you through every trial and adversity.

Don't Be Surprised!

These things I have spoken to you, that in Me you may have peace. In the world you will have tribulation; but be of good cheer, I have overcome the world (John 16:33).

❧ "Surprise!"

A room full of friends have gathered to celebrate your birthday. You are caught off guard; you never expected it.

Christians easily become entrenched in daily routines. Then when trials come, we are all too often bewildered by the sudden interruption. The Scriptures tell us in today's passage that we should never be astonished at tribulation. Travail should never stagger us. We live in a hostile, sinful, decaying world. There are sun and drought, rain and floods, health and disease, food and famine.

We have an adversary, the devil, who is called "the ruler of this world" (John 12:31 NASB). At present, God allows the devil's destructive tactics to continue—aimed at humankind. Together, the power of sin and Satan warp our character and behavior, inciting all manner of evil—jealousy, murder, hatred, greed, slander.

Jesus told us that we would have tribulations.

Responding to Tribulation

He said to her, "You speak as one of the foolish women speaks. Shall we indeed accept good from God, and shall we not accept adversity?" In all this Job did not sin with his lips (Job 2:10).

❧ The reason many of us are surprised by trials is that subconsciously we believe that suffering can somehow bypass us. In *When Life Isn't Fair*, Dr. Dwight Carlson and Susan Carlson Wood relate this concept:

> This assumption that if you live a good life you will be granted immunity from life's difficulties permeates our society. So many people proceed blindly until tragedy strikes, thinking they are immune from disaster because they are good.
>
> I have often noticed that many Christians hold a non-verbalized, unconscious belief that a dedicated follower of Christ should be immune to misfortunes . . . This unconscious belief surfaces quickly when misfortune strikes; the person becomes bitter and may even reject God. But God never promised that He would insulate you from misfortune. God may intervene at His sovereign choosing—but it is not our divine right to demand His intervention.

Your response to tribulation and its effects can be vastly different when you understand the character of God and His purposes.

Understanding God's Character

You have caused men to ride over our heads;
We went through fire and through water;
But You brought us out to rich fulfillment (Ps. 66:12).

❧ You can handle adversity only when you understand several essential truths about God:

God is not the author of evil. God uses adversity to accomplish His purposes, but He does not originate evil.

God is sovereign over all adversity. He can use any pain to honor Him and benefit you because He fits all events—good and bad—into His plan for you.

God is trustworthy. Your pain is not outside His wisdom, love, and power; and He has promised never to fail you or forsake you (Heb. 13:5).

Understanding these truths, you must decide to trust God in your times of affliction. Margaret Clarkson writes in *Grace Grows Best in Winter:* "We set ourselves to believe in the overruling goodness, providence, and sovereignty of God and refuse to turn aside—no matter what may come, no matter how we feel."

Walking Through the Darkness with God

The path of the just is like the shining sun,
That shines ever brighter unto the perfect day (Prov. 4:18).

❧ The *Canadian Home Journal* carried this exquisite poem on the treasures of darkness:

The shuttles of His purpose move to carry out His own
    design;
Seek not too soon to disapprove His work, nor yet
    assign;
Dark motives, when, with silent tread,
You view some somber fold;
For lo, within each darker thread
There twines a thread of gold.
Spin cheerfully,
Not tearfully,
He knows the way you plod;
Spin carefully,
Spin prayerfully,
But leave the thread with God.

God will work your darkness—disease, loneliness, inferiority, pain, divorce—into His masterpiece as you place your times into His skillful hands (Ps. 31:15).

Mounting Up Like an Eagle

But those who wait on the LORD
Shall renew their strength;
They shall mount up with wings like eagles,
They shall run and not be weary,
They shall walk and not faint (Isa. 40:31).

The story is told of an eaglet that fell from his mountain nest into a wooded valley. There he discovered a roving flock of wild turkeys, and since they appeared somewhat like him, he joined them.

He ate like the turkeys, acted like them, and eventually thought like his adopted family. Occasionally he saw a solitary eagle fly majestically overhead and felt a certain kindred spirit. But, of course, turkeys don't fly very high.

Then one memorable evening as he returned to his roost, a golden eagle landed nearby. Seeing the odd behavior of a member of his own species, the golden eagle explained to him that he, too, was a proud eagle and had no business dwelling with turkeys. The youngster decided to trust the elder eagle's advice, so he spread his wings and ascended into the heavens.

Many Christians have been deceived by Satan into acting like miserable, wretched sinners because they do not realize what their identity is in Christ. The truth is this: you are a redeemed child of the Father. Believe it, act upon it, and soar into the abundant life Christ promised to His people.

Darkness Does Not Hinder God

Cause me to hear Your lovingkindness in the morning,
For in You do I trust;
Cause me to know the way in which I should walk,
For I lift up my soul to You (Ps. 143:8).

❧ As a follower of Christ, you are certain to encounter seasons of darkness and difficulty. These times can be confusing: God seems distant; His will remains hidden; His voice is quiet; His presence appears dim.

You can panic; become frustrated; be disillusioned and disappointed; stagger and stumble. In your darkness, however, you must remember that your Guide, Christ Jesus, navigates your way.

As you cling to Him—trusting Him to guide you—and as you confess your dependence on Him, you learn to be confident in His loving care. Christ knows where you are today and where He will lead you tomorrow. The darkness cannot hinder Him.

Surviving Tough Times

Our light affliction, which is but for a moment, is working for us a far more exceeding and eternal weight of glory (2 Cor. 4:17).

❧ The sign next to a new condominium development reads: "For trouble-free living . . ." That certainly would be nice if it were true, but we all know that trials in this life are just as certain as death and taxes.

Physical, emotional, financial, or moral monsoons can strike hard at your foundation of faith in Christ. When (not if) the storms come, you do well to look to Moses' example of standing strong in the face of affliction: "For he endured, as seeing Him who is unseen" (Heb. 11:27 NASB). Moses withstood the intense pressure of both exile and leadership with a fixed focus of faith on God.

The peace that comes from knowing God is in control, the joy that flows from loving Him, and the strength that springs from His presence sustain you in your trouble: In the midst of your affliction, regardless of its nature, Christ is with you. He will never leave you or forsake you.

God Is by Your Side

I, even I, am He who comforts you.
Who are you that you should be afraid
Of a man who will die,
And of the son of a man who will be made like grass? (Isa. 51:12).

❧ The God of all comfort can lovingly touch all heartache, despair, darkness, pain, evil, and desperation. Your tribulations are severe. Your path is hard. Your conditions are bleak. Your outlook is dim. But the God of all comfort—the God who Himself has suffered indescribably at the hands of people—will aid you, encourage you, strengthen you, and guide you.

Because Christ has experienced the ridicule and rejection of people and now stands as the Great High Priest, the throne of grace beckons every believer. If you hurt, let the healing love of Jesus Christ sustain you. He longs to comfort and encourage you with His presence, His promises, His people, and His power.

The God of all comfort will not let you go over the edge or sink beneath the mire. He will come instantly to your aid as you call on His name. One day He will use you to personally carry His comfort to the ailing heart of another—transforming your trouble into His healing balm.

The Pathway of Perplexity

The LORD will guide you continually,
And satisfy your soul in drought,
And strengthen your bones;
You shall be like a watered garden,
And like a spring of water, whose waters do not fail (Isa. 58:11).

❧ The Greek word Paul used for "perplexed" in his letter to the Corinthians was *exaporeo. Poreo* means "a pathway." When Paul added the letter *a* (alpha) in front of the word, it became "no way." When combined with the prefix *ex*, Paul's term became "absolutely no way out."

Have you felt that way? Does it describe your current conditions?

If so, take heart. Even though it appeared to Paul as if there was no way out at times, he never despaired, never lost hope. He never walked out on his divine calling as Christ's ambassador to the Gentiles.

Why? Because he understood that Jesus Christ was his constant Companion in all of his struggles.

When you have Jesus, you have the Way to guide you although there seems to be absolutely no way out.

Facing Winds of Adversity

Be merciful to me, O God, be merciful to me!
For my soul trusts in You;
And in the shadow of Your wings I will make my refuge,
Until these calamities have passed by (Ps. 57:1).

❧ When the winds of adversity whip up swirling whitecaps of stress, you can rely on several calming biblical truths to anchor your inner person.

1. *Recall God's activity in the lives of His people (and yours) in the past:* The lives of Abraham, Moses, Joshua, David, Daniel, Peter, and Paul are illustrations of God's dealing with men. Examine His methods. Investigate their responses.

2. *Count on God's fixed, unfluctuating character:* "Jesus Christ is the same" (Heb. 13:8 NASB). You can depend on God to act consistently with the revelation of Himself through His Word.

3. *Magnify the power of God's grace:* Grace works every time. Grace is His supernatural provision for every need, every problem, every circumstance. Grace overwhelms every obstacle, overflows every failure, overcomes every dilemma.

Crisis or Opportunity?

The LORD God is my strength;
He will make my feet like deer's feet,
And He will make me walk on my high hills (Hab. 3:19).

❧ When crises arise, they appear foreboding—a pink slip at work; a somber look on the face of your physician after seeing test results; an unexpected call with the sad news of a family death. Although you cannot diminish their gravity (the Bible never ignores or attempts to explain away pain), you can take realistic stock of your dilemma and then turn to the ultimate Realist, Jesus Christ.

The danger in facing life's crises is withdrawing into the valley of despair or seeking to surmount it with feeble self-resolve. Both tactics will end in ruin. The opportunity is to trust God to make your feet as "deer's feet" so that through Him, you may see God at work in your problems. Faith in God and His care for you will stabilize your footing and give you a confident grip in His ability.

As God strengthens and equips you, you can ride on the divine winds of faith. The result is renewed hope in God's active presence in your life.

When the Going Gets Rough

He has delivered me out of all trouble;
And my eye has seen its desire upon my enemies (Ps. 54:7).

❧ God has fitted you to navigate through turbulent times. Just as a pilot's confidence during inclement weather is in the instruments, so must your reliance be on God, not yourself.

Your foremost guide in rough times is God's Word. It is always a lamp unto your feet, especially when darkness is at its deepest. If you are in tempestuous circumstances, read His Word voraciously, cling to specific promises tenaciously, and anticipate His gracious response.

You can also count on the unerring help of the Holy Spirit who lives in you. As the third person of the Trinity, He is unaffected by emotional, spiritual, financial, or psychological tumult. He will stabilize you through His divine assistance, upright you when you fall, and constantly gird you through His unfailing strength and love.

God is the Sustainer of your soul. He will see you through when you cannot see at all.

Nothing Is Too Difficult for God

I will say of the LORD, "He is my refuge and my fortress;
My God, in Him I will trust" (Ps. 91:2).

❧ "When the going gets tough, the tough get going" may be an inspiring motto on a gym wall, but it is not applicable for the believer who encounters difficulty. The strong despise the weak, but God's strength is specifically designed for the feeble in spirit, the small in faith, the little in stamina. When you fall on His grace, exhausted and spent, you are revived. You are renewed. You ride on His wings and are borne up by His divine drafts.

God's promises are your hope as you wait on Him. Waiting on God does not mean being idle. It is active, daily obedience in the things you know to do with supreme confidence in His perfect, sovereign answer.

Waiting on God means you know that He is at work when all appears silent and frozen. In His time, in His way, He will meet your needs and bring honor to His name.

Admit your helplessness. In your weariness, cast your burdens on Him. Remember, nothing is too difficult for Him.

Dealing with Destitute Circumstances

Let those who suffer according to the will of God commit their souls to Him in doing good, as to a faithful Creator (1 Peter 4:19).

❧ The circumstances for a Russian inmate were bleak. Incarceration in a Soviet prison was miserable enough. The cold weather, the harsh treatment, the loneliness, and isolation made survival the chief object. Added to his woe was the ravage of cancer.

In the midst of this anguish, the prison physician, Dr. Boris Kornfield, stood in sharp relief. The doctor was a Christian who treated the inmate with kindness and shared his faith regularly. But after reporting the theft of food from a patient by another prisoner, the physician was brutally killed.

The inmate whom the doctor treated survived his bout with cancer and his prison sentence. So taken was he, however, with Dr. Kornfield's faith, that he embraced Christ as his Savior. His name is Aleksandr Solzhenitsyn, the famous Russian author whose literary works are internationally acclaimed.

Your circumstances may be as destitute as Solzhenitsyn's; they may be much less severe. But the same God who worked in a Stalinist prison camp to save an indigent Russian prisoner is at work in your problems. Surrender to His care and trust Him for the outcome. He will never disappoint you.

God's Big Picture

In all this Job did not sin nor charge God with wrong (Job 1:22).

❧ Seeing the "big picture" is crucial if you are to live above your circumstances. Focusing on parts alone, mainly the circumstances at hand, will confuse and discourage you.

God's big picture is this: He is always at work in everything to conform you to Christ's image. God uses both blissful and dismal circumstances to accomplish that task, though you always prefer the former.

When you were saved, Christ came to indwell you so that He could live through you. As He does, you become like Him in character, thought, and deed. When your circumstances press you toward Christ, when they push you to depend on Him, the big picture is being drawn.

Never lose sight of God's sovereign purpose of molding you to Christ's image. It is what life is really about, both now and for eternity. Ask God to help you keep your focus on Him and His purpose in your difficulty. He is quietly but firmly at work on His masterpiece—Christ formed in you.

Nothing Can Thwart God's Purpose

We know that all things work together for good to those who love God, to those who are the called according to His purpose (Rom. 8:28).

❧ God never exercises His sovereignty capriciously. He is never the author of evil, but always uses the vile and the virtuous for His ultimate design—to conform men and women to the image of Jesus Christ.

This is what He died for, to redeem us from sin's curse—death—and work unceasingly in our souls to restore us to our original image—His image—stamped in the Garden and distorted by sin.

As you turn to God and cry out to Him in your affliction, the providence of God is mysteriously at work, accomplishing His intent. Absolutely nothing can thwart that purpose when your heart is bent toward Him. The pressures of life, severe as they may be, drive you only deeper into His divine mold.

Cry Out to God

I cried to the LORD with my voice,
And He heard me from His holy hill (Ps. 3:4).

☙ We like our thermostats set on seventy-two degrees and the wind always at our backs. In other words, we enjoy a level path, sustained contentment, and favorable conditions.

Adversity disrupts our controlled environment. We rise and fall on the doctor's reports, sink and soar on the response to our résumés. Affliction barges into our ordered world, overturning our carefully tailored plans. But the intrusion of difficulty cultivates a ripe climate for spiritual growth.

When bad things happen, we cry out to God. The Psalms in particular are redundant with pleas and petitions for God's help. Crying out to God admits our helplessness and weakness, and confesses our dependence on Him. As nothing else does, adversity causes us to realize our need for Christ.

In turning to God for help, we also learn to listen. Spiritual ears that were dull in contentment and ease become suddenly sensitized to God's Word in a crisis. The Scriptures are personalized to our individual needs.

Are you in a trial? Pour out your heart to God and listen to His encouragement. Nothing is impossible for Him.

Peace in Bad Times

O LORD, You have searched me and known me (Ps. 139:1).

❧ Is peace possible in bad times? Can God truly give the peace that passes understanding in the cancer ward, the bankruptcy court, the funeral home?

Peace is possible only when you accept your adversity. In acceptance there is peace—genuine, deep-seated security. You can experience God's peace and accept your hardships when you realize that your problems are allowed by God to accomplish His purposes in your life.

What happens to you is not outside God's power. It is not outside His wisdom. It is not outside His love. Evil may seem to reign, but God overrules evil for His purposes.

Acceptance is not resignation. It is not denial. It is not passivity. It is conscious awareness that your pain, though not authored by God, has been filtered through His sovereignty and providence and will conform you to Christ's image. You may never discover until eternity why He permits certain adversities. But they come with His knowledge and permission, and He knows all things perfectly.

Depend on Him

Though He slay me, yet will I trust Him (Job 13:15).

❧ Troubles are the earthly gymnasium that exercises our heavenly faith. In the crucible of adversity, God is looking for faith in His goodness, sovereignty, plan, love, and grace.

R. C. Sproul writes in *Surprised by Suffering:*

> God was asking Job to exercise an implicit faith. An implicit faith is not blind faith. It is a faith with vision, a vision enlightened by a knowledge of the character of God . . .
>
> God deserves to be trusted. He merits our trust in Him. The more we understand of His perfections, the more we understand how trustworthy He is.
>
> That is why the Christian pilgrimage is one that moves from faith to faith, from strength to strength, from grace to grace.

Trusting God in the dark when you doubt, when you do not understand, when you are ready to crumble at any moment, is the stamp of true faith. It rests on the faithfulness of God. You can trust Him because He is trustworthy. You can depend on Him because He is dependable.

Tears of Adversity

You therefore, my son, be strong in the grace that is in Christ Jesus (2 Tim. 2:1).

❧ For the peach lover, there is nothing quite like the sweet scent and taste of a ripe peach. However, a peach tree requires a certain number of cold days during the winter to produce quality peaches.

You can advance through your adversities because your afflictions likewise produce spiritual growth. Genuine spiritual fruit is unlikely to fully develop unless you are put into strenuous places. In adversity you grow in grace. Grace, God's undeserved blessing, is hollow apart from suffering. Its richness, its strength, its nourishment, are released in adversity. Grace helps the weak to stand, the bruised to heal, the barren to blossom. In trouble you learn to "be strong in the grace that is in Christ Jesus."

You also grow in your knowledge of God. Paul wanted to know God above all. That intimate relationship blossomed in prison cells, not hotel rooms. Adversity drives you into face-to-face dealings with the Father.

You grow, too, in your love for God's Word. David said, "It is good for me that I have been afflicted; that I might learn thy statutes" (Ps. 119:71 KJV). Spiritual fruit is watered by the tears of adversity.

Make Me a Flame

He delivers the poor in their affliction,
And opens their ears in oppression (Job 36:15).

❧ Amy Carmichael ministered to the poor and oppressed children of India for fifty-five years. She penned the following poem in 1912:

> From prayer that asks that I may be,
> Sheltered from winds that beat on Thee
> From fearing when I should aspire,
> From faltering when I should climb higher,
> From silken self, O Captain,
> Free Thy soldier who would follow Thee.
>
> From subtle love of softening things,
> From easy choices, weakenings,
> (Not thus are spirits fortified,
> Not this way went the Crucified)
> From all that dims Thy Calvary,
> O Lamb of God, deliver me.
>
> Give me the love that leads the way,
> The faith that nothing can dismay,
> The hope no disappointments tire,
> The passion that will burn like fire,
> Let me not sink to be a clod:
> Make me Thy fuel, Flame of God.

He Understands

Surely He has borne our griefs
And carried our sorrows;
Yet we esteemed Him stricken,
Smitten by God, and afflicted (Isa. 53:4).

❧ A woman in Bangladesh holds her limp child and wails—the victim of yet another cyclone.

A son is awakened from his sleep with a call informing him of his father's sudden death. He grieves.

A Kansas wheat farmer looks numbly at his hail-flattened field and buries his weathered face in his calloused hands to hide the tears.

Jesus weeps with you as He wept at the news of Lazarus's death. In your agony He, too, is pained. He is not an automated, austere Sovereign, immune to your suffering, but a merciful High Priest who can "sympathize with [your] weaknesses" (Heb. 4:15 NASB).

Jesus came as the suffering Messiah, the slain Lamb, the tearstained and bleeding Savior. He understands and comforts your deepest sorrows. He not only understands but actually asks you to cast your burdens and place your heartache on His shoulders so that He might sustain you in your anguish. He knows how you feel and comes tenderly to your aid.

Redeeming Your Suffering

To you it has been granted on behalf of Christ, not only to believe in Him, but also to suffer for His sake (Phil. 1:29).

❧ We all want to experience true meaning in life. It is exactly because suffering seems to have no meaning that we seek to recoil from it.

What meaning can there be in another miscarriage? What meaning can there be in still another financial setback? What meaning can be found for the person who has to use a wheelchair because of a drunk driver?

The meaning is this: we were placed on this planet to know and glorify God. As we suffer and turn to Christ, we accomplish both goals—to know Him intimately and to glorify Him. When our chief desire is to glorify God, suffering is only another means to achieve that end.

You can redeem your suffering, give meaning to it, and rescue it from emptiness by realizing that your pain can be used to glorify Jesus.

Your Adversity Is in God's Hands

My times are in Your hand;
Deliver me from the hand of my enemies,
And from those who persecute me (Ps. 31:15).

❧ Joseph emerged from jail as Pharaoh's right-hand man and saved millions from starvation by administering God's wisdom over Egypt's agricultural program.

David came out of the backwoods as Israel's beloved king. His psalms, many written during his exile, comfort and encourage believers in affliction.

Paul's jail terms were the study halls where he penned the Spirit-inspired books of Ephesians, Colossians, Philippians, and Philemon.

Each of these biblical characters advanced through his personal adversity in different fashion, but all of their progress (and yours) in harsh times is built on the bedrock truth of the sovereignty of God.

In other words, God is in charge. Your adversity is in His hands. You are never powerless, for His power works on your behalf to accomplish His purpose.

When Sorrow Flees

God will wipe away every tear from their eyes; there shall be no more death, nor sorrow, nor crying. There shall be no more pain, for the former things have passed away (Rev. 21:4).

❧ Counselor and author Larry Crabb writes about the importance of eternity's perspective on suffering in his book *Inside Out:*

> Modern Christianity, in dramatic reversal of its biblical form, promises to relieve the pain of living in a fallen world.
>
> The message . . . is too often the same: The promise of bliss is now! Complete satisfaction can be ours this side of heaven . . .
>
> The effect of such teaching is to blunt the painful reality of what it's like to live as part of an imperfect, and sometimes evil, community.

Adversity can wreak havoc in this life. But the outcome of suffering, when entrusted to God's kind hand, is always merciful. The sufferings of this life, Paul said, cannot compare to the "glory that is to be revealed to us" (Rom. 8:18 NASB).

April

THEME: The Sheep Gate

REPRESENTING: The work of the Cross,
the final sacrifice

*I am the good shepherd. The good shepherd gives His life for the
sheep. (John 10:11)*

The Cross

To open their eyes, in order to turn them from darkness to light, and from the power of Satan to God, that they may receive forgiveness of sins and an inheritance among those who are sanctified by faith in Me (Acts 26:18).

❧ Although crosses adorn our church steeples and their likeness is printed, woven, or worn in a variety of fashions, there often is only a vague knowledge of the true meaning of the Cross. What really happened at the cross? What does it mean for someone today? Is it all that important?

At the cross of Christ, the three mortal enemies of humankind—sin, death, and the devil—were confronted and defeated by the Son of God. Jesus took your sins on Himself at the cross. He bore God's judgment of death on your behalf, as your substitute. God's uncompromising wrath against sin was satisfied. You have been transferred from the kingdom of darkness to the kingdom of light, from the dominion of sin to the dominion of God.

The next time you look at a cross, wear it around your neck, or see its imprint, remember that sin was judged, death slain, and the devil conquered at Calvary.

What Really Happened at the Cross

Therefore, having been justified by faith, we have peace with God through our Lord Jesus Christ (Rom. 5:1).

❧ The blood, agony, and torture of the cross of Christ are well known, even to unbelievers and adherents to other religions. The Cross, however, was far more than mere historic melodrama. Its significance lies not in the emotional experience of the participants but in the reality of what God accomplished through His Son's death.

At the cross of Calvary, our sins were forgiven. The penalty of sin was death. Christ suffered that divinely decreed punishment on our behalf, thus enabling God to forgive us of our transgressions based on Christ's substitutionary sacrifice.

At the Cross death was defeated. Since Christ tasted the bitter dregs of death at Calvary and rose again three days later, death no longer reigns over those who trust in Him. Christ triumphed over the grave, and we who come to Him for salvation share in that awesome conquest.

Perhaps you have viewed the Cross with supreme sympathy for our suffering Messiah but never understood what His death entailed. If so, realize today that on the cross Christ died for *your* sins and overcame death. Come to Him for forgiveness of your sins, and gain the gift of eternal life.

The Cross: Relevant to Every Age

This Man, after He had offered one sacrifice for sins forever, sat down at the right hand of God (Heb. 10:12).

❧ The cross of Christ appears unimportant to many cultures today mainly because of the time of its occurrence: "How could the death of a Jewish carpenter on a Roman cross two thousand years ago affect my life today?" This reasoning confuses the significance of the Cross.

When Christ died is not the central issue. In God's timing He was crucified about A.D. 30, but He could have died in 100 B.C. or in 1943—had the Father so purposed. *How* Christ died is not the essential meaning either. He died on a cross, but had God desired, His Son could have died another way.

It is *who* was executed on the cross that is significant. Only God Himself was qualified to be our substitute on Calvary. The Cross is relevant for every man, woman, and child in every age because there the eternal God died on our behalf so that we might receive His gift of everlasting life.

The Cross: A New Way of Living

Likewise you also, reckon yourselves to be dead indeed to sin, but alive to God in Christ Jesus our Lord (Rom. 6:11).

🕊 The Cross is removed from a purely historical perspective when we realize that we, too, are involved in its ageless liberation. The apostle Paul informed us that by God's unfathomable working, we were included in the Lord Jesus Christ's death, burial, and resurrection.

We have been crucified, buried, and raised with Christ. Through faith in Christ Jesus, each of us has died to sin and been joined with Him to become "a new creature" (2 Cor. 5:17 NASB).

This concept is difficult to understand. Perhaps this analogy will help: Think of a book mailed to Europe. Inside the book is a three-by-five-inch photograph. Wherever the book is sent, the photograph goes also.

God placed you in Christ in His death, burial, and resurrection. What happened to Jesus also has happened in you. Romans 6:11 tells you "to be dead indeed to sin, but alive to God in Christ Jesus."

You can do so only because of your union with Christ. His death to sin is yours, and His life with the Father is yours. The Cross is the means to an entirely new way of living—now and forever.

The Cross: God's Power and Wisdom

And by Him to reconcile all things to Himself, by Him, whether things on earth or things in heaven, having made peace through the blood of His cross (Col. 1:20).

❧ Modern people scorn the contemporary relevance of the Cross, assailing its intellectual virtue. Despite their skepticism and ridicule, the very core of the Christian faith is the cross of the Lord Jesus Christ. A large part of the four Gospels pertains to the events leading to Christ's crucifixion.

The Cross is the central truth of both Christian doctrine and experience. In the words of Paul, the crucified Christ is both "the power of God and the wisdom of God" (1 Cor. 1:24 NASB). The Cross is God's power and wisdom because it is the only means by which sinful human beings can be reconciled to holy God. Because God became flesh, He could die as our substitute, bearing the divinely decreed penalty of sin.

Through the Cross, the wrath of God the Father was spent on His Son. Through the Cross, the love of God is freely extended to repentant men and women who, embracing Christ and His work, may receive the gift of eternal life, that is, Jesus.

Is the cross of Christ the center of your faith? There is no other way to God except through the Cross.

The Power of the Cross

He has delivered us from the power of darkness and conveyed us into the kingdom of the Son of His love (Col. 1:13).

❧ There has never been—and will never be—anything that rivals the awesome power of the gospel.

The gospel has the power to deliver from death. Because Christ paid the penalty of sin—death—and emerged from the tomb, the gospel is the only power that can liberate humankind from the horror of eternal, spiritual death. The gospel alone can transfer you from the domain of death and darkness into the kingdom of life and light.

It has the power to liberate from sin's bondage. Through the indwelling Holy Spirit, the power of the gospel transforms your behavior, unchaining you from the grip of habits and passions. You are free to obey a new Master.

The gospel also has the power to radically alter every relationship. Instead of your striving for self-dominance or self-protection, the gospel empowers you to reorient your life toward selfless giving, living, loving, and serving.

An Instrument of Eternal Liberty

I determined not to know anything among you except Jesus Christ and Him crucified (1 Cor. 2:2).

❧ The cross of Calvary—where Jesus Christ, the Son of God, died—is the extraordinary instrument of freedom where our eternal liberty was secured.

You see, our freedom cannot be purchased with a social revolution or a majority vote. The source of our oppression is spiritual, not political, economic, or cultural. We are born sinners, separated from the life and liberty of our Creator, God. We are imprisoned by the darkness of sin, chained by its selfish grip and under the influence of the god of this world, Satan.

Our only hope is to be rescued by the One who alone has the power and right to liberate us from sin's reign and rule. That is exactly what Christ did at the cross. He bore the penalty of sin—death—making it possible for us to be reconciled to the Author of spiritual liberty, Jehovah God.

At the cross, Jesus released you from the curse of eternal death. When you receive Christ, you gain the incredible inheritance of eternal life. You still die physically, but your spirit is made alive by God. And you will be with Him forever! The Cross shattered the bonds of sin, making spiritual freedom possible for all who believe in Jesus Christ.

The Symbol of Eternal Freedom

He Himself is our peace, who has made both one, and has broken down the middle wall of separation (Eph. 2:14).

❧ Your freedom from sin's penalty and power do not come cheaply. Your symbol of true freedom—liberty from the chains of sin and self—is a costly one. It is steeped in the blood of Jesus Christ, God's Son.

On Calvary, Christ fought and secured your deliverance from sin. He paid the supreme price, the sacrifice of His divine life. The grace of God is wonderful, marvelous. But it is yours only through the ransom paid by God to God through Christ's torturous death.

Bearing the guilt of your sin, He died in your place, turning aside the wrath of holy God. His sacrifice satisfied God's justice and opened heaven's doors to those who place their faith in Him. There is nothing passive about the Cross. There is nothing cheap about salvation. It is a gift—a costly one.

Have you received Christ as your personal Savior? The gift of eternal life is free if you believe, but it was secured at a most extravagant price.

A Right View of Repentance

Do you despise the riches of His goodness, forbearance, and long-suffering, not knowing that the goodness of God leads you to repentance? (Rom. 2:4).

❧ Repentance includes physically turning away from sin, and also includes a mental or intellectual change in the way you view sin. When you repent of a certain sin, you agree with God that what you did was wrong. Therefore, you willfully choose to step away from sin.

Repentance is not an emotional act. However, it does involve your emotional well-being. True repentance surfaces feelings of both remorse and regret over the obvious breach you have allowed to invade your life. Sin separates you from fellowship with God, while repentance restores your intimacy with Him.

Some Christians think they can enjoy the security of being saved by God's grace while living life with a sinful vengeance. But true salvation denotes a humble spirit and a repentant heart. There is no way to live a victorious Christian life while coveting sin. Ask God to help you come to grips with any sin in your life. His restoration is always available through repentance.

The Enemy's Power Is Broken

Our old man was crucified with Him, that the body of sin might be done away with, that we should no longer be slaves of sin (Rom. 6:6).

❧ As Christians, we often become discouraged when tempted by sinful habits we thought were eliminated at the point of our salvation. The truth is, we still live in a fallen world under the influence of Satan.

Because you are a child of God, the enemy no longer holds the title to your life. Spiritually you are seated in heaven with Christ (Col. 3:3). However, this does not free you from the strife of Satan's disastrous intentions. Salvation only shifts his goal for your life from one of eternal death to one of ineffectiveness.

Sin is his favorite weapon because he knows it damages your relationship with God. However, the Cross eternally broke the power of sin. You no longer have to yield to its temptation. When temptations come, remember the enemy's power has been broken. Jesus is your strong Advocate before the Father. Confess your sins, claim His forgiveness, and continue your life in the light of His grace.

The Barriers Are Removed

The Lord is merciful and gracious,
Slow to anger, and abounding in mercy (Ps. 103:8).

❧ Christians should be the most joyful people on earth. The thrill of victory should dance on our tongues and souls since Christ has borne the agony of sin on His shoulders.

Perhaps the wonder of your relationship with Christ has been obscured by a misplaced emphasis on the character of God. Yes, He is holy; yes, He is a righteous Judge. But He always exercises these attributes within the framework of His mercy and grace.

When you were saved, God became your loving Father. You are His treasured, precious son or daughter. Nothing you do will change His steadfast, fatherly love. Run if you will; rebel against His rule; yet the Father's heart does not turn away from you.

When you were saved, Christ became your faithful Friend. He is always there for you. You can never offend Him or disappoint Him since He knew you perfectly before you were saved and still He brought you to Himself (Rom. 5:6). He wants to help you, regardless of the mess you may have made. You are free to enjoy God because He has removed all of the barriers.

Amazing Grace

If anyone is in Christ, he is a new creation; old things have passed away; behold, all things have become new (2 Cor. 5:17).

In 1736, eleven-year-old John Newton went to sea on his father's ship, beginning a life of rebellion and immorality. An ambitious young man, Newton soon owned a slave ship and was proud of his place in a bloody and cruel industry.

Only when his ship ran into a horrible storm and he feared for his life did he turn to God. In desperation he read a devotional about Christ. Newton came face-to-face for the first time with Jesus' sacrificial love, and it changed his life. He eventually renounced the evil slave trade and became a powerful and bold minister.

Years later, Newton penned the words to "Amazing Grace," the moving story of his conversion. Newton realized that no crime is too big, no deed is too horrible, no thought is too wicked for Christ to forgive.

Christ's amazing grace covers all sin. When you accept His payment on the cross for your sin and make Him the Lord of your life, you are cleansed completely. God washes old things away and makes you a new creation.

The High Cost of God's Grace

I say to you, her sins, which are many, are forgiven, for she loved much. But to whom little is forgiven, the same loves little (Luke 7:47).

❧ Clutching the bottle of expensive perfume, Mary moved through the doorway to where Jesus and the others were seated at the home of Simon the Pharisee. She realized her actions would draw their scorn. Only Jesus would understand the motive of her heart.

As she knelt and broke the seal of the fragrant oil, her eyes met His, and something passed between them. Feelings of love, yes, but not human or emotional love. It was something that was holy and pure. No matter what her past contained, the moment she bowed her heart in repentance, God's forgiveness was hers.

Mary responded in humility and repentance. His grace sufficiently covered and cleansed her sin. Many think the idea of unconditional love cheapens God's grace. But nothing can devalue such an expensive gift. The high cost of God's grace meant Jesus had to die so that you, like this woman, could experience forgiveness and eternal life. Only Christ can save you from your sins, and only He can offer the grace you need to live confidently and securely.

Implementing God's Plan

There were also false prophets among the people, even as there will be false teachers among you, who will secretly bring in destructive heresies, even denying the Lord who bought them, and bring on themselves swift destruction (2 Peter 2:1).

❧ The theories of the modern world—evolution, humanism, secularism—have one basic element in common: they deal in chance, luck, and randomness. But the Christian faith rests on the outworking of a definitive, distinctive plan that God is relentlessly executing. His wise and perfect design, formulated in His omniscient mind, begins with salvation. This is what He unceasingly is up to in the lives of men and women who are still separated from a personal relationship with Him.

Through the death, burial, and resurrection of His Son, Jesus Christ, God seeks to save you from the penalty of sin: eternal death. He uses encounters with Christians and the Scriptures, adversity and success, creation and creatures to testify of the reality of His existence.

All that is necessary to implement His eternal plan is an admission of your sin and personal belief in Christ's forgiveness. Once you make that choice, His plan of redemption is irreversibly ignited.

A Supernatural Change

He made Him who knew no sin to be sin for us, that we might become the righteousness of God in Him (2 Cor. 5:21).

❧ Since we cannot remedy our sinful state or eternal destiny through any actions of our own, we must trust in God's provision for salvation: the person and work of Jesus Christ. When Jesus died on the cross, He bore our sins, paying our sin debt in full through the sacrificial offering of His body. The Father's wrath and punishment for our sin were placed squarely on His Son.

That is the biblical doctrine of justification: Jesus Christ dying on our behalf and rising again to remove our guilt. We can now be reconciled to God through Christ's substitutionary, atoning death. But we are not justified automatically. Rather, each of us must accept salvation by faith, receive the gift, and—not intellectually, but volitionally—trust in Christ.

When you, by grace through faith, believe in Christ as your Savior from sin, a supernatural change of condition occurs. At the moment of your salvation, the very righteousness of God—His holy, moral character—is imparted to you. Christ instantly and permanently transforms your sinful state.

The Blood of Christ

Knowing that you were not redeemed with corruptible things, like silver or gold, from your aimless conduct received by tradition from your fathers, but with the precious blood of Christ, as of a lamb without blemish and without spot (1 Peter 1:18–19).

❧ The sight of blood can make even the strong queasy. It is not so much the color, odor, or viscosity of blood that kindles such a reaction but the nervous awareness that life itself is at stake. The unstopped flow of blood results in death.

But the shedding of Christ's blood is the one truth on which hangs all of Christianity—Jesus died for our sins. Christ's spilled blood led to His death; and through death, the Son of God and the Son of man completed His work on earth—to die on our behalf, pay our sin debt by the sacrifice of His life, and provide the pathway to reconciliation between God and us. Jesus' death enabled God to forgive us of our iniquities by carrying out the punishment of sin on His own Son.

Christ's holy blood allows the Father to declare you innocent of your sins the moment you believe and receive Jesus as Savior. Christ's bloody death is the good news that delivers you from eternal death and makes eternal life a treasured gift from God.

A Personal Invitation from God

> *"Come now, and let us reason together,"*
> *Says the* LORD,
> *"Though your sins are like scarlet,*
> *They shall be as white as snow;*
> *Though they are red like crimson,*
> *They shall be as wool" (Isa. 1:18).*

❧ Throughout time, God has repeatedly appealed to us to step away from our sins and follow His way of righteousness. Sin alters life by taking what God calls pure and distorting it. An iodine stain on white linen ruins the fabric's design and fiber, and nothing can remove its staining power. Sin has the same effect on your life—it stains deeply. Yet God in His mercy has provided a way for its removal through the atoning death of Jesus Christ. Christ is your personal invitation from God to be washed clean from sin's staining power.

Once you have accepted Jesus as your Savior, God clothes you in the righteousness of His Son. Your sins are forgiven, and you are made white as snow. His forgiveness means freedom from sin, freedom from guilt, and peace that passes all understanding. It means living forever in the vital union of fellowship with Christ.

Cleansing from Sin and Sins

You have forgiven the iniquity of Your people;
You have covered all their sin (Ps. 85:2).

☙ We must make a critical distinction if we are to deal successfully with sin and enjoy God's provision for overcoming its deceptive and destructive power. The crucial principle is this: God dealt with sin at Calvary. That was His responsibility that could not be executed by anyone other than omnipotent God.

We, however, must deal with sins. That is a responsibility that God assigns to us as believers. At the cross, God stripped away our sin nature by crucifying it with Christ. That is why we can be new creatures in Christ. The old, corrupt, fallen nature was done away with.

There is still a potential of sin in each believer, but we are no longer under its reign. We are freed from its tyranny, for we have died to its rule. We can freely choose to obey God.

Although God dealt with our sin nature through the Cross, making us saints who occasionally sin, we must deal with sins—habits or activities that violate God's revealed truth. We do so by confessing our particular sins to God. We agree with Him that we have sinned.

You are completely forgiven. You can confess sinful acts to a Father who restores joyous fellowship. You have victory over the sin nature through Christ and cleansing from sins through confession.

Repentance: Complete or Incomplete?

Therefore, King Agrippa, I was not disobedient to the heavenly vision, but declared first to those in Damascus and in Jerusalem, and throughout all the region of Judea, and then to the Gentiles, that they should repent, turn to God, and do works befitting repentance (Acts 26:19–20).

❧ Sometimes repentance can seem a little like commercials in that there is no end. We come before God, confess our sins, express our desire for repentance—and find ourselves in exactly the same condition the next time we approach our Father.

Biblical repentance means forsaking sin, not simply confessing it. To forsake is to leave behind, to abandon. We repent not just with our hearts but with our actions.

You possess power in the person of the Holy Spirit to conquer your sin. You can effectively repent of sin because sin's slayer, Jesus Christ, empowers you. You are not left to your own devices, your own willpower.

Is there a nagging area of disobedience in your life that you are unable to conquer? Face it as sin, count on God's unequaled power each day, and persevere as Christ frees you moment by moment from its grip.

Not Guilty

Seek the LORD while He may be found,
Call upon Him while He is near.
Let the wicked forsake his way,
And the unrighteous man his thoughts;
Let him return to the LORD,
And He will have mercy on him;
And to our God,
For He will abundantly pardon (Isa. 55:6–7).

➦ Guilt afflicts the entire human race. We know the inner gnawing and churning that come with having violated the moral or civil code. It drives some to depression, others to compulsive behavior, still others to suicide.

The foundation for dealing with all guilt is the cross where Christ died. Jesus, the Son of God, became a guilt offering for us. Because Christ bore God's ultimate judgment, we are free to experience the forgiveness of God.

When you receive Christ by faith, God declares you not guilty. The slate is clean—from both its penalty (which is death) and its guilt. Your conscience is cleansed, and your burdens are lifted.

The Resource for Guilt

For if by the one man's offense death reigned through the one, much more those who receive abundance of grace and of the gift of righteousness will reign in life through the One, Jesus Christ (Rom. 5:17).

❧ Why is the Cross the resource for dealing with guilt? Because all men and women one day will stand before God to have their sins judged. Those who have received God's pardon by faith in Christ's atoning sacrifice will not be condemned. Those who have not had their guilt removed through the Cross will be condemned for eternity. The Cross is the basis for dealing with guilt.

For believers, that guilt is the work of the Holy Spirit who seeks to convict us. He does not condemn us. His conviction is to bring us back into fellowship with the Savior. That happens when we admit our wrongs, confess our sins to God, and receive His forgiveness.

Will we still endure the consequences? Yes. But forgiveness of your sins restores your relationship with God and releases guilt's grip on your emotions. Your guilt has been atoned for by Christ, for which you can be eternally grateful.

When You Are Feeling Condemned

Who is he who condemns? It is Christ who died, and furthermore is also risen, who is even at the right hand of God, who also makes intercession for us (Rom. 8:34).

❧ Many Christians fail to grow in their relationship with Christ, not because of indifference or sin, but because of nagging feelings of guilt and condemnation. They feel unworthy of God's blessings. They are convinced He cannot love them anymore because of what they have done or said.

This kind of thinking is false. God has accepted you completely—based on the forgiveness provided by Christ Jesus on the cross. You are no longer under God's wrath, but you are a recipient of His grace, which is given without respect to performance. Grace came to you freely at salvation and continues to flow thereafter. No misdeed can sever your personal relationship with God. If you have sinned, confession and repentance restore total intimacy. Sacrifice or penance in the form of good works or self-denial is useless.

If feelings of guilt have stunted your fellowship with Christ, they can be removed instantly by your humble confession. Never let your performance hinder God's grace.

His Spirit in You

In Christ Jesus neither circumcision nor uncircumcision avails anything, but a new creation (Gal. 6:15).

❧ English author William Temple explained the Spirit-controlled life this way:

> It is not good giving me a play like *Hamlet* or *King Lear* and telling me to write a play like that. Shakespeare could do it; I can't. And it is not good showing me the life of Jesus and telling me to live a life like that. Jesus could do it; I can't.
>
> But if the genius of Shakespeare could come and live in me, then I could write plays like that. And if the Spirit of Jesus could come and live in me, then I could live a life like that. It is not that we should strive to be like Jesus, but that He by His Spirit should come and live in us.

Where Your Victory Was Won

For of Him and through Him and to Him are all things, to whom be glory forever. Amen (Rom. 11:36).

❧ The cross of Jesus Christ is the fulfillment of God's plan for salvation through the death, burial, and resurrection of His Son. That is why the Lord Jesus Christ cried, "It is finished!" (John 19:30) as He drew His final breath on Golgotha. Prophecy was fulfilled; redemption was accomplished.

Also the Cross is the keystone for individual destiny and deliverance. Your eternal state rests on your acceptance or rejection of God's redemptive work on Calvary. There your sins were forgiven; your sin nature was judged and rendered powerless; and your archenemy, Satan, was defeated. God dealt with the old person by crucifying it with Christ so that you may enjoy a new quality of life.

You experience the transforming power of the Cross when your faith is anchored in its truth. You overcome all obstacles, all barriers, all habits, all circumstances, by total reliance on the conquering Christ, who shattered sin's penalty and power on Calvary. Christ's cross secured it all.

God Is for You

The LORD will fight for you, and you shall hold your peace (Ex. 14:14).

❧ Not only is God's Spirit in you, but also God is for you.

Have you blown your marriage due to immorality? If you are a believer, God is still for you.

Have you backed off from your commitment to God? Have you ignored His counsel, refused His direction? As staggering as it seems, God is still for you.

Here's why. When Christ died, God's judgment was fully executed on His Son. His wrath against sin was vented. God's love is steadfast for those who receive the gift of eternal life by faith in Christ Jesus. You may sin and rebel, but His love for you does not change. Yes, He will discipline you; yes, He will chastise you if necessary. But all correction is filtered through His loyal, blessed love.

God is for you, not against you. Because of the Cross, you can abide in His presence permanently and experience His love through personal faith in Jesus Christ. Paul declared that nothing can "separate us from the love of God which is in Christ Jesus our Lord" (Rom. 8:39).

Satisfying Your Greatest Need

Seek first the kingdom of God and His righteousness, and all these things shall be added to you (Matt. 6:33).

❧ What would you list as your single greatest need today? A new house? A better job? A marriage partner? A genuine friend? An increase in income? What if that need were dramatically met today? You moved into a beautiful home, got the job you wanted, found the perfect mate, met a true friend, and came into a healthy inheritance. Would you still have a pressing need in a week or two?

You're never without needs. That's why the answer to the original question—"What would you list as your single greatest need today?"—can only be, "An intimate, steadfast, growing relationship with Jesus Christ." That is your greatest need.

When you know Christ, you can have all of your emotional needs met (Matt. 11:28 NASB). When you make knowing God your chief priority, your physical needs are met (Matt. 6:33 NASB).

To know God is to have a vital relationship with the Author, Sustainer, and End of all things. That is really the only necessary thing. Is it yours?

Clearing Up Conversion Confusion

In Him you also trusted, after you heard the word of truth, the gospel of your salvation; in whom also, having believed, you were sealed with the Holy Spirit of promise (Eph. 1:13).

❧ The most important decision you will ever make is whether to receive or refuse the offer of eternal life through Jesus Christ. Since your eternal destiny depends upon such a determination, do you think God wants you to be in continual confusion concerning the consequences of your decision?

Absolutely not. God is interested in your developing a growing, loving, secure relationship with His Son. As your Father, He wants you to be aware of your indisputable relationship as His child. When you invite Christ in as Savior, He is there to stay. He will never leave you or forsake you (Heb. 13:5). You are sealed with the Holy Spirit. You are a child of God. Jesus abides in you because you are forgiven of your sins through His death. The obstacle to knowing God has been removed through His sin-bearing work at Calvary.

God's Ultimate Intention

For God so loved the world that He gave His only begotten Son, that whoever believes in Him should not perish but have everlasting life (John 3:16).

❧ The attributes of God are many—love, mercy, grace, forgiveness, kindness, goodness. Yet none of these marvelous qualities would be known to humankind without the character-trait–giving God, who by His own choice holds nothing to Himself.

We have life only because He has created us by an exercise of His will. We can receive salvation only because He wills to grant it. The ultimate testimony to the Giver of all good things is, amazingly, the saints, the redeemed ones, "in order that in the ages to come He might show the surpassing riches of His grace in kindness toward us in Christ Jesus" (Eph. 2:7 NASB).

The Supreme Giver's gift to us of salvation through Christ will resound throughout eternity. Believers will be the showcase, the tangible evidence of His ever-giving heart. Thus, while we enjoy the eternal fundamental benefits of salvation, its root lies in the reality that is the preeminent Giver—God. All of the heavenly hosts will marvel without end at that truth.

You Can Win over Sin

[Jesus Christ] whom God raised up, having loosed the pains of death, because it was not possible that He should be held by it (Acts 2:24).

❧ Here is the essence of the crucified life—you can win over sin because you are joined inseparably to the Lord Jesus Christ who has conquered sin. Paul wrote that he wanted to know Christ in "the power of His resurrection" (Phil. 3:10 NASB). He desired to experience the indwelling resurrection power of Jesus Christ day by day.

For you, that possibility is a reality through your indivisible union with the risen Christ. That is precisely why the Christian life is a victorious one. You win not by undying struggle, but by submission to and reliance on the triumphant Spirit of God in you.

Victory is yours. It may not come instantly, but it will come if you walk with Christ in His power. The Christian life can be an abundant one as you shift your focus from self-effort to the all-conquering might of Christ Jesus, within whom is your hope and your victory.

Living the Crucified Life

Now we have been delivered from the law, having died to what we were held by, so that we should serve in the newness of the Spirit and not in the oldness of the letter (Rom. 7:6).

❧ Before salvation, you were captive to the sin of envy—wanting what you could not have, desiring what others had. After salvation, you still experience the same problem, but you are all the more miserable because you realize God condemns the sin of covetousness.

The path to victory lies in the purpose and work of the Cross. You have been raised with Christ—made a partaker of His resurrection power. By faith in what God accomplished by the Cross, you can put on the new person—alive to God, filled with the Spirit, made in the image of God.

Living the crucified life is a bold act of faith. You may feel envious and be mentally assaulted by it. But now with Christ in you and you in Christ, you have a new source of power to cope with the problem. You can overcome; you can conquer; you can be content.

It is supernatural living—to be experienced, not understood—as you choose to present yourself and your affections to Christ each day as one alive from the dead.

May

⌒

THEME: The Horse Gate

REPRESENTING: The believer's spiritual warfare

Fight the good fight of faith, lay hold on eternal life, to which you were also called and have confessed the good confession in the presence of many witnesses. (1 Tim. 6:12)

Be Ready for Conflict

The serpent said to the woman, "You will not surely die" (Gen. 3:4).

❧ One of the surest wake-up calls in the Christian life is realizing that you are in spiritual warfare. The avenues of Satan's assaults vary, but be assured that he will launch spiritual attacks against your mind, emotions, and will. The apostle Peter warned that you should "be of sober spirit, be on the alert. Your adversary, the devil, prowls about like a roaring lion, seeking someone to devour" (1 Peter 5:8 NASB).

Before you received Christ as Savior, you were a captive of sin and Satan, whether or not you were aware of this bondage. You lived, in Paul's words, "according to the course of this world, according to the prince of the power of the air [the devil and his evil angels]" (Eph. 2:2 NASB). However, as a Christian, you have been delivered from "darkness to light and from the dominion of Satan to God" (Acts 26:18 NASB). You are no longer under the devil's dominion or authority. Praise God for your mighty deliverance, but be ready for conflict.

Preparation for the Battle

Fight the good fight of faith, lay hold on eternal life, to which you were also called and have confessed the good confession in the presence of many witnesses (1 Tim. 6:12).

❧ The Gulf War was a highlight film of readiness. Each day's broadcasts usually contained a segment of how tank mechanics, flight crew, soldiers, and other military personnel took extra precautions to clean and repair their respective tools of war.

Like abrasive desert sand, sin clogs your fellowship with the Father, disrupting your clear sense of His direction and creating static in your relationship with Him. The all-important line of communication with the Captain of your salvation is garbled, making victory more difficult.

Repentance will not happen until you are serious about sin. See it as God does. Hate it as He does. Understand its disabling effects on you.

Prepare yourself for the good fight of faith by identifying obvious sin, turning away from its practice, and in faith looking to God for His righteous help. You will be ready for the struggle with a clean and pure heart.

Snares of the Schemer

And that they may come to their senses and escape the snare of the devil, having been taken captive by him to do his will (2 Tim. 2:26).

❧ Many words are used to describe your arch-enemy, the devil: *evil one, tempter, prince of this world, the god of this age, prince of the power of the air,* and *accuser of the brethren.* Whatever his title, you know he works craftily to deceive both people and nations into believing his lies and doubting the truth of God's Word. He deceives unbelievers by blinding them to the truth. Such comments as "The Bible really isn't inspired," and "How can the death of one man thousands of years ago affect my life today?" are just two of his distortions.

He deceives you, a Christian, by working in your mind to cause you to doubt or ignore the truth that is God's Word. The mind is the battlefield, and deception is his primary weapon.

Jesus resisted the devil with God's Word. When you are tempted, the truth of the Bible is still your best defense. If you are under Satan's assault, find the Scriptures that pertain to your battle. Memorize them, meditate on them, and use them against the devil. The truth of God defuses the lie of Satan every time.

Dressed for the Battle

Take up the whole armor of God, that you may be able to withstand in the evil day, and having done all, to stand (Eph. 6: 13).

🕊 Proper dress is essential. If you're a football player, you put on shoulder pads. If you're a state trooper, you wear a uniform and a gun. If you're a Christian, you are in a battle against an unseen foe, and you don't dress casually for warfare. The suit looks like this:

The loins of truth. This is the truth of what God's Word says about you. God accepts you unconditionally. You are His child. You belong to Him forever. This is your guard against deception.

The breastplate of righteousness. This is your standing with God. He has declared you innocent of all sin through the blood of Christ. This is your guard against guilt.

The preparation of the gospel of peace. This is your means for sharing the good news of salvation with others, bringing them the offer of peace through Christ; it is your guard against complacency and self-centeredness.

The shield of faith, helmet of salvation, and sword of the Spirit. These work together as your commitment to and reliance on the Word of God for every circumstance—refusing to yield to temptation or to falter in trials.

Suitable Weapons

For though we walk in the flesh, we do not war according to the flesh (2 Cor. 10:3).

❧ You don't have to be a hunter to know that you can't kill a grizzly bear with a popgun. Success in any conflict requires using weapons suitable to the task.

The mighty arsenal described in Ephesians 6 is the only sure defense against the onslaughts of Satan and a sinful world. When you reach for other means of protection, you lose the fight and possibly make yourself even more vulnerable to attack.

In dealing with rocky relationships, do you put on the sandals of peace, or do you attempt manipulation and harmful compromise? When you confront lies, do you use God's girdle of truth or the authority of people? For times of temptation, are you covered by the shield of faith or by rationalization? When emotions overpower you, do you adjust them with the breastplate of righteousness or with aggression and uncontrolled outbursts?

The choice you make in each encounter decides the outcome. Learn how to take up the arms God provides; He gives the victory every time.

A Conqueror in Christ

The flesh lusts against the Spirit, and the Spirit against the flesh; and these are contrary to one another, so that you do not do the things that you wish (Gal. 5:17).

❧ When asked who their greatest enemy is, most believers would say Satan. He is literally public enemy number one and will continue to rage and battle until Christ throws him into the everlasting lake of fire in hell (Rev. 20:10).

The devil, however, is not the only adversary on whom you must keep a watchful eye. Within the context of this overarching spiritual conflict are two less infamous, but equally notable foes.

Galatians 5:17 identifies your internal enemy: "The flesh sets its desire against the Spirit" (NASB). These sinful desires cannot control you now, yet they still pack a powerful punch in your mind and emotions.

Externally your very position in Christ sets you at odds with the entire world system (1 John 2:15–17). People who don't know Him as Savior have different values, ideals, and moral codes. Even though at times you may feel surrounded by more enemies than you can name, you are never defeated (Rom. 8:35–39). In the turbulence today and the tough times ahead, remember that you are a conqueror in Christ.

Spiritual Alertness

Watch, stand fast in the faith, be brave, be strong (1 Cor. 16:13).

❧ Alertness to the strategy and presence of the enemy is always a fundamental part of winning a war, including the spiritual war Christians fight against the forces of the devil, the world, and sin. Alertness is dulled by pride or self-reliance. The more confident you are in your abilities, the more complacent you are about sin and the less attentive you are to the enemy's efforts. Do you know that you wake up to a spiritual war each morning? Are you aware that the power of the evil one is set against you?

Simply stepping out into the day with a smile and a hearty breakfast may make you feel good but does not prepare you for spiritual combat. Alertness begins with awareness of the conflict and the identity of the enemy. Steeled against his schemes, you will not be caught by surprise.

Eternally Defeated

Watch and pray, lest you enter into temptation. The spirit indeed is willing, but the flesh is weak (Matt. 26:41).

❧ Once you become aware of the severe nature of your spiritual conflict, you must realize God has issued a call to arms.

"Stand firm against the schemes of the devil," Paul told the Ephesian believers (Eph. 6:11 NASB). "Resist the devil and he will flee from you," James wrote the early church (James 4:7 NASB).

God does not ask you to obey an impossible command. If it were useless to resist Satan, why would the Father insist on your defiance?

The devil was met and defeated by Christ in His life, death, and resurrection. On Calvary He dealt a mortal blow to the devil's chief weapon—death—destroying its power for those who believe in the Savior. Although Satan conducts guerrilla warfare and still possesses deadly weapons of unbelief, doubt, and temptation, he has been confronted on the battlefield of the ages—Golgotha—and has been decisively and eternally defeated.

You can resist the devil. You can overcome his temptations and live an abundant, overcoming Christian life.

How to Resist the Devil

To open their eyes, in order to turn them from darkness to light, and from the power of Satan to God, that they may receive forgiveness of sins and an inheritance among those who are sanctified by faith in Me (Acts 26:18).

❧ How do you resist your conquered but still dangerous foe, the devil?

1. *Understand that you fight in God's supernatural strength, not your own.* That strength is yours through the indwelling presence of the "God of all grace, who . . . will Himself perfect, confirm, strengthen and establish you" (1 Peter 5:10 NASB). Your faith in God's might is like a spiritual smart bomb that thwarts the devil's schemes.

2. *Submit and draw near to God* (James 4:7–8). You do not submit to your temptation; you submit to God. When you turn and yield to God instead of your temptations, you place yourself in the "mighty hand of God" (1 Peter 5:6 NASB).

3. *Persevere "with all prayer and petition"* (Eph. 6:18 NASB). You are righteous in Christ, and God hears and answers the prayers of the righteous. Prayer routs the enemy, overrunning his evil command and control system with the power and authority of Jesus Christ. Pray quickly; pray hard; pray confidently. You are already on the winning side.

A Wartime Lifestyle

This occurred because of false brethren secretly brought in (who came in by stealth to spy out our liberty which we have in Christ Jesus, that they might bring us into bondage) (Gal. 2:4).

❧ Realizing you are engaged in hostilities should radically alter your thinking and actions according to Peter Kreeft, a professor of philosophy at Boston College. In an article in *Christianity Today,* Kreeft writes:

When you know you are in a war, your adrenaline flows. You are passionate. You willingly make sacrifices. You don't expect or demand constant comfort, security, enjoyment, and entertainment.

Each day's tasks become a spy mission, an assignment from our Commander. The one thing life never is in battle is the very thing it is for the modern world: boring and purposeless.

When there is a "clear and present danger," life brings a great purpose and a great choice.

The whole reason for the most important event in human history, the Incarnation, was spiritual warfare: God's invasion of enemy occupied territory to redeem his children from captivity to the forces of evil.

Standing Firm in God

Having disarmed principalities and powers, He made a public spectacle of them, triumphing over them in it (Col. 2:15).

❧ In occupied or totalitarian states, resistance movements commonly operate. However, they are usually small in number and vastly inferior to the dominant force. Their actions, while irritating, have little impact.

This is not the kind of opposition God asks of you when He commands you to resist the devil. You are to engage your spiritual adversary "firm in your faith" (1 Peter 5:9 NASB). The same spirit of triumph echoes from Paul, who urged you to "stand firm against the schemes of the devil" (Eph. 6:11 NASB) and "having done everything, to stand firm" (Eph. 6:13 NASB).

"But I am no match for Satan," you say. You are clearly right. Your solidity comes from your confidence in Christ, who routed Satan on the cross. Though your enemy still works, his hour of doom draws near.

A Defective Doctrine

These things I have spoken to you, that in Me you may have peace. In the world you will have tribulation; but be of good cheer, I have overcome the world (John 16:33).

🕊 As the ruler of this world system, Satan has very precise schemes orchestrated to frustrate you, a believer in Christ. Recognizing and understanding his ploys can help you thwart his shrewd tactics and walk in victory.

The devil seeks to impede your spiritual progress by keeping you from prayer. He accomplishes this by propagating a defective doctrine of guilt. When you are overloaded with guilty feelings, you withdraw from God. This is Satan's cruel hoax. Your guilt—all of it—was placed on Christ at Calvary. You are completely accepted by God. If you have sinned, sincere confession instantly restores joyful fellowship.

Satan's other primary stratagem to foil your walk with Christ is causing you to doubt God's promises. The spiritual conflict hinges upon faith. Do you really believe God will do what He says? Will He honor His Word? Absolutely. God's Word was written by Himself. It is His unalterable Word to you.

Reject guilt. Be of good courage and refuse doubt. Satan's chief schemes will be defused and God's truth unleashed for triumph.

A Spiritual Cold War

Assuredly, I say to you, whatever you bind on earth will be bound in heaven, and whatever you loose on earth will be loosed in heaven (Matt. 18:18).

❧ In the time of rebuilding following World War II, a subtle international conflict began. Nations seeking ideological supremacy jockeyed for world position in an ongoing confrontation that has been labeled the Cold War. Diplomacy became even more complicated, however, when leaders did not recognize that such tensions existed. Those who denied its reality formed policies that ultimately threatened their national security.

A cold war is going on right now in the spiritual realm as well. You can't see it, though; no visible shots are fired, no bombs dropped. But the war is real. First Peter 5:8 lays bare the battle plan of your number one enemy: "Be of sober spirit, be on the alert. Your adversary, the devil, prowls about like a roaring lion, seeking someone to devour" (NASB).

In Luke 10:18–20, Jesus said that His children are to expect, but not fear, Satan's schemes. Awareness is the key. God gives you insight into the invisible world so that you will be prepared for every assault.

Test What You Hear

Beloved, do not believe every spirit, but test the spirits, whether they are of God; because many false prophets have gone out into the world (1 John 4:1).

❧ Since his prideful revolt and fall from heaven, Satan has been committed to destruction, deception, and rebellion against God. His tactics have not changed; from the first temptation in the Garden of Eden, his strategy has been the distortion of God's Word (Isa. 14:12–14).

Many are led into error by those who make deceptive changes or additions to God's unerring, eternal truth. The best line of defense against the twisting of Scripture is knowing exactly what it says.

Whenever you hear teaching at church or receive information about the Bible, check it out yourself. Find a good concordance to help you locate pertinent passages quickly, and always compare a verse to other similar verses to verify the context.

Do you test what you hear? Ask God today for a wise and discerning spirit.

The Instrument of Satan's Defeat

Inasmuch then as the children have partaken of flesh and blood, He Himself likewise shared in the same, that through death He might destroy him who had the power of death, that is, the devil (Heb. 2:14).

❧ Some Christians are afraid to talk about Satan or think about spiritual warfare. While we should be careful not to underestimate his destructive arsenal (Jude 9), we should never fear the devil.

Although he is still active by God's permission, the devil has been soundly defeated. He is a rebellious angelic creature on the losing end of a cosmic struggle with Creator God. He knows his fate is the lake of fire from which he will never escape (Rev. 20:7–10).

At the cross, Jesus "disarmed the rulers and authorities [Satan and his demons]" and "made a public display of them, having triumphed over them through Him" (Col. 2:15 NASB). Jesus defeated the devil at the cross by delivering you from sin's penalty, death. Satan is a vanquished foe, and he knows it. You are no longer under his dominion but under the rule and reign of Christ.

Temptation

Jesus said to him, "Away with you, Satan! For it is written, 'You shall worship the LORD your God, and Him only you shall serve'" (Matt. 4:10).

❧ If temptation does not come from God, what is its source? Temptation is a tool of your adversary Satan. He desires to disable your spiritual service, distract your spiritual attention, and disrupt your spiritual relationship with the Father. Since he cannot affect your eternal destiny, he seeks to disable you emotionally, short-circuiting your joy and testimony.

The world system is also a source of temptation. The world system is the prevailing philosophy of the age, devoid of God's wisdom. A quick look at the arts, entertainment, and education reveals an underlying value system ruled by ungodly appetites and reasoning, not God.

Yet another source of temptation is the power of sin still abiding in each Christian. You are freed from sin's penalty by faith in Christ but must be delivered daily from its power through His sanctifying Spirit.

Whatever the source of temptation in your life, Jesus Christ can help you overcome it.

Who's to Blame?

My son, if sinners entice you,
Do not consent (Prov. 1:10).

Temptation. Every believer encounters it. For some, it is an occasional struggle. For most, it is an everyday occurrence, often resulting in failure. When temptation leads to sin, we often explain our conduct by blaming others, our temperament, our environment, or any other acceptable excuse.

The Greek word for temptation is *peirazo*. It means "an enticement or inducement to evil." Although God often tests you in various ways to enlarge your faith, He never tempts you to do evil. That contradicts His absolute holiness. Tests from God are for your spiritual growth. Temptations can be for your spiritual detriment if you yield to them or to your spiritual advantage if you reject them.

Whatever temptations you face, do not accuse God. If you succumb and sin, be honest and hold yourself accountable. His forgiveness always ensures a fresh start.

The Appeal of Temptation

You are of your father the devil, and the desires of your father you want to do. He was a murderer from the beginning, and does not stand in the truth, because there is no truth in him. When he speaks a lie, he speaks from his own resources, for he is a liar and the father of it (John 8:44).

❧ Temptation is the appeal to engage in a form of unholy conduct. Dr. Henry Thiessen described the fundamental components of temptation in *Systematic Theology*: "Satan's temptation may be summed up as appealing to man in this way: it made man desire what God had forbidden, to know what God had not revealed, and to be what God had not intended for him to be."

God establishes boundaries in your personal relationship with Him. He allows you tremendous degrees of personal freedom to think, act, and speak, but His Word clearly defines when your thoughts, deeds, and words transgress His boundaries.

Temptation always entices you to transcend God's borders. It seduces you into thinking something or someone else other than God can meet your emotional, physical, or spiritual needs.

Temptation is a trap of excess and indulgence, tripped by self-gratification. It need not be sprung.

An Appealing Camouflage

I fear, lest somehow, as the serpent deceived Eve by his craftiness, so your minds may be corrupted from the simplicity that is in Christ (2 Cor. 11:3).

❧ How does Satan manage to deceive you, to get you to take the bait of temptation?

His initial thrust works at undermining your confidence in God's goodness and provision. God had bestowed every blessing necessary on Adam and Eve. They wanted for nothing until Satan aroused suspicion of God's faithfulness: "Indeed, has God said . . . ?" (Gen. 3:1 NASB) was and is his opening dialogue.

Has God really said you are to be faithful to your marriage partner? Has God really said you are to speak for the edification of people and not their destruction? The more you entertain doubt, the closer you move to yielding to Satan's temptation.

The next step is believing the tempter's lie: "And the serpent said to the woman, 'You surely shall not die!'" (Gen. 3:4 NASB). Adultery is commonplace today. Words never hurt anybody. What harm can a few pleasurable thoughts do? Everybody else is in debt.

Doubts and lies. Never buy into them. The price is always exacting and never right.

Your Best Defense

Your word I have hidden in my heart,
That I might not sin against You (Ps. 119:11).

➤ Temptation can storm your mind and heart with sudden fury, overwhelming you and leading you into the whirlwind of sin. Your best defense is to willfully brace yourself daily for its assaults, mindful that you are easily conquered when ill-prepared.

You must choose to spend time with the Father, fellowshipping with Him in prayer and feasting on His Word. This is more than mere exercise. It is life and breath, spiritual stamina. Your devotion is strengthened. Your awareness of Satan's subtle strategies is heightened. This is the way you build truth into your life, sensitizing yourself to error and deceit. Apart from regular, concentrated time with God, you are vulnerable to temptation.

You also prepare for temptation by maximizing the rewards of obedience while minimizing the pleasures of sin. Temptation seems sweet. But it leaves a bitter aftertaste. Resisting temptation is arduous, but the fruits of obedience are lasting and fulfilling.

Prepare now for Satan's tempting attractions. When they come, you will be ready, armed with the truth and convinced of the blessings of obedience.

A Passionate Temptation

The thief does not come except to steal, and to kill, and to destroy. I have come that they may have life, and that they may have it more abundantly (John 10:10).

❧ Perhaps the most passionate, potent temptation of all is sexual allure. Even the strongest-willed men and women are overcome by its illicit attraction. Even the best marriages are destroyed by adulterous relationships.

One reason is the enormous emphasis our society places on sexuality. Sensuality permeates our entire culture, titillating us through television, magazines, books, and fashion.

But a more basic reason is the natural, God-given desire for physical relationships. Sex is God's idea but only within the bounds of marriage. Thus, Satan takes a legitimate desire for sexual fulfillment, seeking to twist and distort it, and deceives us through the illegitimate means of adultery, fornication, pornography, and other forms of sexual abuse.

The fierce struggle is to enjoy your sexuality as God intends while resisting Satan's alluring, but devastating temptation. Be thankful that God provides a way of escape.

Overcoming Sexual Temptation

"There is no one greater in this house than I, nor has he kept back anything from me but you, because you are his wife. How then can I do this great wickedness, and sin against God?" . . . She caught him by his garment, saying, "Lie with me." But he left his garment in her hand, and fled and ran outside (Gen. 39:9, 12).

❧ God warns you in the Scriptures that you cannot handle sexual temptation with mere determination or self-discipline. Rather, He provides two clear principles of defense against sensual onslaught.

The first principle is preventive: express daily devotion to Jesus Christ. You cannot simply say no. That leaves a vacuum. For the Christian, that void is always filled with an affirmative yes to Jesus Christ: "Yes, Lord, I do love You and want to follow You. I do realize my frailty and ask You to deliver me from temptation. I am committed to You." This everyday exercise takes up the shield of faith and withstands Satan's ploys.

The second principle is simple: flee temptation and avoid the source. Joseph did. You must do the same. Do not go out to lunch with your secretary. Do not meet your boss for a late night meeting. Do not visit a local hangout.

Joseph loved God too much to sin against Him (Gen. 39:9). He also fled at the peak of temptation. Both principles still work.

A Tool of the Tempter

Whoever causes one of these little ones who believe in Me to sin, it would be better for him if a millstone were hung around his neck, and he were drowned in the depth of the sea (Matt. 18:6).

No one likes to feel used by another person. Yet when we cause other believers to stumble in their Christian walk, we have unwittingly become tools of the tempter. When we spread gossip in the office, dress immodestly, speak coarsely, or allow questionable television programs in our homes, we can be the tempter's agents. Suppose you were asked: "Do you want to be used by Satan?" Surely your answer would be an adamant "No!"

While each of us is responsible for our response to temptation, we can avoid any compliance with the deceiver's tactics as we understand a crucial truth: each Christian is part of Christ's body. Our actions are never in isolation. For good or evil, our behavior affects the health and vitality of other believers. Therefore, it is for your well-being as well as the rest of the body of Christ that you live obediently. God desires that you be a blessing to others, not a curse. Let your love for believers keep you and them from temptation.

Examining Your Lifestyle

Whether you eat or drink, or whatever you do, do all to the glory of God (1 Cor. 10:31).

🕯️ Keeping a close check on your lifestyle is the most reliable means to avoid direct or indirect participation in the tempter's schemes. Jerry Bridges highlights four guidelines in his book *The Pursuit of Holiness:*

"Everything is permissible for me"—but not everything is beneficial. (1 Corinthians 6:12)
Question 1: Is it helpful, physically, spiritually, and mentally?

"Everything is permissible for me"—but I will not be mastered by anything. (1 Corinthians 6:12)
Question 2: Does it bring me under its power?

"Therefore, if what I eat causes my brother to fall into sin, I will never eat meat again, so that I will not cause him to fall." (1 Corinthians 8:13)
Question 3: Does it hurt others?

"So whether you eat or drink or whatever you do, do it all for the glory of God." (1 Corinthians 10:31)
Question 4: Does it glorify God?

MAY 25

What to Do with Temptation

I beseech you therefore, brethren, by the mercies of God, that you present your bodies a living sacrifice, holy, acceptable to God, which is your reasonable service. And do not be conformed to this world, but be transformed by the renewing of your mind, that you may prove what is that good and acceptable and perfect will of God (Rom. 12:1–2).

❧ Martin Luther was a profound reformer and premier preacher of biblical doctrine. Temptation, Luther said, is inevitable. What you do with temptation is a matter of personal choice.

How do you keep temptation from leading you into sin?

1. *Promptly reject temptation's deceptive advertisements:* "I recognize this thought is not from God. I refuse to entertain this uninvited and unwelcome guest."

2. *Replace the thought with a positive promise from God's Word.* Make it applicable to the nature of the temptation.

3. *Think of someone you can help or something constructive you can do.* An idle mind and idle hands are the devil's workshop where he plies his devious trade.

4. *Pray instantly.* Prayer and temptation are incompatible. Sincere prayer will magnify God's presence and leave no place for the devil's nest.

A Way of Escape

And do not lead us into temptation,
But deliver us from the evil one.
For Yours is the kingdom and the power
And the glory forever. Amen (Matt. 6:13).

John Bunyan, the Puritan preacher and writer, said of temptations: "Temptations, when we first meet them, are as the lion that roared upon Samson; but if we overcome them, the next time we see them, we shall find a nest of honey within them."

God is faithful. When temptation presents itself, God always comes to your aid. The temptation is never more than He can handle; therefore, it is never more than you can handle, no matter how weak and helpless you feel. Knowing you can deal with the tempter in God's strength bolsters your spiritual morale.

God provides the way of escape for each temptation. The best way is by faith in the power and truth of His Word—the very tool Jesus used to overcome Satan's snare. Truth defeats error every time you obey.

God also promises that you can endure it. The temptations may not—and probably will not—vanish. But you can bear up under their load, daily casting your burdens on the Lord who will "not lead us into temptation, but deliver us from evil" (Matt. 6:13 NASB).

A Reinforcement for Your Faith

Seeing then that we have a great High Priest who has passed through the heavens, Jesus the Son of God, let us hold fast our confession (Heb. 4:14).

❧ British author C. S. Lewis revealed in his book *Mere Christianity* how God can use our temptations to reinforce our faith:

> A silly idea is current that good people do not know what temptation means. This is an obvious lie. Only those who try to resist temptation know how strong it is . . .
>
> A man who gives in to temptation after five minutes simply does not know what it would have been like an hour later. That is why bad people, in one sense, know very little about badness. They have lived a sheltered life by always giving in.
>
> We never find out the strength of the evil impulse inside us until we try to fight it; and Christ, because He was the only man who never yielded to temptation, is also the only man who knows to the full what temptation means—the only complete realist.

Guilt should never accompany temptation. Turn it away by turning to Christ.

An Accurate Diagnosis

It came to pass, when the judge was dead, that they reverted and behaved more corruptly than their fathers, by following other gods, to serve them and bow down to them. They did not cease from their own doings nor from their stubborn way (Judg. 2:19).

❧ A young boy was assigned the chore of weeding his father's garden. At first glance, the lad appeared to have done a fine job. To the eye, the garden was weed-free. However, after a few days and a good rain, the rows again sprouted with the unsightly greenery. The youngster had superficially achieved his assignment. He had removed the tops of the weeds but failed to uproot them.

The problem was not solved.

We tend to take the same ineffective approach concerning temptation, dealing with the surface symptoms rather than the root cause. We wrestle with drugs and alcohol without identifying the anger driving us to indulgence. We grapple with a critical spirit while ignoring the poison of bitterness that nourishes its presence.

Ask God's Spirit to illumine the root problem pertaining to a particular, persistent temptation. Depend on His grace and His power to pull down its stronghold and defuse its allure. An accurate diagnosis is the first step to healing.

When You Have Failed

You do not desire sacrifice, or else I would give it;
You do not delight in burnt offering.
The sacrifices of God are a broken spirit,
A broken and a contrite heart—
These, O God, You will not despise (Ps. 51:16–17).

You failed. The tempter played his seductive tune, and you danced. For the first time, the third time, the "I don't know how many" times, you failed.

Now what? Do you cower before God, run from Him? Do you drown in your guilt, sink in your sadness, nosedive into mediocrity?

While the Father's desire is resistance to and victory over temptation, He provides a way of escape even when you capitulate. He meets and deals with your failure through forgiveness and mercy. The remedy of the Cross is still effective for a believer who drinks the poison of temptation. Christ's sacrificial death paid your sin debt in full, removing your guilt, and His resurrection grants you His unceasing hope and power.

Confess your sin. Acknowledge that you have grieved God. Humbly and penitently receive His forgiveness. Learn about your weakness and His provision. Cling to His stubborn love that will never forsake you. Do not give up the fight. God is with you and for you, never against you.

Satan Out, Christ In

They overcame him by the blood of the Lamb and by the word of their testimony, and they did not love their lives to the death (Rev. 12:11).

❧ Dr. A. W. Tozer stressed the need for the proper perspective on spiritual warfare in *Born After Midnight:*

> The scriptural way to see things is to set the Lord always before us, put Christ in the center of our vision, and if Satan is lurking around, he will appear on the margin and only be seen as but a shadow on the edge of the brightness.
>
> It is always wrong to reverse this to set Satan in the focus of our vision and push God out to the margin. Nothing but tragedy can come of such inversion.
>
> The best way to keep the enemy out is to keep Christ in. The sheep need not be terrified by the wolf; they have but to stay close to the shepherd. It is not the praying sheep Satan fears, but the presence of the shepherd.
>
> The instructed Christian whose faculties have been developed by the Word and the Spirit will not fear the devil. When necessary he will stand against the powers of darkness and overcome them by the blood of the Lamb and the word of his testimony.

The Victor Lives Within You

He who has an ear, let him hear what the Spirit says to the churches. To him who overcomes I will give to eat from the tree of life, which is in the midst of the Paradise of God (Rev. 2:7).

❧ Although Jesus has conquered Satan and his hosts, they are not yet confined to their final destiny— the lake of fire. In his book *The Cross of Christ,* author John R. W. Stott explains the tension in this manner:

> For though the devil has been defeated, he has not yet conceded defeat. Although he has been overthrown, he has not yet been eliminated. In fact, he continues to wield great power.
>
> On the one hand we are alive, seated and reigning with Christ, with even the principalities and powers of evil placed by God under His (and therefore our) feet; on the other hand we are warned that these same spiritual forces have set themselves in opposition to us so that we have no hope of standing against them unless we are strong in the Lord's strength and clad in His armor.
>
> The tension is part of the Christian dilemma between the "already" and the "not yet." Already the kingdom of God has been inaugurated and is advancing; not yet has it been consummated.

Place your faith in the finished work of Christ on the cross, and you will always be led in His triumph.

June

THEME: The Refuse Gate

REPRESENTING: The old, carnal nature that needs to be changed by God's power

Therefore, if anyone is in Christ, he is a new creation; old things have passed away; behold, all things have become new (2 Cor. 5:17).

The Flesh

If we live in the Spirit, let us also walk in the Spirit (Gal. 5:25).

❧ "Now the deeds of the flesh are evident" (Gal. 5:19 NASB).

"But the fruit of the Spirit is . . ." (Gal. 5:22 NASB).

The distinction here is so critical that it can mean the difference between an enjoyable, profitable, abundant Christian life and a mediocre, vacillating one. Here's why. Your life and journey as a Christian began through the work of the Spirit and, if they are to be successful, must continue through His work in you.

Once saved, the tendency is to revert to established behavior patterns to deal with sin. You do not understand when you fail and try harder and fail again. But resolve and grit could not save you from sin or self, and they will not free you from your problems after you are saved.

What must happen is a transforming dependence upon the power of the Holy Spirit. The victorious life is one that abides and rests in and yields to the Spirit of God. That does not mean that you fail to pray, work, study, read, or accept responsibility. It does mean that you do these things with reliance upon the power of God to liberate you.

How does that happen? By simple faith that God will do it (just as you were saved) and a submissive, obedient heart that looks to and leans on the Spirit of God.

Self-Inflicted Pain

Their sins and their lawless deeds I will remember no more (Heb. 10:17).

❧ "Be easy on others and hard on yourself" is an old saying. To a degree, that commonsense proverb rings true. But when it comes to forgiveness, it can be misapplied.

What if you are the one responsible for a divorce? What if you are the one who spread malicious gossip about another—gossip that proved false? What if you lost your temper and struck your mate?

An inability to forgive yourself can lead to a severe character disorder, plunging you ever deeper into discouragement, bitterness, and hopelessness.

If anyone had a reason to judge himself harshly, it was the apostle Paul. He was a killer, persecutor, and enemy of the Church. What if Paul had allowed his past to haunt him after his dramatic conversion to Christ? Could he possibly have shared Christ so boldly and persistently?

Paul's refusal to forgive himself would have damaged his life and ministry. Being hard on yourself when it comes to forgiveness is a setup for a lifetime of self-inflicted pain.

The Past

Through the LORD's mercies we are not consumed,
Because His compassions fail not (Lam. 3:22).

❧ How can you forgive yourself? How can you stop the pain that comes from knowing you have injured others?

Here is the key: You can forgive yourself because Christ has forgiven you. If Jesus Christ, the most stringent Judge, has declared your sin forgiven through His death on the cross, how can you not forgive yourself? One reason is a false sense of pride. Somehow you feel more spiritual if you continually berate yourself. You feel bad if you feel good. Paul condemned that sort of self-abasement. You can no more earn God's forgiveness than you can earn your salvation. Both are a gift from God.

Another reason is an erroneous view of repentance. Repentance does mean that you say you're sorry, but its ultimate meaning lies in a change of behavior. Repentance doesn't mean that you grovel in self-pity; you deliberately trust God to transform your conduct through His Spirit.

Christ has forgiven you—He loves you as you are. Let Christ handle your past and revolutionize your today and tomorrow.

Guilt

There is therefore now no condemnation to those who are in Christ Jesus, who do not walk according to the flesh, but according to the Spirit (Rom. 8:1).

One of Satan's most potent weapons is the fraudulent use of guilt in your life. He enjoys seeing you wrestle with unnecessary guilt. He understands that if unresolved, it can lead to a miserable Christian existence, destroying joy and peace.

This doesn't have to happen to you or any believer. God has made full provision for the problem of guilt through proper understanding of His remedy and discernment of Satan's deceptive tactics.

When Jesus died on the cross, He paid the penalty of your sin and its condemning guilt. You are forgiven of all your sins—past, present, and future. Your sin debt is paid in full when you receive Christ as Savior. When you sin after salvation, the Holy Spirit convicts you of specific transgressions. Any guilt feelings are the Spirit's loving prompting for confession and repentance.

If you seem to be walking around in a cloud of guilt but you cannot point to a specific act of sin, then it is a lie of Satan. Reject it. Refuse it. God loves you unconditionally and never puts false guilt on you.

Unforgiveness

The woman said to Him, "Sir, give me this water, that I may not thirst, nor come here to draw" (John 4:15).

❧ Jesus' encounter with the woman at the well is a timeless marvel of divine love and forgiveness. But what would have become of His forgiveness if the woman had left without fully receiving and experiencing Christ's healing love? What if she never forgave herself as Christ did? Would she have ever known the miraculous freedom of forgiveness?

Jesus has forgiven us of all sin. He tells us to forgive others as Christ forgives us (Eph. 4:32). If Jesus forgives you and He asks you to freely extend His forgiveness to those who offend you, is there any reason why you cannot forgive yourself?

You must be able to forgive yourself if you are to truly enjoy the liberation that God's forgiveness brings. Perhaps you have done something very bad. God forgives all sins; therefore, no sin should imprison you.

Don't wallow any longer in self-pity or guilt that unforgiveness can beget. Fully receive God's love by forgiving yourself. God has a wonderful plan for your life, and it does not include self-condemnation.

Rejection

He Himself has said, "I will never leave you nor forsake you"
(Heb. 13:5).

❧ A loyal company employee is laid off after twenty
years. A devoted wife is divorced by her husband of
fifteen years. A once faithful friend no longer desires
your fellowship.

The pain of rejection is strong. It attacks the very
foundation of your personality, your concept of self-
worth. If you let the assault continue unbridled, you
suffer spiritually, emotionally, and physically. You can
become a prime candidate for bitterness and depression. Is there a way out? Can you recover your self-
esteem when another has cast you into the ditch of
rejection?

Yes, you can. It is not an easy road out. But there is
a biblical path that can comfort you and restore you
to wholeness. It begins by understanding that even
those closest to you are capable of rejecting you. We
are imperfect people who often wrongly judge and
think. We are all stained by sin. Even believers are
constantly tempted to put self first.

Recognize that your self-worth is tied not to your
performance or another's faulty judgment but to
Christ's evaluation of you. His appraisal declares
you unconditionally accepted and loved.

Worthlessness

Your eyes saw my substance, being yet unformed.
And in Your book they all were written,
The days fashioned for me,
When as yet there were none of them (Ps. 139:16).

❧ The piercing arrow of rejection can be removed and the wounds healed as you understand that your intrinsic worth is forever bound to God's unchanging truth. Joseph Aldrich, author, pastor, and Bible school president, speaks to this issue in his booklet *Self-Worth:*

> Here's the point: If the whole world decided you were worthless, it would not change your essential value. Why? Because as a believer you share both the image and nature of the unchanging God Himself.
>
> Your value is tied to Him. He is the magnetic north pole of your essential worth. The Almighty Creator is the infinite reference point, the ultimate standard, the "cosmic blue book" of your value . . . Your value was written in blood at the cross. And whatever He values is valuable.

If rejection has put you into a slough of despondency, affirm God's love for you. You can eventually put rejection behind you as you place Christ in front of you.

Fear

Whenever I am afraid,
I will trust in You (Ps. 56:3).

❧ Fear seemed to be one of the first abnormal symptoms that the man experienced following the fall from perfect union and fellowship with God: "Then the LORD God called to the man, and said to him, 'Where are you?' And he said, 'I heard the sound of Thee in the garden, and I was afraid'" (Gen. 3:9–10 NASB).

Since then every heart has known the panic and trembling that fear brings. Fear of failure. Fear of today. Fear of the future.

We live in fearful times. The only antidote for fear is trust. David, who knew the depth of fear as few people ever have, came to this conclusion as he was seized by the Philistines: "When I am afraid, / I will put my trust in Thee" (Ps. 56:3 NASB). David did not deny his fear. He did not rationalize it or try to out-man it. He admitted his fear and then affirmed his trust in the Lord.

Identify the source of your fear. Bring it before God. Then confidently assert His ability to handle your fears and His willingness to replace your fears with His courage and peace.

Loneliness

A man who has friends must himself be friendly,
But there is a friend who sticks closer than a brother (Prov.
18:24).

❧ Christians become mired in the murky waters of loneliness for many reasons—an extended illness, a divorce, an empty nest, the death of a genuine friend. The starting place to lift loneliness's enveloping emotional fog is to build intimacy with Jesus as our Friend.

Fellowship with Jesus is sweet friendship with your most loyal Friend. It is coming to Christ with honesty and sincerity. You need not hide your feelings. He understands them and does not condemn you. You can draw as close to Christ as you desire.

Jesus stands ready now to embrace you with the love that died for you and now lives within you. He is no fair-weather friend. He will stand with you and comfort you in your darkest hour.

Alienation

As in water face reflects face,
So a man's heart reveals the man (Prov. 27:19).

❧ The ache of alienation is soothed first by building new intimacy with Christ Jesus as Friend. But it does not stop there, for Jesus knows our needs for mutual love and fellowship as well.

Elijah had Elisha. The disciples traveled in pairs. And Paul always had traveling companions. God knew each person needed the support of a friend as well as His supernatural presence.

Seek to cultivate new depths of intimacy with your family. Pray for your family. Look for creative ways to do things together.

Ask God to provide friends of the same sex with whom you can develop openness and sharing. If you are single, widowed, or divorced, ask God to bring someone into your life who will brighten your day.

Don't force a futile friendship. Let Him guide you. Look for avenues of service to your neighbor, church, or community that will open the door of fellowship.

You need others, and God knows that. As your most noble Friend, He will help you build godly friendships that keep loneliness at bay and sharpen you for His good and blessed purposes.

Anger

Nor give place to the devil (Eph. 4:27).

❧ If you keep your anger within certain acceptable bounds, it is not sin. David's anger is obvious in Psalms. Jesus visibly vented His anger in the temple. Nowhere are these actions described as sin.

But when anger crosses certain boundaries, it becomes sinful behavior. Knowing those emotional and spiritual land lines is difficult, but here are a few helpful guidelines.

Anger is okay as long as it is not a synonym for a constant, irritable temper. If you frequently stew over matters and are quickly irritated, you are not walking in the Spirit. You need His self-control and a mega-dose of biblical love.

Anger is acceptable as long as it is directed at another's behavior and not the person. God does not treat you as your sins deserve; likewise, you must be careful not to attack a person's self-worth. Let your anger be directed at the problem, not the person. Don't always suppress your feelings. Express your ire, but keep it within legitimate bounds.

Volatile Emotions

Now you yourselves are to put off all these: anger, wrath, malice, blasphemy, filthy language out of your mouth (Col. 3:8).

❧ Some boundary markers on handling volatile emotions include the following:

1. *Deal directly with the situation or responsible party who has irked you.* Face conflict head-on. Refuse to spread your anger to other parties.

2. *Resolve your anger as quickly as possible under the leadership of the Holy Spirit.* It is folly to let your anger brew over days, weeks, or months. That is the perfect breeding ground for bitterness and division.

3. *Remember that the temperament and personality of other people can easily provoke you.* If this is the catalyst that makes you angry, your best choice is to accept others as God accepts you—freely and unconditionally.

4. *Make a daily choice to submit to the reign of the Holy Spirit in your emotional life.* Put your focus on Christ and the peace He gives in all circumstances. The sweeter your fellowship with Jesus, the more like Him you will naturally become with the Spirit's help.

Spiritual Paralysis

Fear not, for I am with you;
Be not dismayed, for I am your God.
I will strengthen you,
Yes, I will help you,
I will uphold you with My righteous right hand (Isa. 41:10).

Many times our fears result from imaginary thoughts, things that will never happen or come true. Satan is a relentless adversary, and he loves to fill our minds with fearful thoughts. He knows if he can frighten us enough, he will stand a good chance of paralyzing us spiritually and physically.

When you come up against a fear-producing situation, immediately pray for God's wisdom and protection, admit your inner struggle, and then stand your ground against the enemy's tactics, for God has said He is with you.

Bitterness

Looking carefully lest anyone fall short of the grace of God; lest any root of bitterness springing up cause trouble, and by this many become defiled (Heb. 12:15).

❧ Jesus was specific about forgiving those who hurt us. The reason? He never wants us to become ensnared by bitterness. Members of the early church knew the score when it came to abuse. Many suffered beatings, verbal attacks, and even death, all because they were followers of Jesus Christ.

At first, Jesus' admonishment may appear hard to swallow: "You have heard that it was said, 'You shall love your neighbor, and hate your enemy.' But I say to you, love your enemies, and pray for those who persecute you in order that you may be sons of your Father who is in heaven" (Matt. 5:43–45 NASB).

In praying for those who hurt you, you are not saying you condone their actions, nor do you say you deserve their abuse. No one deserves mistreatment. You focus the attention of your heart on Christ because He is your Source of inner healing and protection.

No matter how difficult your situation appears, Christ is in it with you; and He will make a way of escape. Even the most horrifying incident can become something for His glory when you turn to Him.

Abuse

Be merciful to me, O God, be merciful to me!
For my soul trusts in You;
And in the shadow of Your wings I will make my refuge,
Until these calamities have passed by (Ps. 57:1).

❧ King Saul spent years consumed with the idea of ending David's life. At a time when he should have been basking in the blessings of God, Saul was obsessed with one notion—kill the son of Jesse, so Saul's position as Israel's king would be secure. The issue was not a wrongful act or a betrayal by David. It involved Saul's jealousy and inability to submit to God's authority.

By refusing to react to Saul's anger, David found a place of rest in God's presence. He was not drawn aside by negative thoughts or feelings of inadequacy, but instead sought strength and refuge under the wings of God (Ps. 91:4).

God did not immediately deliver David. Years passed before he sat on Israel's throne. Yet God watched over His servant and protected his every move. The process of molding David's heart into one of godly principle and character began in the brokenness of life.

No matter what you face, God has a plan for you. Ask Him to show you where to go from here.

Inferiority

God said to Moses, "I AM WHO I AM." And He said, "Thus you shall say to the children of Israel, 'I AM has sent me to you'" (Ex. 3:14).

❧ Few of us would think of Moses as having low self-esteem. But read his answer when God told him that he would be the one to lead Israel out of bondage: "Who am I, that I should go to Pharaoh, and that I should bring the sons of Israel out of Egypt?" (Ex. 3:11 NASB).

If you have ever felt this way, you are not alone. However, God has a course mapped out for your life, and all the inadequacies in the world will not change His mind. He will be with you every step of the way. And though it may take time, He has a celebration planned for when you cross over the "Red Seas" of your life.

Moses was right. He had nothing to say on his own. But the moment he trusted the Lord to be his support, things changed—seas parted, pillars of fire rose in the night, and water flowed from rocks.

In God's eyes there are no losers, only lives being changed for His glory. The cure for inferiority is the staff of God's righteousness. Grasp it and move forward to meet the challenge He has placed before you.

Shame

God did not send His Son into the world to condemn the world, but that the world through Him might be saved (John 3:17).

When temptations come and you yield to sin, feelings of shame are sure to follow. Your conscience springs to action any time it is violated. That is one way you know what you have done is not in line with God's will for your life.

There is only one way to handle shame: take it immediately to Jesus Christ. Ask Him to show you what you have done, if anything, and to help you obey His leading in confession and submission to His Word.

As a believer you stand forgiven before His throne. However, there will be times when you make wrong choices, and then you need to be willing to admit the mistakes. Never forget: God's forgiveness was applied to your life at the cross when Christ died for your sins past, present, and future.

When you have Jesus, you need never allow guilt or shame to dominate your life. He accepts you just the way you are. You cannot disappoint Someone who knows all about you and loves you just the same. This is God's love for you.

Depression and Discouragement

For the good that I will to do, I do not do; but the evil I will not to do, that I practice (Rom. 7:19).

❧ You are a believer. The deepest yearning of your heart is to know, serve, and please God. But before you trusted Christ, you had a severe problem with anger. You still do. Before salvation, you grappled daily with depression. Now as a believer, you still are easily discouraged. You commit yourself to study the Bible, pray regularly, memorize Scripture dealing with your particular albatross, read books, and listen to tapes.

Sometimes you have temporary conquest but almost always eventual relapse. It all can lead to a very frustrating circle of resolve and regret. Although you became a new spiritual creation in Christ at salvation, your mind, emotions, and habits were not automatically transformed. Once saved, you realize that these old patterns are not compatible with your new identity. Your natural response then is to do all you can to improve your behavior.

Such effort is admirable and makes you feel a little less guilty, but it doesn't work very well. The root cause requires a radical approach to your familiar problem-solving techniques.

Perfectionism

By grace you have been saved through faith, and that not of yourselves; it is the gift of God, not of works, lest anyone should boast (Eph. 2:8–9).

❧ No one would know it by your appearance, but inside you are frustrated—not with the circumstances beyond your control, but with your performance. Your supervisors at work judge you to be successful, and your family is pleased with your level of involvement at home. Still, you can't shake the feeling that you have not done enough. A standard is out there, but you haven't reached it yet: *Maybe with a little more effort . . .*

If this is frequently a sample of your thoughts, you might be struggling under the weight of perfectionism. Perfectionists drive themselves to do more and be more all the time, in an endless quest to gain approval. In every situation, even noncombative ones, perfectionists seek to have control by coming out on top.

To rid yourself of this consuming drive and put striving for excellence into healthy perspective, you must learn to acknowledge and rest in the acceptance you have in Christ. Remember, He died for you when you had nothing to offer and nothing to prove. You cannot earn His love by good performance, and you cannot lose it when you fail. Learn to rest in His achievement.

Discontentment

I know how to be abased, and I know how to abound. Everywhere and in all things I have learned both to be full and to be hungry, both to abound and to suffer need (Phil. 4:12).

❧ You probably know people who live in a state of constant agitation. Even on a good day, they seem to be slightly irritated. Something isn't quite right—the weather, their hair, their schedule, their plans for the weekend, their bank account. And though they are believers and in general are emotionally well-balanced, it is not unusual for them to voice some kind of complaint. At the heart of their lingering frustration is a basic lack of contentment.

So much of what you deal with on a daily basis are things you cannot change, either problems with people or environments over which you can exert no influence. You can respond in two ways: by grumbling and letting the frustration level rise, or by giving thanks for blessings received and looking ahead with peace and hope.

Hold on to this promise: "I can do all things through Him who strengthens me" (Phil. 4:13 NASB).

Burnout

My yoke is easy and My burden is light (Matt. 11:30).

❧ When an old worn-out tire is left on a car, the result is often a blowout on the highway. You've seen it before—shredded rubber everywhere. If someone had taken care of that tire a little sooner, the whole mess could have been avoided.

Do you ever feel like a tire that is about to burst apart? Or one that already has? If so, you may be headed for emotional, spiritual, and physical burnout. Here are some steps to help you evaluate your situation:

Get away and reappraise your life. Take some time off, as much as possible, and make a list of everything you perceive to be an obligation. Write down how much time and energy each activity takes.

Look for a pattern. Are you more involved in career or hobbies? Do you balance work and play? What preference do you give to spiritual activity?

Ask God to give you insight on His priorities. What other people think doesn't matter; what God wants you to do is of primary importance.

Through His Word and the guidance of the Holy Spirit, He will show you what areas need adjustment. Before pressure makes you pop, go to the One who gives true rest to your soul, and He will steer you away from collapse.

Disobedience

To him who knows to do good and does not do it, to him it is sin (James 4:17).

 Lack of obedience is one of the greatest hindrances to discovering God's plan for your life. If you are seeking to know God's will in a certain matter, but an area of disobedience is present, do not be surprised if God appears silent. Faith and obedience go hand in hand. He wants you to follow in faith what He has taught you up to this point.

All of the Lord's principles and directions have a special function in shaping your life and character to be more like Christ's. In fact, God's ultimate goal is to conform you to the image of His Son. When you choose to ignore some part of what He is trying to teach you, you sin and hinder His growth process and remain unprepared for what He has in store.

The key to understanding His will for you is coming to the point where you want what God wants more than you want what you desire. In other words, you value His plans more than your own. You know that His way is the best way, no matter how good other options look. When you demonstrate this understanding by willing obedience, your ears are tuned to hear His voice.

Grudges

If someone says, "I love God," and hates his brother, he is a liar; for he who does not love his brother whom he has seen, how can he love God whom he has not seen? (1 John 4:20).

❧ In *The Weight of Glory*, C. S. Lewis wrote:

> To forgive the incessant provocations of daily life—to keep on forgiving the bossy mother-in-law, the bullying husband, the nagging wife, the selfish daughter, the deceitful son—how can we do it?
>
> Only, I think, by remembering where we stand, by meaning our words when we say in our prayers each night "Forgive us our trespasses as we forgive those that trespass against us." We are offered forgiveness on no other terms. To refuse it is to refuse God's mercy for ourselves. There is no hint of exceptions and God means what He says.

Not forgiving someone who offends you doesn't mean that you lose your salvation, but your refusal to forgive discolors your experience of God's grace. By not weeding out the roots of bitterness as they spring up, you will soon be controlled by the full-blown fruit of unforgiveness.

Don't let the smallest grudge or littlest insult have room to grow. Take it to the Lord immediately.

Disagreements

Be kind to one another, tenderhearted, forgiving one another, even as God in Christ forgave you (Eph. 4:32).

❧ The Bible instructs us to settle our differences before we part: "Be angry, and yet do not sin; do not let the sun go down on your anger, and do not give the devil an opportunity" (Eph. 4:26–27 NASB). There are obvious reasons why God wants you to solve a disagreement quickly. For one, when you bring the right kind of closure to a hurtful matter, you free yourself and the other person emotionally and spiritually. Those who refuse to extend forgiveness are the losers. Nothing soothes a guilt-worn conscience like the forgiveness and love of God.

When you forgive others, you do what Jesus did for you. You also align your life with His standard of obedience. Forgiveness is not always easy, but it is essential to emotional and physical health. God promises to personally deal with those who have harmed you (Rom. 12:19).

However, many people refuse to wait on Him. They want vengeance, and they want it now. If this is your attitude, ask God to remind you of how your life looked to Him before He saved you. Even if you were six or sixty, you, like all people, deserved death. Yet through the work of His wondrous grace and forgiveness, you were given eternal life.

Envy and Strife

That I may know Him and the power of His resurrection, and the fellowship of His sufferings, being conformed to His death (Phil. 3:10).

᷿ In Luke 10:38–42 we see this scenario: Jesus was in the front room of the house talking to those gathered near Him. Martha was rushing around the cooking area in the back of the house. All was fine until she discovered her sister was missing. A quick check of the courtyard provided no clue to Mary's whereabouts. With her jaw set to reprove her sister, Martha stormed by the doorway to the front room.

When she spotted Mary sitting near the feet of Jesus, envy and jealousy took control of Martha's heart: "Lord, do You not care that my sister has left me to do all the serving alone? Then tell her to help me" (Luke 10:40 NASB).

All of us have fought similar feelings. While God understands our weaknesses, jealousy is intolerable to Him. Why? For one, it proves that we are more interested in taking care of ourselves than in taking care of our love relationship with Him. Jesus told Martha, "Mary has chosen the good part, which shall not be taken away from her" (Luke 10:42 NASB).

Make every effort to rid your life of envy and strife. Set the focus of your heart on Him, and rejoice that He greatly loves you.

Jealousy

David went out wherever Saul sent him, and behaved wisely
(1 Sam. 18:5).

❧ Everything was going well for young David. King Saul had given him a position of authority. He also had access to the king's household and often spent his evenings in the king's presence. Saul was pleased with David's allegiance until one day when he returned from war and overheard the people shouting: "Saul has slain his thousands, / And David his ten thousands" (1 Sam. 18:7 NASB). As a result of their cheers, Saul's need for acceptance evolved into a toxic jealousy that ruled his life until his death.

The only way jealousy can flourish is to have an acceptable atmosphere in which it feels at home and can grow. In reality, jealousy is a symptom of a deeper problem. And while it needs to be dealt with swiftly, you also need to ask God to show you the root cause of any envy that has set up shop in your life. Usually pride is the taproot of jealousy, envy, and strife.

Only Christ can free you from the stronghold of pride and its cousins, jealousy and envy. If this is an area of concern in your life, be honest about it. Tell the Lord you want nothing to do with anything that keeps you from enjoying His fellowship. Pray that He will remove any hint of jealousy so that you may live free in Christ Jesus.

Doubt

My brethren, count it all joy when you fall into various trials (James 1:2).

⌁ Scholars believe the book of James was one of the first New Testament books to be written. The apostle James wrote to believers forced to live outside Jerusalem. Because of the political and religious unrest of the city, Roman officials banished the early Christians.

Peter, James, and John had been with them on a daily basis—teaching and encouraging them in the faith. James knew that their exile would become a point of discouragement and doubt. Therefore, he dealt with those issues immediately in the opening of his letter.

When trouble comes, one of the first things you want to do is to guard against doubt. Faith helped those believers get through such horrendous times, and many times that is all you and I have to combat discouragement. Through Jesus Christ, it is more than enough.

The church survived those dark times to become what it is today. Without those tenacious believers, we would not have the heritage of faith we so richly enjoy. Who is the beneficiary of your faith? Is it a son or daughter, a niece or nephew? Maybe a grandchild needs to see your faith in Christ. When you place your trust in the Lord, He always comes through in a mighty way.

Confusion

He who calls you is faithful, who also will do it (1 Thess. 5:24).

❧ Is there something you have been praying about for a long time? You know that your request is in keeping with God's will. You've checked the Scriptures to make sure you are on target, and God has confirmed that you are. Each verse the Holy Spirit brings up underscores God's faithfulness and ability to answer your prayer. However, your request seems to go unanswered.

God anointed David king over Israel when he was a lad and fresh out of service in his father's sheep field. Yet he did not assume the kingship until several years later. God may give you a promise and then allow you to go through a time of waiting for Him to bring it to completion. That is when you face the greatest temptation to doubt Him. You wonder what He is doing, and you question His reasoning. Thoughts such as *Has God forgotten His promise?* run through your head as you worry over doing the right thing. Doubt is the breeding ground for confusion and fear.

Faith is the atmosphere in which hope and joy flourish. If God has promised to do a certain thing, it will be done. Never give up; with God all things are possible.

Irritation

A servant of the Lord must not quarrel but be gentle to all, able to teach, patient (2 Tim. 2:24).

❧ What bugs you? Whether it's a neighbor who enjoys mowing his lawn at 7:30 on Saturday morning or a coworker who snaps her gum all day or a mate who always forgets to pick up after himself or herself, you are forced to deal with nagging irritations.

The most important principle to remember if you are to deal with minor irritants successfully is to view them as helpers in your spiritual growth. Each time you confront an abrasive person or circumstance, you must either lay down your personal rights or enforce them. That involves a denial of self and a yielding to the lordship of Christ. Your choice in such situations advances your growth in godliness or neutralizes it. You choose the way of humility and servanthood as Jesus did, or you proclaim your selfishness.

Irritations reveal the true nature of self. If accepted as God's agents for maturity and obedience, they will scrape away the layers of pride, ego, and selfishness and reveal the pearl of genuine spiritual beauty.

Compromise

No one can serve two masters; for either he will hate the one and love the other, or else he will be loyal to the one and despise the other. You cannot serve God and mammon (Matt. 6:24).

❧ A veteran U.S. senator humorously tells how his late father used to describe fence-sitters: "My daddy told me there isn't anything in the middle of the road except dead skunks and a yellow line."

His reference was obviously political, but the same principle applies in the spiritual dimension: compromise with worldly, fleshly standards does not please us or God.

And that is exactly where the carnal Christian finds himself: trying as best he can to walk a spiritual middle of the road where he can blend his bent toward self with faith toward God. God described such a state in more graphic terms: "I know your deeds, that you are neither cold nor hot . . . So because you are lukewarm, and neither hot nor cold, I will spit you out of My mouth" (Rev. 3:15–16 NASB).

Why such disgust? Because Jesus must be acknowledged as Lord of all. Receiving Christ is the step on a brand-new course of life, where we allow Christ to express His life through us.

If you are attempting to hold on to a lifestyle that denies the absolute lordship of Christ, realize the danger and ask Him to take total possession and control of your life.

July

THEME: The Fish Gate

REPRESENTING: Christian witness

He said to them, "Follow Me, and I will make you fishers of men"
(Matt. 4:19).

The Call to Commitment

When the LORD saw that he turned aside to look, God called to him from the midst of the bush and said, "Moses, Moses!" And he said, "Here I am" (Ex. 3:4).

❧ God called Moses to a task that required a tremendous commitment. Once he accepted the challenge, there was no turning back. He could not lead the nation of Israel out of Egypt and then decide he had made a wrong decision.

True commitment changes a person's life forever. It changed Moses. Once he committed himself to God's call, everything else became insignificant.

However, it was not always that way. It took forty years of molding and reshaping Moses' character before he was ready for the mission God had for him. Then one day a flash of light on the side of Mount Horeb caught his eye. A bush was ablaze; yet the fire did not consume it. When Moses stepped toward the burning bush, he took a step toward a lifelong commitment. Before that moment, his eyes were on his flocks, his family, his hurts, and his desires.

Has God placed a burning bush in your life, but you are afraid of the commitment? Moses could have avoided the call, but he never would have known the wonder of the holiness of God. Nothing is worth missing God's wonderful plan for your life.

Step Out in Faith

Now therefore, go, and I will be with your mouth and teach you what you shall say (Ex. 4:12).

❧ Moses thought he was the wrong man for the job. Why should a pharaoh listen to a man who had spent the last forty years tending sheep?

However, God reminded Moses of his true identity: "Who has made man's mouth? Or who makes him dumb or deaf, or seeing or blind? Is it not I, the LORD?" (Ex. 4:11 NASB). In other words, God put Moses' attention and focus back on Him.

You can understand your identity and the unique works that God has planned for you only when you identify yourself fully with Jesus Christ. You are an eternal part of God's family. Insecurity, emptiness, and purposelessness have no place in your life—the Lord provides fulfillment and direction.

Do you feel inadequate or unprepared for a specific challenge? Is the threat of failure eroding your faith? Remember that God is sovereign and gives you the strength and wisdom for what He asks you to do. He calls you to step out in obedient faith, letting Him handle the details.

Equipped for Service

When Jesus heard it, He said to them, "Those who are well have no need of a physician, but those who are sick. I did not come to call the righteous, but sinners, to repentance" (Mark 2:17).

❧ Jesus told us in Mark 2:17 that He did not come to the healthy but to the sick. In the Greek, *sick* is used metaphorically of mental ailments.

The people of Jesus' day were in need of much more than a physical touch. They were in need of a Savior. They struggled with depravity. Instead of worshiping God in purity, they often were bound to the darkness of their day. Paganism and legalism were just two of the infirmities plaguing them.

Once they were set free, Jesus commissioned them for service. He told them to go and share what God had done for them.

That was how the gospel spread, by the testimony of those Jesus touched and healed. It is also how God equips us for service. Believers, once mentally insensitive to the things of God, are freed to share the hope of Jesus Christ.

Your life is a living testimony of the healing power of God. Ask Him to show you how you can share His victorious truth with someone today.

Developing a Servant Spirit

So the last will be first, and the first last. For many are called, but few chosen (Matt. 20:16).

❧ It wasn't easy for Peter to restrain himself. He was a natural leader, and leaders lead others. However, the events of Christ's last week on earth shattered any dreams Peter might have had concerning self-glory and leadership.

He watched in frustration as the Savior wrapped a towel around His waist and began washing the disciples' feet (John 13). When He approached Peter with the basin of water, the disciple recoiled: "Lord, You shall never bathe my feet!"

Jesus was firm in His reply, "Peter, don't you understand? Unless you allow Me to do this, then you will have no part of Me."

A restless silence stood between them. God was confronting the motive of Peter's heart. Peter didn't understand the ways of God, and he wasn't ready for service. It takes both humility and grace to serve others. It also takes the same to allow others to serve you. Peter's life was still on the drawing board. Soon he would learn firsthand of God's grace through the painful trial of humility.

Jesus said to the disciples: "If you want to be first, you must first learn to be last." The only way you will develop a servant's spirit is to treasure this truth deep within your heart.

Channels of Reconciliation

If anyone is in Christ, he is a new creation; old things have passed away; behold, all things have become new (2 Cor. 5:17).

❧ Those who meet Jesus are changed eternally. No one meets Jesus and remains the same. Even Judas after the betrayal cried, "I have betrayed an innocent man" (Matt. 27:4, author's paraphrase).

Either you accept Jesus as the Messiah and become reconciled to God, or you reject Him and live a life of separation and denial. No matter how you view it, anyone who encounters Christ is changed.

Sin once separated you from God; but Jesus, being God's Son, broke the power of sin through His death, burial, and resurrection. When you accept Him as your Savior, God reconciles you eternally to Himself. Reconciliation is the goal of salvation.

Yet the message of reconciliation does not stop here but continues through you to reach others who have never heard the truth of the gospel. Nothing has changed since the call of the Great Commission. God reconciles you to Himself that you might have a ministry of reconciliation.

The words He spoke to His disciples at the Resurrection are the same words He speaks to you today. You are His channel of reconciliation to a lost and dying world.

Here I Am—Send Me!

I heard the voice of the Lord, saying:
"Whom shall I send,
And who will go for Us?"
Then I said, "Here am I! Send me" (Isa. 6:8).

❧ The days in which Isaiah lived were filled with sinful peril. Israel worshiped many gods and adhered to all kinds of evil. It is true; Isaiah should have known better than to overlook Israel's compromise. He was a priest of God and served daily in the temple. He knew the value of holiness. Yet sin in its quiet deception had stolen a place in his heart.

The day he stood in the presence of God with heralds of seraphim hovering above him was his day of reckoning. God was looking for one man, one voice, to carry His truth to the people. Who would go for Him? Who would answer His call?

Has God called you to a certain task, but the memory of past failures holds you back? Take heart; He is near. Get on your face before Him. Tell Him the ways you have failed, and He will cleanse you.

One of the most wondrous attributes of the heavenly Father is His mercy in forgiveness. Will you, like Isaiah, answer His call?

The Call to Serve

By this all will know that you are My disciples, if you have love for one another (John 13:35).

❧ If given a choice to serve or be served, most people would opt for the latter choice. The notion of servanthood, though not a repulsive idea, is certainly not a natural affinity. Yet the call to servanthood is distinctly Christian; for Christ Himself, the Sovereign of the universe, came to serve, even to the point of death.

A clue to His mission of suffering and service is found in John 13:1–5, where Christ stooped to wash the dusty feet of His disciples: "Jesus, knowing that the Father had given all things into His hands, and that He had come forth from God, and was going back to God, rose from supper, and laid aside His garments; and taking a towel, He girded Himself about" (John 13:3–4 NASB).

Jesus was secure in His identity as God's Son and in His destiny. The mantle of servanthood was not a threat but a fulfillment of His mission.

You can serve others when you are secure in your relationship with the Father. When you minister to others, you do so in His name and demonstrate the reality of Christ in you.

A True Servant

He who is greatest among you shall be your servant (Matt.23:11).

❧ Those who chose roles in our nation's government during the colonial days did so on the noble basis of public service. Compensation was small, and recognition was not the determining motivation.

How interesting that our notion of public service has eroded through the centuries. Now those elected to govern are usually motivated by greed or power. Once they are in office, their energies are focused on the maintenance of their position, not service to their constituency.

However, biblical servanthood is always cloaked in the garment of true humility. It is not self-seeking. Its real value lies not in pleasing or helping the one served, but in honoring the Master and reflecting His character.

Do you serve others so that you can be recognized for your efforts? Do you serve to gain position or acknowledgment?

You can maintain such humility only by cultivating an intimate relationship with the servant heart of Jesus Christ. The dearer Jesus is to you, the more you are enveloped in His holy humility. The more in awe you are of God, the less likely you are to succumb to pride.

The Key to Servanthood

If I am being poured out as a drink offering on the sacrifice and service of your faith, I am glad and rejoice with you all (Phil. 2:17).

❧ Oswald Chambers wrote of the importance of serving God in the small, often unnoticed realms of life in *My Utmost for His Highest:*

> Are you willing to be offered for the work of the faithful—to pour out your life blood as a libation on the sacrifice of the faith of others? Or do you say "I am not going to be offered up just yet, I do not want God to choose my work. I want to choose the scenery of my own sacrifice; I want to have the right kind of people watching and saying, 'Well done.'"
>
> It is one thing to go on the lonely way with dignified heroism, but quite another thing if the line mapped out for you by God means being a doormat under other people's feet. Suppose God wants to use you to say, "I know how to be abased"—are you ready to be offered up like that?
>
> Are you ready to be not so much as a drop in the bucket—to be so hopelessly insignificant that you are never thought of again in connection with the life you served? Are you willing to spend and be spent; not seeking to be ministered unto, but to minister? Some saints cannot do menial work and remain saints because it is beneath their dignity.

Applying for Greatness

For the LORD does not see as man sees; for man looks at the outward appearance, but the LORD looks at the heart (1 Sam.16:7).

❧ A former military commander spoke of the dignity and honesty that should grace the life of any individual. "When I stand before God," he said, "He won't ask me for my résumé."

His remark is profoundly simple and relevant. While we tirelessly work at enhancing our performance, God is concerned with a far more accurate barometer—the heart.

This should give hope and inspiration to any man or woman who wants to be used by God. You don't have to possess a college degree, attend a megachurch, or master the Greek and Hebrew languages of the Bible. God's requirement is a pure heart, a hunger and thirst to know and serve Him without consideration of reward.

Whoever you are, God can and will use you in an eternal, meaningful way if you maintain childlike faith and dependence on Him. That is His primary requirement for spiritual greatness.

The People God Uses

Now therefore, go, and I will be with your mouth and teach you what you shall say (Ex. 4:12).

❧ Have you ever thought about the people God uses? If you took a heavenly roll call, the group would include an Egyptian castaway turned sheepherder, a shepherd boy whose best friends were criminals, an abandoned widow and her mother-in-law, a carpenter whose hands were cracked and calloused, a common Jewish girl, a brawny fisherman, a tax collector, a prostitute, and a prideful Pharisee.

You may be thinking, *What a group! Looks as if God would have chosen people of nobility.* The truth is, He chose those very people, common in social status but uncommon in spirit, to change the course of history. They may have appeared foolish by the world's standards, but they were wise by God's. He takes the world's hand-me-downs and molds them into precious instruments of His loving grace.

Common people doing uncommon things. God isn't looking for polished social giants; He is looking for people who are available and willing to trust Him.

Whatever your past holds, it is no match for God's grace. Tell Him you are available to be used by Him, and you will be surprised at the work He gives you to do.

The Requirements of Servanthood

The Son of Man has come to seek and to save that which was lost (Luke 19:10).

☙ The most striking feature about Jesus during His earthly ministry was His unceasing servanthood mind-set. Though He was full deity, His life was a pure reflection of a humble servant.

Since you are created to be conformed to the image of Christ, you should increasingly demonstrate the attributes of a genuine servant. That will occur as you take on the following characteristics:

Awareness. Are you alert to the needs of others around you? Are you sensitive to their hurts, dreams, problems?

Availability. Do you take so much time meeting your own needs that you have no time for others? You have to make time to serve.

Acceptance. One reason you don't serve lovingly is that you have a hard time accepting others. You look at their faults instead of seeing them through the eyes of the Father.

Abiding. You can give time and love to others only as you depend on Jesus daily and draw your strength and wisdom from Him.

Abandonment. Jesus said that if a man is to find his life, he must lose it (Matt. 10:39). What He meant was that you should cease trying to call attention to yourself and instead concentrate your concern on others.

Pea-Sized Christianity

He Himself is the propitiation for our sins, and not for ours only but also for the whole world (1 John 2:2).

❧ In his book *In the Gap*, David Bryant looks at the Christian's reluctance for missionary involvement:

> Underneath disinterest in world outreach, underneath small missions budgets or limited personnel and the scandal of billions yet unreached, hides a culprit I call "pea-sized Christianity."
>
> There is a pea-sized box called convert Christianity—life in Christ gets no bigger than making it safely inside the kingdom. Or there's character Christianity—life in Christ gets no bigger than pulling one's own spiritual act together.
>
> When life in Christ is no bigger than the warm, secure fellowship I have each week with my good Christian buddies, I'm in a box of cloister Christianity. Or when life in Christ is no bigger for me than getting nicely settled in a good paying job after graduation, then I'm trapped in career Christianity . . .
>
> In summary, when my Christian experience expands no further than my salvation or small group or church or future, it's pea-sized. When my activities don't link me to the reaching of the earth's unreached people, I've succumbed to pea-sized Christianity.

Disturbing Your Comfort Zone

Do you not say, "There are still four months and then comes the harvest"? Behold, I say to you, lift up your eyes and look at the fields, for they are already white for harvest! (John 4:35).

🕊 Francis Schaeffer, the late Christian thinker and theologian, said the two greatest enemies of the modern church in America are "personal peace and affluence." He was describing the prevailing indifference that envelops the body of Christ today. Christians become complacent when they are preoccupied with meeting only their needs instead of reaching out to others.

The church in America is wealthy and prosperous. But believers in many countries are imprisoned for their faith or punished with loss of their jobs. Christians in Africa and developing countries are poor. Wherever we live, there are emotional, spiritual, and physical needs, but we must first lift our eyes to the fields (John 4:35).

Complacency is also nurtured when we settle for the wisdom of our age instead of becoming "fools for Christ's sake" (1 Cor. 4:10 NASB). Paul said he had "become as the scum of the world, the dregs of all things" (1 Cor. 4:13 NASB).

Following Christ calls for radical discipleship— denying self and discarding the wisdom of this world for the wisdom of God. Have you allowed God to disturb your comfort zone?

Spiritual Readiness

When I call to remembrance the genuine faith that is in you, which dwelt first in your grandmother Lois and your mother Eunice, and I am persuaded is in you also (2 Tim. 1:5).

ᵇ We all endure seasons of spiritual idleness when our service for Christ appears slack. Opportunities seem few; demand for our input is slight. If we allow such occasions to dull our spiritual fervor, however, we will not be ready to minister when the door of service opens.

Spiritual readiness in the dry season is necessary for usefulness later, meaning you cultivate your relationship with Christ Jesus through daily prayer and searching of the Scriptures. Your purpose is to know and glorify God. That should be your passion, regardless of your ministry opportunities.

Spiritual readiness also means you daily apply the truth you discover through fellowship with the Lord and study of the Scriptures. You apply publicly what God's Spirit teaches you in your private devotions.

You are faithful in the little things. Then when the demand arises, you will be fully prepared—equipped for the task through Christ's presence within you.

The Power of Your Personal Testimony

Men shall speak of the might of Your awesome acts,
And I will declare Your greatness (Ps. 145:6).

❧ Your personal testimony of knowing Christ as Savior and Lord is an effective tool for evangelism and edification. To many, the Bible is antiquated and irrelevant. But people can relate to what God has done, and is doing, in your life.

Whether your conversion to Christ was a quiet living room or Damascus Road experience is insignificant. What matters is that you had an encounter with a personal God that changed your way of thinking and your life.

That encounter is a tangible means of personalizing and manifesting the reality of Christ and His Word—one that the Holy Spirit can use to authenticate the message of the gospel. Even other Christians can be encouraged through your testimony. Many can identify with your struggle of unbelief and doubt. Still others can relate to your continuing discovery of God's truth as a growing Christian, motivating them to continue the race begun at salvation.

Never be shy about telling someone else what God has done for you. God may use it in ways you never dreamed.

A Light to the World

You are the light of the world. A city that is set on a hill cannot be hidden (Matt. 5:14).

❧ Most Christians are engaged in very ordinary occupations in everyday circumstances. But in each commonplace and average day, we have an opportunity to achieve greatness, to let the light of Jesus Christ illumine our usual circumstances.

Jesus said, "You are the light of the world."

"Me?" you reply. "Plain, simple, struggling me—the light of the world?"

Jesus is never wrong. You are the earthly radiance of the presence of Jesus Christ because the Light of the World, Jesus, indwells your spirit with His. The Light of life resides in you from the moment of salvation. It is the light of truth. It is the light of hope. It is the light of peace. It is the light of love. It is the light of joy. It is the light of confidence.

Why? Because Jesus is all of these things and more, your responsibility is to let your light shine before others (Matt. 5:16). Let the light out. Do not bottle it up in unbelief, irritability, doubt, anger, bitterness, and other such stifling emotions.

Jesus will make His presence known to others around you in a very real way. Just abide in Him daily, and He will make Himself known.

The Enthusiastic Christian

Knowing that whatever good anyone does, he will receive the same from the Lord, whether he is a slave or free (Eph. 6:8).

❧ Many fine, moral, nice people in the world bring good cheer to others, but leave no divine imprint. The interesting thing about Christians is that our light— our good works and words—is to shine in such a way so as to "glorify [our] Father in heaven" (Matt. 5:16).

Your light, your witness, should reflect on the person and character of Jesus Christ, attracting others to His uncommon presence. Your works should bring attention not to yourself but to God, casting His ways in sharp relief to the familiar ways of the world.

Your enthusiasm in your tasks should reflect your passion to serve God. That zeal should spring forth in the mundane projects, the obscure times, and the relatively boring jobs. Your enthusiasm points to the origin of the zest, a desire to glorify Christ in all you do.

Your light also shines uniquely when you do your work with excellence. You are faithful in the little things that others ignore; you go above the mediocre and walk the second mile.

Your enthusiasm and excellence in the familiar routine unveil the inner presence of Jesus Christ for the world to see.

Your Passing Opportunity

Whoever confesses Me before men, him I will also confess before My Father who is in heaven (Matt. 10:32).

❧ Today, as you shop at the grocery store, work in the office, volunteer at school, or do any other routine activity, you will encounter many different people. Each one is a unique individual with an astounding array of personal needs—love, money, friendship, wisdom, courage, among others.

But every human being has one need in common: a personal relationship with Jesus Christ—Savior, Lord, and Friend of all who believe in Him. The joyous truth is that every believer possesses the Person who can meet that universal need.

You may not be able to help people financially. You may not live in close proximity to establish friendships. You may not have the material resources to supply their practical needs. But you can introduce them to Jesus Christ, the only One who can provide for every need, meet every demand, care for every hurt.

Jesus is the Answer. If you know Him, you can tell others about Him in a variety of ways: over a cup of coffee, through a tract, a suggestion to attend church or listen to a religious broadcast.

Everybody needs the Lord. Share Him as His Spirit leads you, and He will meet their needs as no other can.

Essentials of a Fruitful Witness

"For all those things My hand has made,
And all those things exist,"
Says the LORD.
"But on this one will I look:
On him who is poor and of a contrite spirit,
And who trembles at My word" (Isa. 66:2).

❧ Humility is the key to an effective witness for Jesus Christ. You may think that you can dazzle a person into God's kingdom with your Bible knowledge and memorized verses. However, if you fail to have a humble spirit, God cannot bless your efforts.

People need to see Jesus Christ—not a perfect saint, but a Christian who has been saved by His grace and who wants to share a humble testimony with others. If you will open yourself up to be used of God for His witness, in His way, you will be surprised at the opportunities He will bring to you. Ask Him to give you basic tools from His Word. Lean on Him to provide the strength to overcome any fear the enemy may use to prevent you from telling others of His love.

There is only one message the world needs to hear: Jesus Christ our Savior, Jesus Christ our Lord, Jesus Christ our life, Jesus Christ our sufficiency for all things. May He lead you in your witness for Him today.

So Send I You

Jesus said to them again, "Peace to you! As the Father has sent Me, I also send you" (John 20:21).

❧ God gave Jesus a very clear mission—to seek and to save those separated from Him by sin. It was the same mission Christ gave His disciples, and it is the one He gives us today.

Many people spend a lifetime trying to understand their calling, but God's call is clear. We are to be missionaries of His love and grace to a world bound by sin and shame. When you accepted Christ's death as payment for your sins, you also accepted the Father's call—to tell others of His forgiveness. It may take you across the country, around the world, or across the office or neighborhood.

The mission and its message are clear—freedom from the penalty, power, and presence of sin for all who place their trust in Jesus Christ. Christ never calls you to fulfill His mission in your own strength. As the Father sent Jesus with a clear understanding of His purpose and power, He sends you with the same understanding.

Lack of knowledge of the gospel is the greatest hindrance to God's mission. Ask Christ to give you a love for His Word that comes from the Holy Spirit. The insight you gain will serve as a beacon of hope not only to you but also to those the Father brings your way. May you know the wonder of His call today.

Committed to the Task

Jesus said to him, "No one, having put his hand to the plow, and looking back, is fit for the kingdom of God" (Luke 9:62).

❧ Jesus was committed to the Father's mission, even to the point of death. If you plan to answer the call of Christ, you must be committed to His mission. Lack of commitment may cause you to waver, become fearful, and eventually quit. Peter sank while walking on the water because he took his eyes off the Savior and became consumed with his surroundings.

Jesus told His disciples that no one who puts his hands to the plow and then looks back at what might have been is fit for the kingdom of God. Commitment is everything to Him. If you are not fully committed to Christ, you will never be committed to His mission.

Many people fail to answer God's call because the commitment seems too great—the requirements too stiff. You may never understand God's motive in calling you to a certain task, but you can be sure He has a purpose and a wonderful plan in store for you. Obedience is always the prelude to blessing.

Jesus was and still is fully committed to you. Are you committed to Him and His call? If so, praise Him for His work in your life, and then ask Him to give you wisdom and insight into your personal mission.

God's Plan and Power

Now the LORD came and stood and called as at other times, "Samuel! Samuel!" And Samuel answered, "Speak, for Your servant hears" (1 Sam. 3:10).

❧ You have probably known people who insist on serving God on their own terms. Before they even ask God in prayer what He wants them to do, they already have their plans mapped out. Before long, otherwise good and noble projects go wrong, and they don't understand why. Charging ahead without seeking the Lord's will, or ignoring His counsel, almost always brings negative consequences.

Samuel learned how to listen to God's voice and how to respond. Just as Eli had told him, when Samuel heard God's call in the night, he answered, "Speak, for Thy servant is listening" (1 Sam. 3:10 NASB). Samuel was ready to hear and obey whatever his Master told him; he waited for the Lord's command.

Do you seek God's instruction, or do you try to do His work in your own strength? For whatever He asks you to do, He provides the plan and the power to accomplish it. God's work done God's way means sure success.

A Passion to Serve Him

My sheep hear My voice, and I know them, and they follow Me. And I give them eternal life, and they shall never perish; neither shall anyone snatch them out of My hand (John 10:27–28).

❧ The young convert shook his head in disbelief. He thought becoming a Christian would somehow inoculate him from future trouble. Christianity does not provide immunity from heartache and trouble. However, in the heartache, God promises never to leave us. His protection and wisdom are available to all who are His.

In 2 Corinthians 11, Paul provided an extensive list of the personal trials he faced as a result of his love for Christ. Several times he was beaten to the point of death. Many times he was rejected and ridiculed for his desire to further the kingdom of God.

What was the driving force behind his life? What kept Paul from giving up? A passion for God—the very thing that sustains you when fear and adversity threaten your existence.

A passion for God goes beyond fondness. It is a love for God that is constant, regardless of circumstances. With a passion for God you never want to walk away from what God has given you to do. But if you should, you know you can come home because God has a passion for you, and God's love never grows cold.

A Passion to Proclaim Him

Him we preach, warning every man and teaching every man in all wisdom, that we may present every man perfect in Christ Jesus (Col. 1:28).

❧ In Colossians 1:28, Paul wrote, "We proclaim [Christ]" (NASB). The word *proclaim* means "to tell others" about Jesus. But how can you effectively do this if your heart is divided and you lack a true passion for God?

The world is filled with various passions—a passion for sports, food, personal achievement, money, recognition—the list could go on. Many people reason that God is not interested in what they do outside church. But Jesus had a different answer: To love the Lord your God with all your heart is the greatest commandment (Matt. 22:36–37).

Do you have a true passion for God? Is He your first thought in the morning, your constant companion throughout the day, and your last thought at night? Do you consider what He wants for your life above your personal desires?

You may achieve good things, but you will never fully experience Christ until your passion is for Him and Him alone.

Stars and Servants

You, brethren, have been called to liberty; only do not use liberty as an opportunity for the flesh, but through love serve one another (Gal. 5:13).

❧ Philip Yancey, an insightful Christian author, reflected in a *Christianity Today* article on the discrepancy between those who bask in the limelight and those who toil in seeming obscurity:

> My career as a journalist has afforded me opportunities to interview diverse people. Looking back, I can roughly divide them into two types—servants and stars.
>
> The stars include NFL football greats, movie actors, music performers, famous authors, TV personalities, and the like. These are the ones who dominate our magazines and our television programs.
>
> I have also spent time with servants. People like Dr. Paul Brand who worked for twenty years among outcasts—leprosy patients, the poorest of the poor in rural India . . . Or relief workers in Somalia, the Sudan, Ethiopia, Bangladesh, or other such repositories of world-class suffering.
>
> But as I now reflect on the two groups—stars and servants—the servants clearly emerge as the favored ones, the graced ones. They work for low pay, long hours, and no applause, "wasting" their talents and skills among the poor.
>
> But somehow in this process of losing their lives, they have received the peace that is not of this world.

Stewards of God's Mysteries

The purpose of the commandment is love from a pure heart, from a good conscience, and from sincere faith (1 Tim. 1:5).

❧ Paul described both himself and Apollos in this humble way: "servants of Christ and stewards of the mysteries of God" (1 Cor. 4:1). That is, in essence, what every Christian is—regardless of the level of spiritual maturity. We are servants because Jesus is Lord and Master of all. Those who aspire to leadership in the body of Christ have a divine prerequisite: ever-increasing servanthood. None of us should labor with the idea that others will admire us. We are stewards because Jesus is the Owner and Giver of all: "For who regards you as superior? And what do you have that you did not receive? But if you did receive it, why do you boast as if you had not received it?" (1 Cor. 4:7 NASB).

Jesus has given us abundant and eternal life in His name. As our Maker and Redeemer, He has endowed us with natural and spiritual gifts. He has equipped us with the Holy Spirit and His Word. He teaches us, leads us, and reveals His ways to us. He is the Source of all. That removes all grounds for haughtiness and bragging in the Christian life.

Called to the Marketplace

Whatever you do, do it heartily, as to the Lord and not to men (Col. 3:23).

❧ In a watershed survey dealing with moral and ethical behavior for the *Wall Street Journal*, a 1983 Gallup Poll uncovered some astonishing results. The survey stated: "The results show the churched to feel somewhat more likely than the unchurched that charging a company for a cab ride is wrong, but other differences are of only marginal significance . . . In the case of other types of behavior—lying, cheating, and pilferage—the differences are not significant or of marginal significance." It's no wonder that the business world sees little compelling evidence that Christianity is a practical, valid faith for all of life, not just Sunday morning.

Because He is Lord of our lives, God's wisdom, grace, and counsel are available for all of life, making us salt and light through the methods and quality of our work. God has given work supreme dignity. It was His idea. He has called you to work. Whatever the nature of your job, the reality of your faith is communicated.

Christianity works in the workplace. Ask Christ to equip you to be His witness to your coworkers, and your job will become not just a career, but a calling.

Making Your Life Count

Having your conduct honorable among the Gentiles, that when they speak against you as evildoers, they may, by your good works which they observe, glorify God in the day of visitation (1 Peter 2:12).

❧ A great deception of our media-saturated age is that a person has to be prominent or visible to be influential. Jesus taught quite the contrary. Standing on a rural hillside with a few thousand farmers, fishermen, carpenters, and other men and women of humble background, He pronounced them as the "salt of the earth" and the "light of the world."

Jesus brings the same message to you. You are valuable and worthy in His eyes, created as His workmanship for a lifetime of good works that will demonstrate the reality of the kingdom of God to a blind and captive world.

Realize your worth in Christ. You were not created or saved by accident but by His design, to be used for His purposes, which will have eternal consequences.

Whoever you are, whatever you do, wherever you are, Christ can use you today. Accept your worth to Him and your value to others. Your life is a fragrance of the indwelling Christ.

Carry the Light

In Him was life, and the life was the light of men (John 1:4).

❧ John described Jesus as the Light of the World, for "in Him was life, and the life was the light of men" (John 1:4). In actuality, Christ was God's first missionary. He was the bearer of redemption, of sins forgiven, and of God's grace for all humanity. His words of acceptance and love moved men and women to immeasurable points of commitment to God. Their lives were changed, their hopes renewed, and their hearts made pure, all because they heard the gospel message and believed in God's Messenger.

When Jesus died on Calvary, His earthly mission was complete. Salvation's pathway was no longer closed. Instead, all of heaven was opened to everyone who would trust in God's Son.

As a Christian, you are His chosen light of hope to a world bound in the darkness of sin. You cannot escape the call of His commission. You may not be called to an overseas mission field, but as a child of God, you are called to carry the light of the gospel to those around you. You are a missionary to the people in your office, in your family, on the commuter train, on the airplane, and in the garden club. Wherever there is darkness, Jesus wants you to shine His light of love and salvation.

Will You Answer the Call?

You shall receive power when the Holy Spirit has come upon you; and you shall be witnesses to Me in Jerusalem, and in all Judea and Samaria, and to the end of the earth (Acts 1:8).

For a moment he studied the crowd moving toward the front of the church. Then with sweaty palms and a nervous feeling in the pit of his stomach, he stepped out into the aisle. As he walked to the front of the church, the words of "Have Thine Own Way" comforted him.

Standing at the altar, he suddenly felt a small hand slip inside his. In looking down he saw the face of his seven-year-old daughter. "I will go for Jesus, too, Daddy," she said and beamed a smile. As he lifted his eyes, he saw his wife holding their eighteen-month-old son. She said, "Darling, we'll all go for Him." He knew the moment meant total surrender to the will of God.

But so much had happened in the past. So many tears. So many words spoken in haste and anger. Could Jesus see past the years spent in sin and denial? Could God really be calling them to carry the light of His gospel halfway around the world?

Yes. God uses people with hearts turned toward Him. Past sins and failures are forgiven. He abides in the immediacy of the moment. When we open our hearts in obedient faith to His will, He uses us. Jesus has a job for you to do, and no one else can take your place. Will you go for Him? Will you answer His call?

August

THEME: The Fountain Gate

REPRESENTING: The work of the Holy Spirit

On the last day, that great day of the feast, Jesus stood and cried out, saying, "If anyone thirsts, let him come to Me and drink. He who believes in Me, as the Scripture has said, out of his heart will flow rivers of living water." But this He spoke concerning the Spirit (John 7:37–39).

The Holy Spirit

When the Helper comes, whom I shall send to you from the Father, the Spirit of truth who proceeds from the Father, He will testify of Me (John 15:26).

🕊️ Although the Holy Spirit is defined to a degree by His various roles—teacher, guide, and helper—His identity rests on three truths:

1. *The Holy Spirit is God.* In several instances, the Holy Spirit is referred to as "the Spirit of God."

2. *He is one with God, the third person of the Trinity.* As such, He possesses the inherent nature and character of God. The Greek word for "another" in John 14:16–17 is literally translated "another of the same kind." Thus, the Holy Spirit is God Himself, omnipotent (Job 33:4), omnipresent (Ps. 139:7–10), and omniscient (1 Cor. 2:10–12).

3. *Since the Holy Spirit is a person, He is God.* The Holy Spirit likewise is marked by a distinct personality. He is not an "it." He has a will (1 Cor. 12:11), emotions (Eph. 4:30), and intellect (Rom. 8:27).

As a person, the Holy Spirit can be resisted, lied to, and grieved. The Holy Spirit is life. The Holy Spirit helped birth the universe (Gen. 1:2). Christ was conceived by an act of the Holy Spirit. The believer is given God's life through His indwelling, and the abundant life is possible only through His activity.

The Holy Spirit's Identity

He answered and said to me:
"This is the word of the LORD to Zerubbabel:
'Not by might nor by power, but by My Spirit,'
Says the LORD of hosts" (Zech. 4:6).

❧ A sense of enigma often surrounds the biblical teaching on the Holy Spirit. Our concept of God the Father is firmly established. Our perception of the Son, Jesus Christ, is clear. But when it comes to identifying the Holy Spirit, our description and understanding are often muddled.

However, apart from a firm grasp of the Holy Spirit's identity and function, it is unlikely we will make any visible progress in the spiritual realm. Ignorance of His work and ministry has stymied the growth and joy of millions of Christians through the ages. Misconceptions of His activity have led equal numbers down the disillusioning path of false doctrine.

Defining Him in the context of personal experience has diluted and distorted His unchanging nature and function. Examining the Scriptures, you can discover the identity and work of the Holy Spirit. In the process, you can lay a foundation for a new dimension in Christian living that transforms your thoughts, motivations, and behavior through His supernatural influence.

The Advocate

And I will pray the Father, and He will give you another Helper, that He may abide with you forever (John 14:16).

❧ In John 14:16, Jesus called the Holy Spirit a Helper. In the Greek this word is *Parakletos*, or "Comforter." It suggests the giving of aid much like a legal counselor or advocate would do. The sense in which *Parakletos* is used means "to come alongside another while giving strength and encouraging support." The Holy Spirit is God's personal representative here on earth. He is the third person of the Trinity.

Jesus knew the void within the hearts of His disciples would be great after He returned to the Father. Therefore, God in His greatness and compassion sent the Holy Spirit to comfort the followers of Christ, and He is still with us today. He is our Guide to all truth and our personal Advocate and Comforter before the throne of God. This is your peace and strength—knowing that whatever you face, God faces it with you through the Holy Spirit.

The Essential Spirit

You are not in the flesh but in the Spirit, if indeed the Spirit of God dwells in you. Now if anyone does not have the Spirit of Christ, he is not His (Rom. 8:9).

🕊 A. T. Robertson writes in *Word Pictures in the New Testament:* "The entire earthly life of Jesus was bound up with the Holy Spirit from His birth to His death and resurrection." Seriously consider this truth: If the presence of the Holy Spirit was essential for the birth, ministry, and resurrection of God's Son, then how essential is the Spirit's presence in the believer's life?

Apart from the Holy Spirit's active participation, a person cannot be born again (John 3:5–6). The Holy Spirit's presence authenticates an individual's membership in God's family (Rom. 8:9).

The power of God's Spirit is the only means by which you can live a consistently productive spiritual life. The Spirit of God produces Christlikeness, enabling you to experience the supernatural life of Christ in your practical world of relationships, obligations, conflicts, and challenges (Gal. 5:16).

Jesus was conceived, anointed for ministry, and raised by the power of the Holy Spirit. Likewise, your spiritual conception, life, and eternal destiny are all secured by the Holy Spirit. Are you depending daily on Him?

Unconditional Presence

Do you not know that you are the temple of God and that the Spirit of God dwells in you? (1 Cor. 3:16).

❧ The incarnate Jesus was Immanuel—God with us. As His crucifixion neared, He spent His last hours with the disciples explaining that the gift of the Holy Spirit would be the divine agent of God's presence following His death and ascension.

Because you are a believer in Jesus Christ, God is with you always through the indwelling presence of the Holy Spirit. You are never alone. You are never helpless. You are never comfortless. The presence of the Holy Spirit is unceasing. Once you are saved, His residence is permanent. The Holy Spirit will never be taken from you.

The presence of the Holy Spirit is unconditional. His presence does not depend on your performance. When the joy of the Lord fills you to the rim or when the depths of despair overwhelm you, He is there.

Knowing that, you should feel great security in the Spirit's unceasing and unconditional presence. It should also encourage you. Through the Holy Spirit, God is intimately involved with every detail of your existence.

The Divine Helper

As they ministered to the Lord and fasted, the Holy Spirit said, "Now separate to Me Barnabas and Saul for the work to which I have called them" (Acts 13:2).

❧ A friend asks you to pray for her deteriorating marriage—you really do not know how to pray.

A telephone call comes in the night with distressing news about your father's illness—the words are lost in tears.

When you do not know what to say, how to pray, or what the needs are, the Holy Spirit is your greatest ally.

In His omniscience—He knows the need.

In His omnipotence—He is able to help.

In His omnipresence—He is involved in their lives.

The Holy Spirit also knows the mind of the Father. He can pray according to the will of God for every person, in every circumstance. Your part is to present the person or petition to the Father, admitting your ignorance and helplessness.

You must also deeply desire God's answer for the dilemma. When you do, the Spirit of God can take your vague requests and intercede before the Father on others' behalf (and yours). If something has baffled or perplexed you, trust in the supernatural, intercessory ministry of the Holy Spirit.

The Intercessor

There is a spirit in man,
And the breath of the Almighty gives him understanding (Job
32:8).

❧ Catherine Marshall in her book *The Helper* provided keen insight into the Holy Spirit's intercessory role:

Unquestionably, all of us need massive help with praying aright. So set is our flesh against praying at all that the Helper's first task is to create in us even the basic desire to pray. He is the One Who also spotlights for us the prayer-need or topic for prayer by creating a "concern" within us.

Then the Helper has to uncover for us the essence, or kernel, of what it is we really want. Usually, the true desire at the heart of our prayer petition is buried under debris that obscures and muddles the real issue.

It is also the Helper's task to show us the blockages in the way of a given prayer-petition: any self-seeking, our desire to control, any resentments and unconfessed sin, etc.

He is also the One who gives us His own prayer faith; also His fervor to replace our tepid love and caring.

As we recognize our ignorance about praying aright and our helplessness, and actively seek the Spirit's help, our prayer life becomes the anteroom to amazing adventure.

Quenching the Spirit

Do not quench the Spirit (1 Thess. 5:19).

❧ The fire of the Spirit burns continuously to work the will of the Father. However, His flame is not often seen in our behavior because of a "quenching" of His activity. The Spirit can be resisted. His promptings can be ignored. His inner stirrings can be doused.

How do you quench the Spirit?

The Spirit is quenched when you fail to spend consistent time in God's Word. The Scriptures were authored by men under the inspiration of the Holy Spirit. The primary way that the Spirit communicates to you is through the Bible. How can you hear His voice, understand His ways, or carry out His desires if you neglect His Word?

The Spirit is also quenched when you stubbornly cling to a bad habit, a willful sin, or a carnal desire. The Spirit seeks to make you holy. That is why He is the *Holy* Spirit. Holiness, however, is not attained unilaterally. It involves your cooperation and your obedience to His cleansing and conviction.

Are you resisting Him at a point? Have you turned a deaf ear to His urgings? His fullness, blessing, and power are yours the instant you obey.

The Voice of His Spirit

It is said:
"Today, if you will hear His voice,
Do not harden your hearts as in the rebellion" (Heb. 3:15).

❧ The Holy Spirit nudges you to avoid gossip and grumbling. You listen, but fail to obey. He brings Scriptures to your mind repeatedly; you are convicted, but gradually lapse into your habit. Over time, your spiritual sensitivity is dulled. The Word of God no longer penetrates your soul, much less brings pangs of conscience.

A hardened heart and numbed conscience are the dangerous consequences of regularly muffling the Holy Spirit's persistent voice. If you procrastinate or have disobeyed so consistently that God's Word no longer convicts or delights you, then you are in the perilous process of quenching the Spirit.

Quickly repent. Confess your sin, your habit, your neglect, and thank God for His restored fellowship. Surrender your rights to His lordship, asking Him to shape you into His image. Listen and respond instantly to the Spirit's voice.

Abiding in the Vine

I am the vine, you are the branches. He who abides in Me, and I in him, bears much fruit; for without Me you can do nothing (John 15:5).

➤ Have you considered why a peach tree bears peaches, not apples, or why a pear tree bears pears, not bananas? It is because the life of the fruit is inseparably bound up in the tree itself. The sap that flows through the vine and into the branches determines the identity.

Just as surely, God's life within each believer produces Christlike character. We are the branches that live in union with the Vine, Jesus Christ.

The life within that determines the godly fruit you bear is the Holy Spirit. He is the divine sap that seeks to reproduce the spiritual qualities of godliness.

You can be kind to ungrateful people because the Holy Spirit is unfailingly kind. You can love all people because the Holy Spirit is love. You can be patient in trials because the Holy Spirit has boundless patience.

"I want to experience the life of the Holy Spirit, but I cannot. I try, but I fail!" you exclaim.

Do not despair. Failure is the first step to victory. Abiding in the Vine, allowing the Holy Spirit to reproduce Christ's character, begins with humble surrender and dependence.

Christlike Character

I say then: Walk in the Spirit, and you shall not fulfill the lust of the flesh (Gal. 5:16).

🐦 Notice Jesus' words when He described the abiding life:

"If anyone does not abide in Me . . ."
"If you abide in Me, and My words abide in you . . ."
"If you keep My commandments . . ."

Bearing Christlike character is not automatic. You are in union with the Vine and indwelt by His Spirit, but the process of developing godly fruit is conditional.

Christ's character is reproduced in you as you not only live by the Spirit, but also "walk by the Spirit" (Gal. 5:25 NASB). "Walking by the Spirit" is consciously depending on the power of the Holy Spirit. Dependence on the Holy Spirit is unabashed anticipation that He will conform you to the image of Christ.

"Walking by the Spirit" is turning over each area of your personality to His control. You do not become Christlike all at once. It is a process that allows the Spirit of God to transform your thoughts and conduct. The Holy Spirit will not overwhelm you. Rather, He will reveal a specific area that He desires to change. Your responsibility is to obey at each step.

The Giver of Gifts

In fact the body is not one member but many (1 Cor. 12:14).

❧ Imagine that someone asked you to build a home and provided you with the architect's drawing and all the necessary building materials: bricks, wiring, Sheetrock, and so forth. Only the proper tools were missing—no hammer, nails, saw, or pliers.

Sometimes, the Christian life can seem as frustrating. God's Word tells us what to do—outlines His plans for living—but we do not seem able to get the job done.

At this juncture, we must depend on the indispensable ministry of the Holy Spirit. As our divine Helper, God's Spirit gives us the tools to accomplish the Father's will in one significant area—spiritual gifts.

Just as there are a variety of workers involved in building a home—plumbers, electricians, roofers, framers, carpenters—so there are a variety of Christians involved in building up the body of Christ. God has a place for you in His church. He has a job for you to do. He has provided you with the heavenly tools to do it right. Do you know your spiritual gift? Are you enjoying your part in building His body, using His special enablement?

Your Spiritual Gift

Having then gifts differing according to the grace that is given to us, let us use them (Rom. 12:6).

🕊 Discovering your spiritual gift is the first step toward a lifetime of rewarding service in God's kingdom. This discovery is not mysterious, arduous, or convoluted. God does not work to confuse you. He wants you to know and exercise your spiritual gift.

Your spiritual gift (or gifts) is usually in accord with your unique set of personal inclinations. If you like helping others, service is probably your motivational gift. If you enjoy study and investigation, teaching is more than likely your gift. If others consistently benefit from your counsel and correction, the gift of exhortation is a good place to start in your search.

The second best indicator of your spiritual gift is the verification of others. If you like teaching, but no one learns, you had better reconsider. If you enjoy leading, but no one follows, leadership and administration are not your calling.

Ask God today to reveal your spiritual gift or gifts. Examine your likes and dislikes, and seek the input of others. Above all, remember your gift is given and determined by the Spirit and is to be used to bring glory to God.

The Power of the Spirit

You shall receive power when the Holy Spirit has come upon you;
and you shall be witnesses to Me in Jerusalem, and in all Judea
and Samaria, and to the end of the earth (Acts 1:8).

❧ Immediately before Jesus' ascension, the disciples eagerly asked the resurrected Savior His intentions for Israel: "Lord, is it at this time You are restoring the kingdom to Israel?" (Acts 1:6 NASB).

Jesus never answered their query, informing them instead of the imminent, personal ministry of the Holy Spirit (Acts 1:8).

We all have piercing questions we would like answered. But we are not to be overly occupied with them. Our real need is for power to enjoy and experience the abundant Christian life. Our most pressing demand is the divine enabling to know and follow Jesus Christ.

Jesus made it clear. What the apostles needed and what we need today is the power of the Holy Spirit.

Are you experiencing the power of the Holy Spirit on a consistent basis? Are you aware of His equipping and enabling in matters that are too difficult for you?

As God's child, you are indwelt by the Holy Spirit. He will release His power through you to meet every demand, every problem, every emergency, every circumstance. Just call on His name.

A Supernatural Tool

That He would grant you, according to the riches of His glory, to be strengthened with might through His Spirit in the inner man (Eph. 3:16).

❧ As Great Britain faced the German might alone in the initial stages of World War II, Prime Minister Sir Winston Churchill sent this urgent but concise message to President Franklin Roosevelt: "Give us the tools, and we will finish the job."

The power of the Holy Spirit is the supernatural tool God has given to equip and enable each believer. The power of the Holy Spirit is to do the work God calls you to accomplish. Serving others, loving even your enemies, building up one another in the faith, sharing Christ, and exercising your spiritual gifts are possible only through the Holy Spirit's enabling ministry. Trying to do such tasks in your own wisdom and strength and by your own methodology will eventually lead to failure and burnout.

The power of the Holy Spirit is also available for you to become the person God wants you to be. How can you possibly be loving, kind, gentle, patient, joyous, self-controlled, or peaceful apart from the Spirit's help?

Depend daily on Him, and the task of becoming Christlike and building His kingdom can be achieved.

Walking in the Spirit

He who sows to his flesh will of the flesh reap corruption, but he who sows to the Spirit will of the Spirit reap everlasting life (Gal. 6:8).

❧ You are driving on a long trip to visit your folks for Thanksgiving. In the backseat, friction is rising between your ten-year-old and twelve-year-old. You have a decision. Will you lose your temper and discipline the children, or will you firmly correct them with your emotions under the Spirit's control?

Such are the constant choices each individual makes to "walk in the Spirit." It is not a mystical experience but practical submission to God's will in everyday circumstances. Walking in the Spirit is thus a cultivated lifestyle, learning to act and react under His direction and influence rather than being controlled by temperament or personality.

Each day brings increasing cooperation with the Spirit's will and power. You can walk in the Spirit one trusting step at a time. Begin with the next decision you must make.

Tenets of a Spiritual Walk

That you may walk worthy of the Lord, fully pleasing Him, being fruitful in every good work and increasing in the knowledge of God (Col. 1:10).

🕊 Walking in the Spirit certainly is not as simple as one, two, three; but a pyramid of biblical truth can help you keep step with His cadence.

When you walk in the Spirit, you are consistently reading and hearing God's Word and obeying His commands. You progressively discover what the spirit of truth reveals through the Scriptures.

When you walk in the Spirit, you are doing what God says to do and how He says to do it. Learning God's methods comes only through systematic, persistent study of God's Word. It is not enough to read His truth. You must investigate, explore, and examine His principles.

You also walk in the Spirit when you do what God says, how He says to achieve it, and why He says to accomplish it. You apply the why through deliberate meditation on God's Word. You read and study, but then you delight in, revel in, and ponder the awesome truths designed to glorify Christ that it reveals.

Keep these cornerstone tenets in focus each day, and walking in the Spirit will become natural for you.

In Step with the Spirit

If we live in the Spirit, let us also walk in the Spirit (Gal. 5:25).

❧ Have you ever held someone's hand as you walked along together? You surely noticed how important it is to maintain the same stride. You can't walk too slowly and you can't walk too fast, at least not without pulling your hand away.

That is what Galatians 5:25 is talking about when it says "walk in the Spirit." The New International Version captures the original Greek flavor of the word *walk* here: "Since we live by the Spirit, let us keep in step with the Spirit." The word picture is one of "walking in line with." When you are not following your fleshly urges to walk at your own pace, you feel the direct guidance of the Holy Spirit step-by-step along the way.

When you walk in harmony with the Spirit, the fruit of this relationship is evident. It makes sense that the fruit of the Spirit is the subject of other verses of Galatians 5. Which of these do you see in your attitudes and behavior: love, joy, peace, patience, kindness, goodness, faithfulness, gentleness, and self-control? It is truly an awesome list. As you think through these attributes, it's crucial to remember that they are not products of a decision to try harder. God keeps your feet on His good path when you keep in step with Him.

The Pursuit of Holiness

God did not call us to uncleanness, but in holiness (1 Thess. 4:7).

❧ You are born again by God's Spirit when you believe in Christ's atonement for your sins. That is salvation, a singular decision with eternal permanence.

You are also sanctified by the same Spirit of God. But unlike salvation, sanctification is a lifelong process. In *The Pursuit of Holiness,* Jerry Bridges describes the joint venture of holy living:

> The farmer knows that unless he diligently pursues his responsibilities to plow, plant, fertilize, and cultivate, he cannot expect a harvest at the end of the season. In a sense he is in a partnership with God and he will reap its benefits only when he has fulfilled his own responsibilities. Farming is a joint venture between God and the farmer. The farmer cannot do what God must do and God will not do what the farmer should do.
>
> We can say just as accurately that the pursuit of holiness is a joint venture between God and the Christian. No one can attain any degree of holiness without God working in his life; but just as surely, no one will attain it without effort on his own part.

The Change Agent

As newborn babes, desire the pure milk of the word, that you may grow thereby (1 Peter 2:2).

❧ The moment you embrace Christ as Savior you become holy and blameless in God's sight; your sins are forgiven by the blood of Christ. Yet salvation is only the starting block for a life of holiness. Your holy state, or position, as a new creature in Christ must be continually appropriated.

As you grow in holiness, you demonstrate the reality of your new identity as a saint, or "holy one." Although you must apply all your faculties to experience growth in holiness, the Holy Spirit is always the Change Agent for holy living. External observance of religious traditions will not make you holy. Good works will not make you holy. Avoidance of certain activities will not make you holy.

Do you want to be holy? Remember that God has already accepted you as His holy child, and then depend on the Holy Spirit to dynamically and continuously make you a partaker of God's divine, holy nature.

The Teacher

I will instruct you and teach you in the way you should go;
I will guide you with My eye (Ps. 32:8).

❧ The most vital area of truth into which the Holy Spirit guides you is the knowledge of God Himself. His holiness, love, faithfulness, wrath, judgment, mercy, grace, patience, power, and numerous other attributes are unveiled for you. Without the Spirit's aid you could never see God for who He is.

The Spirit also reveals the truth about humankind. The Spirit of God convicts the unbeliever of sin and the estrangement from God. The Holy Spirit underscores human depravity and the desperate need for a Savior. Apart from the Spirit's enlightenment, you are blinded by pride and conceit. After you become a Christian, the Spirit continues His ministry of conviction and illumination, not to condemn, but to enlighten and correct.

In addition, the Holy Spirit highlights God's truth about His specific instructions for living. He clearly shows you the pattern for family harmony, the proper motives for business, the guidelines for getting along with neighbors and enemies, and the principles for ethical and moral conduct. Let the Holy Spirit guide you into His truth for your special need today.

A Common Objective

God did not send His Son into the world to condemn the world, but that the world through Him might be saved (John 3:17).

❧ C. S. Lewis wrote in *Mere Christianity* that God has a common objective in each Christian's life:

> Salvation is the changing from being confident about our own efforts to the state in which we despair of doing anything for ourselves and leave it to God. I know the words "leave it to God" can be misunderstood, but they must stay for the moment. The sense in which a Christian leaves it to God is that he puts all his trust in Christ: trusts that Christ will somehow perfect human obedience which He carried out from His birth to His crucifixion: that Christ will make the man more like Himself and, in a sense, make good his deficiencies.
>
> In Christian language, He will share His sonship with us, will make us, like Himself, sons of God.

This is what God is up to in good and bad, adventure and drudgery, favor and misfortune. He wants you to be like Christ, and He equips you with the Holy Spirit to make you progressively so.

The Guide

All these things happened to them as examples, and they were written for our admonition, upon whom the ends of the ages have come (1 Cor. 10:11).

❧ A major function of the Holy Spirit is to guide God's children. But too often the leadership of the Spirit is ascribed to methods and sources of which the Father has no part.

In *Knowing God*, J. I. Packer helps us to understand the fundamental error and make the proper course correction:

> Earnest Christians seeking guidance often go wrong about it. They look for a will-o'-the-wisp; they overlook the guidance that is ready to hand, and lay themselves open to all sorts of delusion.
>
> Their basic mistake is to think of guidance as essentially inward prompting by the Holy Spirit, apart from the written Word.
>
> The true way to honor the Holy Spirit as our guide is to honor the Holy Scriptures through which He guides us. The fundamental guidance which God gives to shape our lives . . . is not a matter of inward promptings apart from the Word but of the pressure on our consciences of the portrayal of God's character and will in the Word. . . .
>
> The Spirit leads within the limits which the Word sets, not beyond them.

Facing the Future

You are my rock and my fortress;
Therefore, for Your name's sake,
Lead me and guide me (Ps. 31:3).

❧ Each Christian has an infallible guide within, the person of the Holy Spirit. He is responsible to navigate you in God's direction.

You are completely ignorant of the future, but the Holy Spirit is all-knowing. He knows how your decisions today fit into His will for your tomorrows. The Holy Spirit wants to guide you into a more intimate relationship with Christ. His express purpose is to glorify the Son of God (John 14:26). He also desires to guide you into the truth of God. The truth sets you free, and God's Word is truth. It should come as no surprise then that the Spirit uses Scripture as His primary tool of guidance.

Do not worry or fret. Gather information, pray, search the Word, and ask God to lead you. He will not fail you.

The Power Within You

God has chosen the foolish things of the world to put to shame the wise, and God has chosen the weak things of the world to put to shame the things which are mighty (1 Cor. 1:27).

❧ God has equipped you for every good work. The presence of the Holy Spirit is His guarantee that no matter what you face, He is committed to providing the power and strength you need to accomplish the task, get through the hurt, and end up victorious in Him.

D. L. Moody had only a fifth-grade education, but he became one of the greatest evangelists of our time. He was never ordained to the ministry, yet God used him to lead thousands to the saving knowledge of Jesus Christ. The book *More Than Conquerors* tells us that "the evangelist spoke to at least 1.5 million in London during four months in 1875, long before radio and television."

God chooses the weak things to shame those who think they are strong (1 Cor. 1:27–29). There is only one way God can be glorified in your life, and that is through your willingness to lay aside your ability, talent, and personal desires in order to follow Him in obedience. Sacrifice and submission lead to a life of tremendous hope, freedom, and eternal joy.

The Power to Stand

Peter, standing up with the eleven, raised his voice and said to them, "Men of Judea and all who dwell in Jerusalem, let this be known to you, and heed my words" (Acts 2:14).

❧ The night of the Lord's Supper, Peter told Jesus: "Lord, with You I am ready to go both to prison and to death!" (Luke 22:33 NASB). A short time later as Jesus struggled in prayer in the Garden of Gethsemane, Peter could not stay awake long enough to pray for the One he called Master. With the betrayal and Jesus' arrest, Peter found himself hovering beside a small courtyard fire outside Caiaphas's house. There three times he denied knowing Jesus.

Hours earlier, Peter said he would die for Jesus. Yet when the time came for him to stand beside the Lord, he denied knowing Him. It was not within Peter's ability to withstand such an attack of the enemy. Jesus knew Peter would rely on his own ability and fail.

In the book of Acts, Peter was completely transformed. God's Spirit was alive within him. The power you have in Christ is all you need to stand securely in the midst of the fiercest battle, the deepest sorrow, the longest wait. What Peter could not do on his own, he did mightily in the Spirit of God, and you can too!

The Fruit of the Spirit

(For the fruit of the Spirit is in all goodness, righteousness, and truth), finding out what is acceptable to the Lord (Eph. 5:9–10).

❧ What kinds of sounds do you hear in a grape arbor or other fruit orchard? You can probably hear birds chirping, the wind rustling through leaves, and many other usual outdoor sounds.

What you do not hear is the sound of the vines or trees groaning and straining. The plants are not laboring to produce their fruit; the fruit comes out of their branches naturally as a part of the growing process. The vine does not have to concentrate on producing grapes. When the vine is healthy and has all the water and nutrients it needs, the grapes come forth.

The secret to fruit producing is as basic for you as it is for a real grapevine: stay planted in the Vine, and focus all of your energy and attention on being there, or abiding, in Christ. Worship Him, praise Him, meditate on His words, seek solitude in Him, and let yourself be absorbed into His purposes. Your fruit is a direct reflection of the quality of your relationship with Christ.

Pruning the Branches

Search me, O God, and know my heart;
Try me, and know my anxieties (Ps. 139:23).

❧ If we are honest, we must admit that at least subconsciously, if not overtly, we prefer the pleasant over the painful, the comfortable over the distressful. Despite this decidedly normal human disposition, we will stumble badly through the Christian journey if we adopt these longings as our chief aim.

Christ's goal for your life transcends this limited perspective. He has something far more sublime in mind for you—to make you productive in the work of His kingdom. This involves a process Christ termed *pruning*, a continual trimming of your character and habits that are unproductive for your personal growth as a believer.

It can be painful at times, even severe, when the pruning lops off sensitive areas. But whatever God sees as detrimental to your fruitfulness and well-being, He will seek to sever. The tools of Providence may be sharp, but loving hands hold them.

The Liberty of the Spirit

Stand fast therefore in the liberty by which Christ has made us free, and do not be entangled again with a yoke of bondage (Gal. 5:1).

❧ In every dimension of our lives, the Holy Spirit releases power within us to be witnesses to God's truth, and only by submitting to the Lord's leadership through the Spirit do we find wholeness.

Jack Hayford observes in *The Power and Blessing:*

In the judgment of some, "a life of submission" sounds like a page out of a handbook for membership in a religious order . . . In fact, in much of today's church, many have almost sanctified the notion of autonomy, of independence, of "I can do just about whatever I want, because of my freedom in Christ."

In terms of spiritual reality, we are made free. But our liberty in Christ isn't a program of perpetuating self-rule in the soul. Our "freedom" is (1) to free us from practicing sin, (2) to free us from smallness of soul, and (3) to free us from a "Lone-Ranger" order of independence which proposes "me" as the single-handed controller of everything in my life.

The spirit of submission, lived out in biblical terms, proposes that God could, in fact, use other people to teach me . . . I'm exposing myself to the possibility that at times these "others" will adjust and correct me in the spirit of love.

Your Thought Life

The weapons of our warfare are not carnal but mighty in God for pulling down strongholds (2 Cor. 10:4).

The power of the imagination—it has created the greatest inventions of all time, the most heartwarming stories, and the solutions to countless everyday problems. The imagination can also be a source of trouble, even as every aspect of your life is touched by the urge to give in to sin. Have you ever found yourself contemplating ideas you knew were not pleasing to the Lord? What was your response?

The Lord knows all too well how your thought life can lead you astray of His purposes and desires. That is why the Bible has so much to say about where you allow your mind to be and the concepts with which you fill it. If you struggle in this area—and we all do—write down the following verses and commit them to memory: 1 Peter 1:13 and Philippians 4:8. Then when certain alluring notions threaten to overcome your thoughts, you will have God's truth to conquer them.

Controlled by the Spirit

Do not be drunk with wine, in which is dissipation; but be filled with the Spirit (Eph. 5:18).

❧ Many people find it important to maintain the feeling that they are in control of their lives and all decisions, and the chance of losing any of that autonomy is scary.

Yet when the Bible speaks of being controlled by the Holy Spirit, the meaning is entirely different. Being controlled by the Spirit is not something to be afraid of; you do not become a robotic creature unable to think or act independently. The Spirit indwells you and fills your spirit, but He never insists on control. In fact, by deciding not to listen and pursuing your own course, you can effectively drown out His gentle voice.

Paul told the Ephesians: "Be filled with the Spirit, speaking to one another in psalms and hymns and spiritual songs, singing and making melody in your heart to the Lord." Yielding to the Spirit's control results in beautiful praise to God and a spirit filled with joy and renewed purpose, and that's nothing to be afraid of.

September

THEME: The Prison Gate

REPRESENTING: Deliverance

I will go before you
And make the crooked places straight;
I will break in pieces the gates of bronze
And cut the bars of iron (Isa. 45:2).

Birth Pangs of a Miracle

My soul clings to the dust;
Revive me according to Your word (Ps. 119:25).

❧ We usually do not seek freedom until we are miserable in our bondage. Sin's pleasures can control us for many years, decades, even a lifetime. It is not until we realize the extent to which sin controls us that we cry out for release.

Some would say it is too late to be delivered from the bondage of such masters as lust, alcohol, drugs, fear, anger, and/or inferiority. But with God our helplessness is our first step on the road to freedom.

Too many of us do not fully receive our freedom in Christ because we will do almost anything to avoid such a predicament. We enjoy the feeling of control. We detest the notions that we cannot stop our drinking, cannot halt our immorality, cannot conquer our fears, cannot heal our marriages, and cannot discipline our children.

Perhaps you view helplessness as weakness—as admission that you are inadequate to solve your dilemma or to do anything apart from Christ, who said, "Apart from Me you can do nothing" (John 15:5 NASB). But in God's eyes and along His route to spiritual freedom, your feelings of helplessness are the birth pangs of a miracle.

Freedom Worth Pursuing

God forbid that I should boast except in the cross of our Lord Jesus Christ, by whom the world has been crucified to me, and I to the world (Gal. 6:14).

❧ The winds of freedom blow hard in our world today. Politically oppressed, Communist bloc countries continue to demolish imprisoning walls and topple the icons of brutal dictators. Countries are dropping the shackles of ideologies that have padlocked individual freedom for the sake of state control. Yet even when freedom is achieved, the once golden promises of liberty are tainted by painful new realities. Democracy is not a panacea. New leaders are not messiahs. The gains of social crusades are often short-lived. In each case, freedom is defined as what allows a nation, a group, or a person the right to pursue and obtain selected goals. It involves the removal of external barriers to self-fulfillment.

But true freedom is spiritual, within the human heart. It is the removal of the universal oppressor—sin—whose great infection lies in the bosom of every man and woman. It cannot be earned or legislated; it can be received only as a gift from God.

God's freedom, liberation of the soul from sin's tyranny, can be enjoyed behind barbed-wire walls, within prison camps, or in the midst of injustice. It cannot be stifled, regulated, or imprisoned. That is freedom worth pursuing.

The Great Emancipator

The thief does not come except to steal, and to kill, and to destroy.
I have come that they may have life, and that they may have it more
abundantly (John 10:10).

❧ Christ Jesus was and is the Great Emancipator. He came to set men and women free, not from political or military tyranny but from the far worse grip of sin. When you embraced Christ as your Savior, Lord, and Life, you were liberated immediately from the penalty of sin—eternal death. Its mastery over you was shattered instantaneously and permanently.

That was only the beginning. Christ came not only to loose you from sin's penalty but also to unshackle you from its power that still seeks to enslave your emotions, will, and personality. "I came that they might have life, and might have it abundantly," Jesus declared (John 10:10 NASB). Was He only joking? Did He really mean that you can attain a life that is free from the chains of habits and fears and worries?

Did Christ ever speak a false word? No, He wants you to be free to experience the most wonderful life you can imagine—His life expressed through your personality. Are you ready to learn how?

Three Dimensions of Freedom

I know that the LORD saves His anointed;
He will answer him from His holy heaven
With the saving strength of His right hand (Ps. 20:6).

🕊 In his book *Living Free in Christ,* Neil Anderson discusses our freedom as God's children:

> *First, we are free from the law.* The law says "don't do this" in order to be righteous, but Galatians 5:1 says, "it is for freedom that Christ has set us free. Stand firm, then, and do not let yourselves be burdened again by a yoke of slavery."
>
> *Second, we are free from the past.* "Because you are sons, God sent the Spirit of His Son into our hearts, the Spirit who calls out, 'Abba, Father.' So you are no longer a slave, but a son." As children of God, we are no longer products of our past; we have a new heritage.
>
> *Third, we can be free from sin.* The only means by which we are capable of doing this is to realize that we have been bought with a price and that the Holy Spirit now lives in us, enabling us to live our lives for Him, free from sin's bondage.
>
> But the choice is still ours. Say no to sin, and you will experience a freedom that our lost world can only dream of knowing.

How Freedom Comes

So that you come short in no gift, eagerly waiting for the revelation of our Lord Jesus Christ, who will also confirm you to the end, that you may be blameless in the day of our Lord Jesus Christ (1 Cor. 1:7–8).

❧ Sin had infiltrated the ranks of the Corinthian church. Members of the congregation knew of the situation, yet they had done nothing to right it. Paul wrote his letter with the purpose of correcting the sin before it became a stumbling block.

But instead of condemning and lashing out at the church, notice how Paul chose to address the congregation: "To the church of God which is at Corinth, to those who have been sanctified in Christ Jesus, saints by calling, with all who in every place call upon the name of our Lord Jesus Christ" (1 Cor. 1:2 NASB). Paul expressed the truth about God's love for His people. He reminded them of their position in Christ and how they had been sanctified and separated by their faith.

It was also a reminder of God's personal love for us. Each of us at some point will fall short of God's plan. This, in fact, is the very definition of sin: missing the mark that God has set as a standard for us to live by. When sin enters our lives, we suffer.

Freedom comes when you turn to Him and ask Him to apply His forgiveness to your life.

Freedom Through the Power of the Spirit

Jesus said to him, "Thomas, because you have seen Me, you have believed. Blessed are those who have not seen and yet have believed" (John 20:29).

❧ One of the reasons Jesus came to earth, apart from humankind's need of salvation, was to correct our view of God. He came to change our perspective of our Father's love. The disciples had tremendous freedom in His presence. They witnessed His miracles and felt secure whenever they were with Him.

After the Crucifixion, their view changed. Suddenly fear gripped their hearts. It was only at the sight of Jesus that their fears subsided. One of the greatest truths you can learn, in addition to God's eternal, unconditional love for you, is that He will never leave you.

The freedom the disciples gained in the presence of the risen Lord is something you, too, can experience. Christ lives in you through the power of the Holy Spirit. Every need, every question you have, can be answered. He is available and longs for you to come to Him. What glorious freedom this brings! Someone is near who cares about your every struggle.

The Truth That Sets You Free

Enter by the narrow gate; for wide is the gate and broad is the way that leads to destruction, and there are many who go in by it (Matt. 7:13).

❧ A highway designed to exacting specifications gives us the freedom to drive. Medicine formulated with precise chemical components gives us the freedom to enjoy its benefits. In every instance the truth—accurate, unbending—is the foundation for lasting success.

It is the same with the spiritual realm. The eternal, unchanging, applicable, divine truth sets us free to enjoy God and experience His blessings. That truth is Christ and His Word. When you have Christ within and when you abide in (live in, meditate on, internally assimilate) His unerring Word of truth, you are on the road to freedom in your emotions, will, intellect, family, job, relationships, and future.

Your constant battle is against the deceiver, the devil. His tactics always are to distort and twist the truth. He is the cursed liar who seeks to enslave the inner person. The devil tells you, "You are no good. God cannot possibly be pleased with you. You will never amount to anything. You cannot measure up to others. You cannot overcome this habit." This master liar can be overcome only by the truth of God as revealed in His Word and applied by the Holy Spirit.

The Foundation for Freedom

Behold, You desire truth in the inward parts,
And in the hidden part You will make me to know wisdom
(Ps. 51:6).

❧ God's truth, woven richly into your innermost being, is the foundation for freedom. God wants His truth to sink deep to establish His perfect wisdom in your mind and heart.

When you understand the truth of your position in Christ, you understand that you are sealed by the Holy Spirit—that you are secure in the family of God. No act or thought can ever alienate you from the love of God. You belong to Christ; You are His and He is yours.

When you understand the truth of your personhood in Christ, your feelings of inferiority can dissolve. You are of infinite worth to God, who died on your behalf. It is not your income level or social status that determines your value; it is God's estimation of your life. You are so valuable to Him that He desires your company for all eternity.

When you understand the truth of your possessions in Christ, any incompetency or inadequacy you may feel is overcome. You have everything you need in the indwelling Christ. He makes you adequate for every demand.

Embracing God's Truth

You were once darkness, but now you are light in the Lord. Walk as children of light (Eph. 5:8).

❧ Satan is always at work, seeking to blind the minds of men and women. His darkest work is to obscure our lost condition caused by sin and our need for Jesus Christ as our Savior, Lord, and Life. When he fails in this endeavor, he does not retire. Rather, Satan is operating constantly to cause us to exchange "the truth of God for a lie" (Rom. 1:25 NASB). We do so when we allow the wrong thoughts of our childhood years to influence us.

Perhaps you could never please your father. Now you have a difficult time understanding how you can please your heavenly Father.

You exchange the truth of God for a lie when you adopt the distorted cultural views of society rather than the authority of the Scriptures. The world endorses the concept of rights; God talks about responsibility. The world sees sex as a mere physiological function without moral implications; God created sex for pleasure and procreation within the context of marital fidelity.

Is there any area of your past or present life in which you have accepted the lies of others about yourself instead of agreeing with God's standard of truth about you? If so, embrace God's truth.

Internalizing Truth

Faith is the substance of things hoped for, the evidence of things not seen (Heb. 11:1).

❧ The reality of our physical existence is undeniable. Each day we awaken to a world that is filled with pain and joy, clouds and sun, failure and success, problems and opportunities. One of the greatest troubles we have with internalizing the freedom that comes from God's truth is comprehending the reality of the spiritual world. We know our problems are real. Cancer makes us sick. Our work makes us angry. Our children rebel. Comprehending the reality of the spiritual world and how it can affect our problems is the real test.

Listen to the insight of A. W. Tozer offered in *The Pursuit of God:*

> Our trouble is that we have established bad thought habits. We habitually think of the visible world as real and doubt the reality of any other.
>
> We do not deny the existence of the spiritual world, but we doubt that it is real in the accepted meaning of the word.
>
> The world of sense intrudes upon our attention day and night for the world of our lifetime. The world of sense triumphs. The visible becomes the enemy of the invisible; the temporal, of the eternal.

Two Crucial Principles

As the heavens are higher than the earth,
So are My ways higher than your ways,
And My thoughts than your thoughts (Isa. 55:9).

❧ The truth does not liberate us automatically. All of us can testify to knowing the truth but failing to experience its power.

When Jesus said the truth would set His hearers free, He preceded that declaration with: "If you abide in My word, then you are truly disciples of Mine" (John 8:31 NASB). Two crucial principles are involved in the emancipation of your spiritual being.

1. *You must abide in the Word of God.* To abide means "to continue in." Bondage to sin and deception did not come overnight, and neither will your sense of liberty. You have to allow the Spirit of God to pour His truth into your inner person over time. He will free you with His truth, but you must be exposed to it repeatedly.

2. *You must be a learner.* That is the meaning of the Greek word for *disciple.* Since God's ways are higher than yours (Isa. 55:9), you have to humble yourself, admitting that you lack the wisdom or strength to save yourself.

Truth is learned in all fields of endeavor, and it is no different in the spiritual realm. The truth will set you free as you look to God and in His Word with an eager, open heart, wanting all He will provide.

The Power That Sets You Free

Let my supplication come before You;
Deliver me according to Your word (Ps. 119:170).

❧ Behind the generation of electricity for a home or business is the power of nuclear physics. Behind the power of an automobile engine is the power of spontaneous combustion. In each instance the power of the truth substantiates the action.

For the Christian, behind the truth of the Scriptures is the power of the living God. His power saved you. The same power of God underwrites every word of the Scriptures. When you believe His Word for handling everyday obstacles, His same divine power works on your behalf.

When Jesus spoke, things happened—diseases healed, demons vanquished, sins forgiven, seas calmed. His power can conquer every fear, every doubt, every habit, every inordinate passion, every trembling heart, every lonely soul.

Whatever holds you in bondage cannot withstand the power of the Warrior of the Ages. You can have hope this very hour because the power of God is behind His truth and will work on your behalf as you embrace and cling to the Lord Jesus Christ. The risen Christ can and will liberate you from any bondage if you call on His all-powerful name.

The Doorway to Freedom

Jesus said to him, "If you can believe, all things are possible to him who believes" (Mark 9:23).

❧ You must receive the truth of the Scriptures in order to be free from the bondage of insecurity and inadequacy.

You have to receive God's truth into your inner person. Pride in your resources can hinder that reception. God is a Gentleman; He will not force His ways upon you. You must open the door of your mind and heart to Him.

You must believe the truth of the Scriptures. Believing means that you trust God enough to step out on His promises. You cannot just assent to the Word of God; you must rely on, lean on, and let Him implement His Word in your life so that Christ Jesus—who is the truth (John 14:6)—can set you free.

You must act on your belief. Since God tells you in His Word not to worry (Phil. 4:6), you must stop fretting. Since He says you are valuable in His eyes (John 3:16), you must lay aside your ideas about a lack of self-worth. When you receive and believe God's authoritative, liberating truth, you have entered the doorway of freedom.

Who You Are in Christ

God said, "Let Us make man in Our image, according to Our likeness; let them have dominion over the fish of the sea, over the birds of the air, and over the cattle, over all the earth and over every creeping thing that creeps on the earth" (Gen. 1:26).

❧ Imagine this scene: a young boy lives in a small frame house in the inner city. He is surrounded by poverty and crime. His days are filled with emptiness and despair. There seems to be no way out. He does poorly in school because he has no motivation.

One afternoon a gentleman knocks on the door. He shares staggering news—the young boy is a direct descendant of a writer of world renown. From that moment on, the boy is never the same. He studies hard; he goes to the library; he helps his parents. Yet all that is changed is his view of himself.

Do you see why it is so important to see ourselves in the light of God's truth? We are not plain Joes and Janes; we are God's sons and daughters. We are not rescued sinners with streaks of goodness; we are saints—the holy people of God. You are now an heir with Christ. All that God has is yours as you receive His blessings humbly by faith (John 16:13–15).

How do you see yourself today? Lonely, inadequate, defeated, afraid? The truth of who you are in Christ will set you free.

Freedom from Manipulation

As iron sharpens iron,
So a man sharpens the countenance of his friend (Prov. 27:17).

🐦 The art of being a friend is a delicate one. Scripture is full of admonitions concerning how we are to treat one another in love and respect. Besides the obvious ways of hurting one another, there are other traps to avoid. Pamela Reeve discusses a major one in her book *Relationships:*

> Another common problem in friendships develops when one person tries to control the other. The deeper the friendship grows, the more vulnerable we become at any level. But the intimate relationship in particular provides fertile ground for the stronger personality to control the one who yields more easily.
>
> This type of manipulation can occur on both conscious and subconscious levels. Yet whatever form that control may take, it's poison in a relationship.

What kind of friend are you? Are you so afraid of losing a relationship that you attempt to manipulate the other person into liking you? Do you give the person space to make his or her choices? It's important to evaluate these issues honestly and ask the Lord to make you a selfless and supportive companion.

Freedom from Feelings

Sanctify them by Your truth. Your word is truth (John 17:17).

A formidable enemy of the truth of Christ is feelings. You feel unworthy—even though God says you are made in His image (Gen. 1:26–27) and called by His name (Acts 2:21). You feel insignificant—even though everything you do can be done to the glory of God and used by Him to accomplish His sovereign purposes (Col. 3:17). You feel unloved—even though God says He cares for you as a shepherd cares for his sheep (John 10:11).

You must learn sooner or later to move past your feelings and instead lean on the indisputable fact of God's Word. How can you do that?

The best way is to compile a list of Scriptures dealing with the troubling emotions that beset you. If you are depressed, take a week or so to find Scripture passages dealing with God's joy and His comfort. Tell the Lord Jesus Christ that you choose to believe His truth rather than your emotions. Then praise Him for His answer.

Refuse to budge. Your feelings may linger, but they eventually will crumble under the weight of God's mighty truth.

Your Internal Programming

For as he thinks in his heart, so is he (Prov. 23:7).

❧ Christians, persons who have received the Spirit of God at salvation, have entered God's kingdom. They are new spiritual creatures (2 Cor. 5:17), but they retain the memory banks of previous years. Habits, thoughts, inclinations, and affections can still influence behavior as before.

That is exactly why too many Christians live in such a miserable state. They do not want to return to their former state, but on the other hand, they cannot enjoy their new standing as children of God.

Yet there is hope. Your internal being—mind, emotions, will—can come under the influence of the Holy Spirit, who now indwells you. Your old mental grid system can be replaced by an entirely new set of thoughts and behavior through the power of God's truth.

A new way of living is possible when you view life from God's perspective and His truth takes up residence in your inner being. Real victory and genuine godliness take root and bear the unmistakable fruit of a Christ-filled life.

The Limits of Liberty

You, brethren, have been called to liberty; only do not use liberty as an opportunity for the flesh, but through love serve one another (Gal. 5:13).

❧ When you receive Christ as your Savior, you instantly step into marvelous liberty. No longer are you dependent on the approval of others for your worth. No longer do you seek to be justified by good works. Rather, you are free to worship and serve Christ as His child.

Such emancipation can be intoxicating. However, freedom is not without boundaries. Your actions must be aligned with the Father's loving will, and they must not be a hindrance to other Christians.

Responsible freedom as a child of God means you must view others as more important than yourself. Your actions may be scripturally permissible, but they may cause trouble for less mature believers. You must have genuine concern for their well-being even if it means discontinuing a particular activity or relationship.

Your salvation brought you into a new relationship with the body of Christ. You must always use your freedom responsibly for the growth and harmony of the entire body. You are free to do not as you want but as you ought under the constraints of agape love for Christ and for your brothers and sisters in Christ.

Freedom to Forgive

If you bring your gift to the altar, and there remember that your brother has something against you, leave your gift there before the altar, and go your way. First be reconciled to your brother, and then come and offer your gift (Matt. 5:23–24).

❧ The woman was always one of the first to walk through the church doors on Sunday morning and one of the last to leave. Despite her regular giving to God's work, her consistent attendance, and service on various committees, there was an unmistakable coolness surrounding her. An incident that happened between her and her best friend fifteen years before left her bitter, resentful, and angry. Time was not a healer. Neither was distance. Thinking that both could begin again, her friend had moved away, but that did not happen.

Unresolved emotions filter into the cracks and crevices of our hearts, spilling over to those around us. Before we know it, they have not only stolen our joy, but also blocked our view of God.

Forgiveness is the only force strong enough to break the bondage of anger or any other unresolved emotion. Jesus knew that in order for us to enjoy our relationship freely with the heavenly Father, there would have to be forgiveness. It cost Him everything, but He paid the price.

Is there someone in your life you need to forgive today?

A Supernatural Change Agent

Being confident of this very thing, that He who has begun a good work in you will complete it until the day of Jesus Christ (Phil. 1:6).

❧ What's your attitude toward life? About people, work, and family? Whatever your disposition, it comes from your thought processes. And how you think and what you think about have a tremendous influence on your outlook.

Part of the fantastic good news of salvation is that Christ has come into your life to give not only a new destiny, but a new disposition as well. The apostle Paul wrote that you are "transformed by the renewing of your mind" (Rom. 12:2 NASB). God desires to revolutionize your mind as well as your soul! Why? Because He knows that your thoughts are the breeding ground for behavior and attitude. Change your thinking and you'll ultimately change your ways.

You're not hostage to your past or to your current conditions. The Holy Spirit is a supernatural Change Agent who can surmount any and all entrenched mental configurations. God is now, even at this moment, at work in you to bring about the transformation. If you are willing, God will make it happen.

Freedom from Temptation

But fornication and all uncleanness or covetousness, let it not even be named among you, as is fitting for saints (Eph. 5:3).

❧ Even in Old Testament times there was a variety of cultures, and each had its own value system. The Israelites were to worship God alone. Other nations worshiped anything from the stars to the sun and moon. Their lives were polluted with all kinds of immorality. God knew if Israel disobeyed Him, their moral and spiritual purity would be compromised.

Paul discussed the same subject in Ephesians and instructed members of the early church to be imitators of God. As seen in Ephesians 5:3, Paul's instruction was clear: there was not to be even a fraction of impurity among them.

You are surrounded by temptation. Most of it comes to you in quiet ways—what you watch, what you hear, what you do when no one else is around.

The enemy's goal is much more than to mar God's creation. He wants to destroy your witness for Christ. As a believer, you are no longer bound by sin's power. Christ put an end to sin's reign at Calvary. Don't hesitate to call out His name whenever you face temptation of any kind (1 Cor. 10:13).

Freedom from the Past

I will run the course of Your commandments,
For You shall enlarge my heart (Ps. 119:32).

All Paul had known as a boy growing up in a slum neighborhood was pain. Merciless beatings by his father, who ordered him never to cry, left him too bloody to crawl. By the age of ten, he was an accomplished thief and a hard drinker. At twelve, he murdered a woman as he took her money. It took the consistent nurture of a Christian couple and a friend who invited him to a Christian youth rally to help turn his life around. In his book *Too Tough to Cry*, Paul Powers tells about the night his screams of anger at God were met with unconditional love:

> At that instant, all of the hurt and pain of thirteen years that had been held inside welled up in my throat. "Oh, God, no, I'm going to cry . . . I'm going to cry . . . but real men don't cry."
>
> I couldn't hold it in any longer. I fell to the floor and began to cry. I wept and wept and continued to weep. It was like a dam had burst inside, and the tears poured out of me. I kept moaning, "Forgive me, forgive me . . ."

Do you feel incapable of loving or reaching out for help? Jesus is the only One who can heal that kind of crushing hurt and restore emotions.

Freedom from Enslavement to Sin

The Lord knows how to deliver the godly out of temptations and to reserve the unjust under punishment for the day of judgment (2 Peter 2:9).

❧ Part of the deception of sin is the lie that you're in too deep to ever get out. You can feel so dirty, so soiled, so mired in its clutches that you begin to believe sincerely that there is no way out for you. With each small step toward freedom that you take, your feet seem to slide backward even more.

You must cling to God's power to free you from the bondage of sin. Self-effort is useless, and your human abilities of reason and emotion are clouded by the consequences of the very sin you are trying to escape.

God knows how to rescue you from the temptations you face right now. Through the power of Jesus Christ, you don't have to say yes to what you know is wrong. That is the liberating message of the Cross.

Freedom from Inadequacy

There is therefore now no condemnation to those who are in Christ Jesus, who do not walk according to the flesh, but according to the Spirit (Rom. 8:1).

❧ Many people are bound by feelings of inadequacy. They struggle with low self-esteem and unworthiness. Your sense of self-worth comes from only one Source, the Lord Jesus Christ. He would never want you to view your life as being less than the very best in Him.

That is what He has in mind for you—the best. When God thinks of you, He thinks of His Son and what He did for you at Calvary. He never considers all the mistakes of the past or even those that will come in the future. Instead, God focuses on your potential.

He does this because His love and forgiveness are greater than any sin. The Lord hates sin, but He certainly does not look at your life and think, *There's no way for Me to bless him or her because of what he or she has done.* God does not operate that way.

Is this a license to sin? Certainly not, but it is truly an invitation to love and be loved by the One who loves you the most.

When you fall, God provides a way of forgiveness. He lifts you up and gives you a new opportunity at life. Only Jesus Christ can truly set you free.

Truth Demands One Way

Jesus said to him, "I am the way, the truth, and the life. No one comes to the Father except through Me" (John 14:6).

❧ A movie celebrity remarked during an interview that he had been reared in a Christian environment but he rejected Christianity as an adult. His rationale was: "There are billions of people on this earth. How can any one group of people make a claim that their way is the only way? I just can't believe that."

He is not alone in his thinking. Multitudes reject the notion that faith in the person of Christ is the only means by which they can approach God. "Surely," they reason, "the diverse throng of tribes, cultures, and nations cannot all be expected to walk the same spiritual path. They must have their own unique staircase to the heavens."

Logically carried to its conclusion, the way to God depends on individual preference. God then is approached in millions of ways, each way right in the eyes of the seeker. Absolute truth then is nullified. God is whatever we make of Him.

The Bible strikes at the heart of such nonsense. It claims Christ is the only way because He is the true way, available for all people everywhere. Truth demands one way. Jesus is the Way.

True Freedom

You did not receive the spirit of bondage again to fear, but you received the Spirit of adoption by whom we cry out, "Abba, Father" (Rom. 8:15).

❧ Throughout the ages men and women have fought for what they believed was freedom. Now that we have obtained a higher level of national security, the theme has shifted to how we can remain free. But are we really experiencing true freedom? Everywhere we turn there are evidences of freedom granted and freedom abused.

Jesus told us there is only one way to experience true freedom—by abiding in His truth. Freedom without moral restraint is not freedom; it is chaos. When we reject God's moral values, we trade freedom for bondage. We run the risk of becoming so comfortable in our sin, we refuse to take the way out when it is given.

Are you experiencing Christ's freedom, or are you living in bondage to the world's sin? When you come to Jesus, placing all your needs and expectations on Him, He grants freedom the unsaved only dream of knowing.

Your First Day of Freedom

In Him we have redemption through His blood, the forgiveness of sins, according to the riches of His grace (Eph. 1:7).

In today's Scripture reading, the apostle Paul summed up our position in Christ. We are chosen of God, sealed by His grace through the redemption of our souls.

There is a freedom that comes from being loved and accepted by another. But for this to take place, you must first have an understanding of just how much God loves you. During your lifetime, you have probably experienced some form of rejection. A parent who walked away when you were young, abuse that came at the hands of another, or a spouse who suddenly lost interest and filed for divorce—each represents deep emotional hurts that can keep you bound in fear.

However, difficulties such as these also carry a tremendous opportunity for spiritual growth and freedom, especially when you refuse to become bitter and angry. God knows the hurts you have felt, and He wants to heal your life. Every heartache can be used to teach you more about His unconditional love and acceptance.

Today can be your first day of true freedom. Give Him your hurts and failures, and He will set you free.

Your Emancipation Proclamation

If the Spirit of Him who raised Jesus from the dead dwells in you, He who raised Christ from the dead will also give life to your mortal bodies through His Spirit who dwells in you (Rom. 8:11).

   ❧ When Jesus sets you free from sin, you are no longer held captive by sin's impulses and desires. You do not have to heed them, but many times, however, you may give a knee-jerk reaction when those desires assert themselves. Old habits die hard, and it's difficult to shake off living patterns that may be entrenched after a period of years.

Paul expressed this frustration in Romans 7:15–19: "For that which I am doing, I do not understand; for I am not practicing what I would like to do . . . For the good that I wish, I do not do; but I practice the very evil that I do not wish" (NASB).

Living in the liberty that Christ gave you by His death at Calvary is a result of understanding that He gives you the power to say no to old ways. The call of sin is the empty shout of false bondage; Jesus' dying cry of "It is finished!" is your emancipation proclamation (John 19:30).

You can say with Paul: "Thanks be to God through Jesus Christ our Lord!" (Rom. 7:25 NASB).

Complete Transformation

Peter, standing up with the eleven, raised his voice and said to them, "Men of Judea and all who dwell in Jerusalem, let this be known to you, and heed my words" (Acts 2:14).

❧ Can you remember the first time you were truly excited about learning something new? The disciples knew that feeling. Jesus had spent three years with them. His crucifixion had left them despondent and lonely. But the Resurrection changed their view. For the first time they grasped what He had been saying. Can you imagine what it was like to be with Peter when he finally understood?

Acts 2:14–36 provides this account. The man who stood up and spoke on the day of pentecost was not the same man who had denied Christ on the night of His arrest. What changed Peter was not merely being around Jesus; the indwelling of Christ's Spirit made the transformation complete.

Make Christ the focus of your days and the emphasis of your praise. He knows where He is leading you, and He is aware of all that is needed to make your life complete. Neither should you become discouraged over the times you fall short of your expectations. Allow God to be in control, and you will discover freedom unlike any you have ever known.

Freedom That Will Endure

He who has died has been freed from sin (Rom. 6:7).

The truth of God alone sets you free (Eph. 2:13–16). Only God can penetrate the invisible boundaries of your spirit and soul and thereby rescue you from sin's rule.

As you relinquish your area of bondage to God, remember that the freedom you find in the Lord Jesus Christ will endure. It will stand fast.

The benefits of freedom in Christ may not be visible for a time. Anger may still flare; fear may still lurk in your mind; passion may still burn. But as you trust the Spirit of God to work in your life, results will come. The battle is yours to endure, yet the Holy Spirit will bring the victory. He is at work in your innermost being, even when you think all is lost. He will triumph as you trust in His strong arms to carry you.

Begin now to operate on the basis of God's truth as revealed in the Scriptures and as you are empowered by the Holy Spirit. The truth can set you free forever.

October

THEME: The Foundation Gate

REPRESENTING: Spiritual foundations

According to the grace of God which was given to me, as a wise master builder I have laid the foundation, and another builds on it. But let each one take heed how he builds on it. For no other foundation can anyone lay than that which is laid, which is Jesus Christ (1 Cor. 3:10–11).

A Well-Built Life

He shall be like a tree
Planted by the rivers of water,
That brings forth its fruit in its season,
Whose leaf also shall not wither;
And whatever he does shall prosper (Ps. 1:3).

❧ When looking for a builder to construct your home, your most important question is: "Are his homes well built?" The Scriptures refer to the importance of a well-crafted Christian life that can withstand the pressures of living.

The well-built life follows God's design. The solid Christian seeks to do the Father's will, not his own. Do you walk in the paths God has ordained, or do you continually insert selfish changes of direction?

The well-built life has a solid foundation. That foundation is a love for and obedience to the Word of God. Anything built on personal preference will crack eventually. Adherence to biblical principles always brings lasting results.

The well-built life is faithful in the little things. The attention to detail distinguishes a good builder. A loyal disciple of Christ is steadfast and careful in small as well as large things: the tone of your voice, your reactions to frustration, and what you watch on TV.

By having your heart bent toward God, your convictions based on God's Word, and your actions consistent, you will withstand the tests of time.

Building on a Firm Foundation

No other foundation can anyone lay than that which is laid, which is Jesus Christ (1 Cor. 3:11).

❧ The fifty-five-story skyscraper began to sway and vibrate as the earth tremors grew more intense. The quake climbed to 7.0 on the Richter scale. Smaller buildings crumpled into unrecognizable heaps of rubble. When the shaking stopped and the thick dust cleared, the skyscraper was still standing.

Developers and contractors had planned for the worst, and their foresight paid off. Fortifying the structure with extra steel beams and a special shock-absorption coil system had cost thousands of additional dollars. But when the ultimate test came, their investment stood firm.

In His parable of the wise builder (1 Cor. 3:5–15), Jesus made this very point: the foundation is everything. A life built on self-reliance and self-seeking motivations is destined for collapse. But a life based on the lordship of Christ and obedience to God's principles is unshakable.

Are you a wise builder, or have you settled for the sinking sands of convenience? Sometimes, following the Lord's direction may appear to be unprofitable, especially when you are criticized or ridiculed for doing so. But when the storms come, temporary rewards are blown away, and unwise builders are left with nothing.

A Foundation for Forgiveness

The next day John saw Jesus coming toward him, and said, "Behold! The Lamb of God who takes away the sin of the world!" (John 1:29).

❧ When convicted serial murderer Ted Bundy publicly shared his religious beliefs days before his execution, many Christians doubted the reality of his conversion. "How could someone who perpetrated such murders possibly be forgiven?" was their fundamental question.

This thinking fails to understand the complete inability of anyone to receive God's forgiveness apart from a personal faith in Christ's work on the cross. Humankind's greatest need is forgiveness of sin because all of us are guilty and separated from God. Good people are lost; bad people are lost. Moral people are guilty; immoral people are guilty.

When Christ died as our substitute at Calvary and paid sin's penalty, which is death, our righteous Judge was free to forgive us based on Christ's full payment. With the sin debt paid, humankind can receive God's pardon and gift of eternal life based completely and solely on Christ's redeeming work.

God saves a Ted Bundy or a good Sam on the same grounds: personal faith in Jesus Christ, who shed His blood for the forgiveness of our sins—no matter how despicable they may be.

The Journey of Faith

Jesus answered and said to them, "Have faith in God" (Mark 11:22).

❧ Although we may wish otherwise, the Christian life is a journey of faith. We like tangible evidence. We are comfortable with proven cause-and-effect scenarios. We turn the key, and the engine starts.

Faith is intangible. It is not so predictable. Yet faith is the unseen dynamic for Christian growth and living. It is the indispensable core of a vital spiritual existence. And for good reason. Faith in God is His requirement for fruitful, enduring ministry. Faith is the barometer of genuine Christianity, which is a personal relationship with the Lord Jesus Christ.

When you express your faith in Christ for your particular needs or desires, you acknowledge your dependence on God. You are drawn intimately near Him as you believe in His purpose and provision. God wants your being—your entire personality—committed to Him, not to a cause or religion or philosophy.

Thus, faith is the highest expression of your allegiance to the Lord. When you place your faith in God, you confess your absolute trust in His personhood.

The Lord wants to fellowship with you. Do you place your faith in Him because you seek results or because you know Him and love Him?

The Foundation of Faith

Our heart shall rejoice in Him,
Because we have trusted in His holy name (Ps. 33:21).

One significant problem concerning faith is reliance upon personal experience. Although the Lord's answers are cause for celebration, you must be careful not to base your confidence on individual cases.

You were created to glorify the Lord, but not all of your requests are designed to honor Him. God alone knows how to answer you so that His provision magnifies His name above all else. That is why He meets your needs often in unusual or unexpected ways. In such instances you know the Lord has worked sovereignly, and your praise is amplified. God always responds to your faith so that you are conformed to the image of Christ.

Though marred by sin, you are being molded into Christlikeness. Thus, God's focus is greater on transforming you into Christ's image than on answering your requests. That explains why your prayers sometimes seem to go unanswered. The omniscient Lord understands exactly how you can be shaped into Christ's image. When you place your confidence in God, your faith depends on His criteria, not yours.

The Shield of Faith

Above all, taking the shield of faith with which you will be able to quench all the fiery darts of the wicked one (Eph. 6:16).

With an increasing emphasis on the occult evident in society, it is easy to forget that Satan's most effective weapons are two ancient foes—doubt and discouragement. How many Christians have been spiritually defeated because they lost heart by the sabotage of these evil ambassadors? Too many fail to press on in their relationship with Christ because they give in to the insistent demands of doubt and discouragement.

Although doubt and discouragement are strong enemies, in Ephesians 6:16 God has given you the means to resolve this problem. Firm, unwavering confidence in the Lord keeps the powers of darkness at bay. Satan is thwarted when the shield of faith is raised against him.

Doubt says, "I don't think so." Faith says, "God is able."

Discouragement says, "It's hopeless." Faith says, "With God, all things are possible."

You may be in a situation where you have almost given up. Your strength is failing; your outlook is grim. Take up the shield of faith. Put the matter squarely into the Lord's hands and believe that He is in control. When Satan attacks, the shield of faith will rout him.

Nourishing Your Faith

If you faint in the day of adversity,
Your strength is small (Prov. 24:10).

❧ We often hesitate when we face a challenge, allowing the obstacles to frighten and even immobilize us. We don't reach our objectives, and our faith sags instead of stretching us.

The key to a growing, confident faith is a consistent focus on the power and might of God. Caleb and Joshua saw imposing giants—as did the rest of the Israelite spies—but they measured them against the power of the most high God (Num. 13–14).

The focus that develops faith to tackle life's challenges comes from sustained, concentrated meditation on the Word of God. Remember God's instructions to Joshua: "This Book of the Law shall not depart from your mouth, but you shall meditate in it day and night" (Josh. 1:8).

Joshua and Caleb kept their gaze on God in an unwavering faith in His Word. Then when the challenge came, they drew their conclusions on the basis of God's unlimited resources, not theirs.

Nourish your faith for tomorrow's challenges by renewing your mind in God's Word today.

Reinforcing Your Faith

Rooted and built up in Him and established in the faith, as you have been taught, abounding in it with thanksgiving (Col. 2:7).

❧ Massive concrete buildings are imposing structures. However, the inner, invisible steel reinforcement rods provide the strength and sturdiness. Without this internal network, concrete would crumble and collapse.

Similarly most often unseen practices and habits reinforce faith in Jesus Christ. It begins by being faithful in the small things and building a foundation for the more pressing situations you encounter. It is nurtured in private seasons of prayer. Communion with God is a vital link to expectant faith.

Loving God is yet another interior bar of authentic faith. If you obey God only out of a sense of duty, you will do well. But if you obey Him because you love Him deeply and long to please Him, your faith will issue from an artesian well of passion that never runs dry.

Regular times of prayer are the rods of a sturdy faith. Confession, repentance, worship, and petition undergird any meaningful life of faith.

Build your faith each day with the disciplines that give your trust true stoutness and solidity.

Is There a Flaw in Your Faith?

Seek first the kingdom of God and His righteousness, and all these things shall be added to you (Matt. 6:33).

✺ A flaw in a product can go unnoticed for long periods of time before the defect finally emerges. Likewise, many believers can grow quite rapidly in their faith before a dormant spiritual fault is revealed in a time of testing. It is then that the most common defect is discovered—operating on personal agendas.

The goal of the Christian life is to exalt and worship the person of Jesus Christ. Faith in anything but His will is idolatry. Substituting your plans for His purposes is idolatry. Faith practiced solely for achieving your personal objectives, as noble as they may seem, is idolatry.

Paul's overwhelming ambition was to know and please Christ, to do everything to His glory. Is that your passion? Do you enter His presence with gratefulness, excitement, and reverence for Him?

It is all right to pray for personal needs and guidance, but all such requests are secondary to faith's primary aim—experiencing God's will for your life and personal communion with the Father. If God is accomplishing that purpose in your life, your faith will not be shaken even when the going gets rough. You will depend on God not to grant your every desire but to fulfill His purposes, whatever they may be.

Mustard Seed Faith

The Lord said, "If you have faith as a mustard seed, you can say to this mulberry tree, 'Be pulled up by the roots and be planted in the sea,' and it would obey you" (Luke 17:6).

❧ Would you like to have greater faith in God? The disciples did. They said to the Lord, "Increase our faith!" (Luke 17:5 NASB). The Master's reply to His disciples—and to every Christian who desires to please Him—was: "If you had faith like a mustard seed . . ."

A mustard seed is very small. The contrast in Jesus' response was curious: His disciples wanted more faith, and Jesus used this seed as an example. The Savior communicated that they needed to use the faith they already had.

The road to a growing faith is to trust Christ each day for the small things of life. Are you trusting the Lord for the seemingly mundane things: help in the office and home, guidance in financial purchases, strength and a cheerful spirit for chores?

God has given you the fullness of His Son, Jesus Christ, through the indwelling of the Holy Spirit. As you learn to express your faith in His love and in His provision for life's daily grind, your faith will increase for the bigger challenges that await you.

Unshakable Faith

The LORD has established His throne in heaven,
And His kingdom rules over all (Ps. 103:19).

❧ An unshakable faith is anchored in a living, unchanging, sovereign God. Your faith works because you trust in a personal, living God who hears your pleas and works on your behalf. The living God never sleeps or slumbers. There is no hour, day or night, when you cannot instantly and confidently approach Him. He lives: "For He is the living God and enduring forever . . ." (Dan. 6:26 NASB).

Your faith is firm because God is from everlasting to everlasting. He is the same for every man, woman, and child of every generation, of every culture. His ways never change; His character is unalterable. He is the stability of our times: ". . . And His dominion will be forever" (Dan. 6:26 NASB).

Your faith is steadfast because God is sovereign, ruling over people and affairs to achieve His purposes. God is in control even when everything seems out of control. He overrules all evil, using even bitter, painful moments for divine good.

God lives. He lives forever. His kingdom and rule on earth are being established now and will be permanently installed upon His return. You can trust God without reserve or regret.

The Mind-Set of Faith

Set your mind on things above, not on things on the earth (Col. 3:2).

The apostle Paul spent a great deal of time writing to the early church about the mind-set of faith, how they should think as new believers in Christ. The message he shared with the church in Colosse was no exception. Because of its location, Colosse was a hub of activity and cultural expansion. Various philosophies dictated religious views and doctrines while young believers faced many challenges concerning their belief in God and His redemptive provision through Christ.

Paul exhorted them to set their minds on the things above, not on the things of this world. The reason was simple. When you focus on Jesus Christ and His truth and plan for your life, you are not easily swayed. You are firmly fixed and established in light of God's victory. Therefore, when disappointments, doubts, or temptations come, you know God is in control because your mind is set on His truth and principles.

Many believers at Colosse struggled spiritually because they allowed their minds to be drawn aside by false doctrines. Paul told them to think with their minds set on Jesus Christ. The same is true for you today. When your mind is focused on Christ, you have His perspective. That is your security and hope.

How Well Do You Know Him?

I know whom I have believed and am persuaded that He is able to keep what I have committed to Him until that Day (2 Tim. 1:12).

❧ A stranger approaches you at the bus stop one morning and asks you to invest $5,000 in his new business venture. Your swift response is negative, for you are unaware of the individual's identity or integrity. You will not place your trust in someone you do not know.

The same principle is at work in the spiritual realm. The more you know about Jesus, the more you will entrust into His care. How well are you acquainted with Jesus Christ? Do you know as much about Him as one knows about mountain climbing by reading books on the subject? Or do you know Jesus as intimately as one who knows mountain climbing by ascending the summit of Mount Everest?

You can know Jesus for yourself by investigating the Word of God regularly, praying habitually about small and common needs, and obeying in the trifles of life. A vital faith in Christ is forged in the tiny corners of the home and heart. You see answers to prayers and observe Him at work in your life.

If you want great faith in Christ, set your heart to know and obey Him in the little tasks. Your faith will increase because you will "know whom [you] have believed."

Mighty in Spirit

If any of you lacks wisdom, let him ask of God, who gives to all liberally and without reproach, and it will be given to him (James 1:5).

❧ Jim Elliot was a bright, articulate young man who left his home in the United States for the jungles of South America. In his mid-twenties he was killed by Indian spears, leaving behind his wife, Elisabeth, and a daughter.

Elisabeth used her deceased husband's diary as the source for her stirring book *The Shadow of the Almighty.* Thousands have testified to the book's influence in motivating them for mission service. By secular values, her husband accomplished little, dying young in a remote forest. But in God's eyes he was successful. He was one mighty in spirit, allowing the Holy Spirit to direct, guide, and energize his life.

People who are mighty in spirit can build enduring, rewarding lives whether they live in a high-rise or in the slums, whether they earn much or little money, whether they are known by many or few.

God's presence and reign in your life give you eternal significance. You can enjoy the gracious blessings that God gives without partiality to His children. Wherever you are—even if it is in the remote reaches of a tropical forest as Jim Elliot was—you can impact your world by being mighty in spirit.

The Spirit-Directed Life

Let us know,
Let us pursue the knowledge of the LORD.
His going forth is established as the morning;
He will come to us like the rain,
Like the latter and former rain to the earth (Hos. 6:3).

❧ You do not become mighty in spirit by setting your inner person on automatic pilot to drift through life. You must employ several basic disciplines if you are to experience the rewards of a Spirit-directed life:

The discipline of rejection. The Holy Spirit is opposed to the flesh, and the one who is mighty in spirit must constantly reject the competing values and passions of the world system, which is devoid of godliness.

The discipline of relationship. Wisdom flows from a pure, honest relationship with the Lord Jesus Christ. Above all you must guard your heart and keep Jesus as your first love—singularly devoted to Him, not a cause.

The discipline of obedience. Obedience is always the path to growth and blessing. Are you obeying what you know? The riches of heaven are yours when you obey the Word of God and the leading of the Holy Spirit.

The motivation for each of these disciplines is love of the Lord Jesus Christ. You want to be mighty in spirit because you adore Him.

Confident Decision Making

My times are in Your hand;
Deliver me from the hand of my enemies,
And from those who persecute me (Ps. 31:15).

◦❧ Watching a football player lie motionless on the turf after a vicious hit is sobering. Almost universally feared, but usually unspoken, is the possibility of an injury that results in paralysis. Often these fears are relieved when the player is escorted off the field.

Far more damaging and much more prevalent is another kind of paralysis that sets in when we are faced with a decision. Multitudes are frozen in fear and confusion in the decision-making process. It is a form of bondage that God certainly does not desire.

You can be confident in any form of decision making because your trust is ultimately in the Lord Jesus Christ. You are responsible to gather facts, analyze them, and weigh alternatives. People hold you responsible for results also.

Having done your part, you can rest because the Lord is in control. You do not know the future; He does. Your times and decisions are in His hands as you trust in His guidance (Ps. 31:15). Even when the consequences of your decision are not what you envisioned, you still know that God works all things together for good to those who love Him (Rom. 8:28).

Loyalty

Most men will proclaim each his own goodness,
But who can find a faithful man? (Prov. 20:6).

🕊 In certain sections of the country, a morning fog is almost a daily occurrence. The day begins with a heavy mist that dissipates within a few hours. The prophet Hosea described the Israelites' relationship with God in a similar way: "For your loyalty is like a morning cloud, / And like the dew which goes away early" (Hos. 6:4 NASB).

Loyalty is an essential ingredient in the relationship between us and God. In the Old Testament the Hebrew word for loving-kindness is translated as "loyal, faithful, steadfast love."

Despite our rebellion and sin, God kept His covenant love for us through the generations, fulfilling His eternal plan for reconciliation through the cross of Christ. In return, God expects the whole-hearted allegiance of His followers.

Are you actively demonstrating your loyalty to Jesus Christ? Has your devotion to the Lord slackened over the years? Do you question God's care?

The Lord Jesus Christ is not as interested in your money or time or activity level as He is in your heart. He wants your wholehearted devotion that is not diminished by time or circumstances.

Responsibility

His lord said to him, "Well done, good and faithful servant; you were faithful over a few things, I will make you ruler over many things. Enter into the joy of your lord" (Matt. 25:21).

❧ The fast track for success is faster than ever. Employers complain that young people want to rise to the top as quickly as possible without any time-consuming layovers in areas they consider unnecessary.

Success in any area, however, does not come easily; and it is no different in the spiritual realm. If you want to do great things for God, you must be willing to endure the small things with patience. There are often seasons when the Lord prepares you faithfully for future challenges.

Responsibility is learned in the little things. Can God entrust a pastorate to one who is inconsistent in teaching a Sunday school class? Can He send someone overseas to the lost if he has not labored among the unsaved where he lives?

Responsibility is best learned on the backstage where you are diligent and faithful because you want to please the Lord, not other people. As you learn to labor consistently out of the limelight, God can challenge you with progressively more demanding opportunities.

Are you faithful where He has placed you, or do you clamor for more? Persevere, and your future is bright.

Order

When He had sent the multitudes away, He went up on the mountain by Himself to pray. Now when evening came, He was alone there (Matt. 14:23).

❧ Sociological studies show that despite increased leisure time, Americans feel more pressured than ever. With increased freedoms and opportunities come more choices; with more choices, more decisions are required. The key to living an orderly life in the midst of such frenzy is an established prayer life in which you can present your needs and agenda to God.

Nehemiah understood this foundational principle. In Nehemiah 1, we see that when he heard the news of Jerusalem's plight, he did not immediately organize a rescue squad or launch a new organization. He prayed: "I sat down and wept and mourned for days; and I was fasting and praying before the God of heaven" (Neh. 1:4 NASB).

For four long months, Nehemiah interceded on Jerusalem's behalf, asking God for direction and wisdom. Then when the time came to petition King Artaxerxes, Nehemiah's request was granted miraculously (Neh. 2:1–6).

Order in your life begins with the rule of the Holy Spirit and the outworking of God's plan. The discernment to implement His plan comes as you spend time in fervent prayer, seeking His mind and purposes.

Demolishing Spiritual Strongholds

The Lord will fight for you, and you shall hold your peace (Ex. 14:14).

⮞ We have to admit that we cannot be successful in eliminating an area of habitual sin, even with strong wills, discipline, and perseverance (John 15:5). That puzzles us because we think we usually can arrive at a successful conclusion. We think, *Why should this problem of lust or jealousy or greed be any different?*

The first step toward progress is a recognition that the battle is spiritual, not rational or behavioral (Eph. 6:13–20). You have allowed the power of sin to establish a spiritual stronghold, a fortified position in your inner person. You cannot conquer this stronghold by futile, ordinary means (2 Cor. 10:3–4).

You can be free by relying on these spiritual weapons—the living Word of God and the Holy Spirit's power. Since the battle is mainly in your mind, reading God's Word attacks the stronghold by infusing His truth, which will always prevail (1 Cor. 10:13; Eph. 4:12).

The Spirit of God, who brought you from death to life, also can demolish spiritual strongholds. His power is available as you depend upon His super-natural resources (Ex. 14:14; Rom. 15:13).

Identify your spiritual stronghold. Recognize that you are in a spiritual battle, and use the spiritual weapons the Lord gives you. They work!

Saved and Sure

Knowing that a man is not justified by the works of the law but by faith in Jesus Christ, even we have believed in Christ Jesus, that we might be justified by faith in Christ and not by the works of the law; for by the works of the law no flesh shall be justified (Gal. 2:16).

๛ People who doubt their salvation are miserable Christians and confusing witnesses to the unbelieving world. They are not portraits of "the abundant life" that Jesus Christ gives those who trust Him for the forgiveness of their sins.

How then do you slip into this anxiety-producing mind-set?

Once saved, you may drift into a performance-based mentality, thinking your relationship with the Lord depends upon your conduct. This is heresy. Only God's grace saves you and keeps you saved (Eph. 2:8). Your basis of acceptance before Him is the Cross where God the Father justified you (declared you not guilty) through His Son's death. You are accepted not on your merit but wholly on Christ's substitutionary death on Calvary. Once for all, Jesus died for all your sins for all time. When you are saved, your sins are forgiven—past, present, and future.

If you are wrestling with doubt over your salvation, look to the Cross. If you have received Christ by faith, you are eternally secure in the Savior. Nothing can alter that fact.

The Divine Link

He said to them, "Where is your faith?" And they were afraid, and marveled, saying to one another, "Who can this be? For He commands even the winds and water, and they obey Him!" (Luke 8:25).

❧ Some people confuse the concept of faith with positive thinking, which it is not. Others project faith as the intense effort to attain something. "If he just had enough faith, he could have what he asks," they say.

These descriptions are foreign to the biblical portrait of faith, which is a confident reliance upon the faithfulness of God. It is not worked up by individuals but grounded in the very character and being of our Father in heaven.

Our faith is in God. When we are weak, we look to Him for strength. When we are afflicted, we look to the Lord for comfort. When we are in need, we look to Him for provision. When we want to see someone saved, we count on God's saving power.

Faith is the divine link that taps into the inexhaustible resources of eternal God, relying on His perfect wisdom, power, and love. God looks for men and women who will place faith in Him, depending on His sufficiency and adequacy.

Where is your faith placed today? Trust in the Lord Jesus Christ alone, and you will never be disappointed.

The Faith to Hold Out

Humble yourselves under the mighty hand of God, that He may exalt you in due time, casting all your care upon Him, for He cares for you (1 Peter 5:6–7).

❧ You have prayed daily for your alcoholic son. You have trusted God for your spouse's salvation for many years. You have sought the Lord for healing from a serious disease for several months.

But your son still drinks, your spouse is still unsaved, and your illness still lingers painfully. How do you hold on to your faith?

First, you must believe that God is at work. You may not see any evidence, but the Holy Spirit unceasingly labors for you. The Lord is changing you in the process, developing Christlike qualities in you.

Second, you must not forget that God cares. The Scriptures assure you that the Lord cares so much that He executed His Son on your behalf (Rom. 5:6). His love toward you is unfailing. Because the Lord cares, you can cast your burdens on Him daily.

Third, you must rest in the assurance that God knows best. His wisdom is sure, even when it runs totally against your logical grain. He knows when, how, what, where, and why. If you are to hold on to faith during trials, you must renew your trust with fresh, daily reminders of the Lord's absolute faithfulness, power, wisdom, and care.

Faith on Trial

That the genuineness of your faith, being much more precious than gold that perishes, though it is tested by fire, may be found to praise, honor, and glory at the revelation of Jesus Christ (1 Peter 1:7).

❧ Face it. You never will receive all you ask from God.

You will experience suffering that cannot be explained. You will be buffeted by volatile affliction. While on earth, you never will fully understand why you must go through trials. Your faith must be anchored in the eternal. You are assured that one day—maybe not on earth—your faith will be rewarded by your just Lord: "That the proof of your faith, being more precious than gold which is perishable, even though tested by fire, may be found to result in praise and glory and honor at the revelation of Jesus Christ" (1 Peter 1:7 NASB).

Faith sees past the physical world into what is invisible and eternal. Faith that rests on visible evidence is not faith at all.

You understand that sin has marred the world and that things will not be set straight until Christ Jesus comes again to establish His reign on earth. When you meet Jesus face-to-face, your wounds and sorrows will be replaced by His perfect peace and joy (Rev. 21:4).

Your faith will be rewarded one day—if not now. It is precious to the Lord, and it is your most valuable weapon in persevering on earth.

God Will Answer

"For My thoughts are not your thoughts,
Nor are your ways My ways," says the LORD.
"For as the heavens are higher than the earth,
So are My ways higher than your ways,
And My thoughts than your thoughts" (Isa. 55:8–9).

❧ Have you prayed about a sick child, financial problems, or your struggling marriage? God will answer. The Lord always hears the prayers of His children and responds to our petitions. Of course, we do not know how He will reply or what His answer will involve. Our faith must rest in God's love, grace, and wisdom.

The test of your faith is that you have expectations but God has His heavenly plan. His ways are higher than yours, and they are always for your welfare. Will you wait for His answer, or will you manipulate the circumstances to achieve your goals? Will you be satisfied with His response, or will you grow bitter and rebel because you did not get your way?

Burn this truth into your heart: God will answer. His ears and eyes are open to your requests and problems. Your faith can withstand the strongest doubts and unbelief when you are assured of His loving answer.

Confident Courage

Then all this assembly shall know that the LORD does not save with sword and spear; for the battle is the LORD's, and He will give you into our hands (1 Sam. 17:47).

❧ David's courage in facing Goliath came from his steadfast focus on the might of Jehovah God: "You come to me with a sword, a spear, and a javelin, but I come to you in the name of the LORD of hosts, the God of the armies of Israel" (1 Sam. 17:45 NASB).

Putting your fears aside is not simple. Sometimes the more you look at the risks or possibilities, the more fearful you become. Only when your fears are placed in perspective against the background of a holy, powerful, caring God can they be dispelled and your courage bolstered.

Identify the task, person, or issue that frightens you. Run through the scenarios that might happen. Then consider the vastness of your infinite, merciful, mighty God. Can He help? Is He bigger than your problem? Does your foe trouble Him?

With a faith focused on the person of Jesus Christ, courageously tackle your Goliath—not in your might but in His. The battle is God's to win.

The Word of the Lord

*Then the word of the LORD came to him [Elijah], saying . . .
(1 Kings 17:2).*

❧ When we think of Elijah, we usually focus on his exceptional faith in God. Such believing faith is not the exclusive domain of prophets or disciples. Every Christian is called to live and walk by faith.

For believers today, "the word of the LORD" is not delivered by angels or dreams or given orally. Rather, God's word is His revelation of truth in the Bible. Scripture is filled with the same divine significance that Elijah experienced when he heard "the word of the LORD."

Your faith is anchored in the eternal principles of God's Word, whose Author is the Holy Spirit. That should bring an awesome sense of reverence and new anticipation as you approach this supernatural communication of God.

As such, it is the cornerstone for life-changing faith. Believe the Word, and you are saved from sin's penalty. Believe the Word, and you can be delivered from sinful strongholds. Believe the Word about any issue, attribute, or problem, and your faith in His truth will work miracles in your life.

Obedience

By faith Abraham obeyed when he was called to go out to the place which he would receive as an inheritance. And he went out, not knowing where he was going (Heb. 11:8).

❧ Two children play in a yard. One mother cries, "Johnny, it's time to come home." Johnny hurriedly tells his friend good-bye and runs home. His companion Bill continues to play. Why did Johnny respond but not Bill? Because Johnny was related to the one speaking, while Bill was not.

Similarly your obedience to God's leadership is a validation that God is your Father and you are His child. When He requires your obedience to His conviction, guidance, and reproof, your compliance is evidence of your relationship with Him. You are still His if you do not obey, but God desires obedient children who are submissive to His will.

Also Johnny responded to his mother's command because of his love for her. When you obey the Father, you likewise give evidence of your devotion to Him. Loving God involves your consistent adherence to His Word and means your glad, prompt obedience.

Knowing that God seeks your obedience only for your benefit is the grounds for your loving allegiance. Even in correction, God's motivation is His love for you. If He is speaking to you about a specific action, let your obedience demonstrate your love as His child.

The Cost of Compromise

*Great is our L*ORD*, and mighty in power;*
His understanding is infinite (Ps. 147:5).

When we compromise on God's clearly stated truth, we dilute His standards. God knows best. Rationalize as we might, compromise is simply an attempt to bring God down a notch, to say that we really know what is best, which always leads to distasteful consequences.

When we compromise our convictions, we settle for less than biblical excellence. Obedience to revealed truth in the Bible allows us to maximize our God-given potential. Compromise reduces our effectiveness as God's servants and is the pathway to spiritual mediocrity.

Likewise, compromise is the precursor to entanglement and enslavement to sin. Compromise seems easy at first, but its long-term consequences are severe. Sin still seeks to master us, and what starts as a minor concession can become a major problem later.

If you are thinking about compromising on any of God's commandments, think again. You always lose when you compromise, for God will never change His Word.

Walking in Holiness

And that you put on the new man which was created according to God, in true righteousness and holiness (Eph. 4:24).

❧ Oswald Chambers wrote in *Our Brilliant Heritage,*

> The one marvelous secret of a holy life lies not in imitating Jesus, but in letting the perfections of Jesus manifest themselves in my mortal flesh. Sanctification is "Christ in you." It is His wonderful life that is imparted to me in sanctification, and imparted by faith as a sovereign gift of God's grace . . .
>
> Sanctification means the impartation of the holy qualities of Jesus Christ. It is His patience, His love, His holiness, His faith, His purity, His godliness, that is manifested in and through every sanctified soul. Sanctification is not drawing from Jesus the power to be holy; it is drawing from Jesus the holiness that was manifested in Him, and He manifests it in me. Sanctification is an impartation, not an imitation.

The key to living like Christ is found not in striving but in letting go of aspirations and seeking the Lord above all else.

When you pray to be holy, pray to be like Jesus. His holiness and purity were natural overflows. He drew people to Himself not by being mechanical in His worship of the Father but by being a light of hope to a darkened world.

Simple Trust

If indeed you continue in the faith, grounded and steadfast, and are not moved away from the hope of the gospel which you heard, which was preached to every creature under heaven, of which I, Paul, became a minister (Col. 1:23).

❧ We think our world today is volatile, but the world in which the early church existed was under constant attack from outside forces. Paul could not be everywhere at once. Timothy and Silas and others did much to uphold the faith, but even they could not meet all the spiritual needs.

It came down to a matter of faith. Congregational minister Horace Bushnell commented, "If you go to Christ to be guided, He will guide you; but He will not comfort your distrust or half-trust of Him by showing you the chart of all His purposes concerning you. He will show you only into a way where, if you go cheerfully and trustfully forward, He will show you on still farther."

The foundation of your faith begins and ends with simple trust. Outside that there is no other truth.

November

THEME: The Gates of Praise

REPRESENTING: Thanksgiving, praise,
and worship

Enter into His gates with thanksgiving,
And into His courts with praise.
Be thankful to Him, and bless His name (Ps. 100:4).

Preparation for Praise

It is good to give thanks to the LORD,
And to sing praises to Your name, O Most High;
To declare Your lovingkindness in the morning,
And Your faithfulness every night (Ps. 92:1–2).

❧ Hudson Taylor, who founded the China Inland Mission, is considered the founder of modern faith missions. The key to his faith and perseverance as he labored for many years in a foreign, hostile environment was a commitment to daily worship. Early each morning, whether at home or on a journey, he would strike a match, light a candle or lantern, and proceed to enter God's presence with thanksgiving and praise. It was said of Taylor that before the sun ever rose on China, he was worshiping God.

If you are to cultivate the spiritual art and intimacy of worship, there must be a setting of the will. Until this happens worship will remain a mystery— an enigma. Add to that the weariness of the flesh, and worship will never flame into godly passion unless you, like David, desire this one thing: "To behold the beauty of the LORD, / And to meditate in His temple" (Ps. 27:4 NASB).

Prepare your heart for worship by an initial setting of your will. As you continue, you will ride the crest of swelling devotion to a majestic God.

Why You Run Dry

I will bless the LORD at all times;
His praise shall continually be in my mouth (Ps. 34:1).

❧ In her daily devotional book *Edges of His Ways,*
Amy Carmichael noted,

> I believe that if we are to be and to do for others what
> God means us to be and to do, we must not let adora-
> tion and worship slip into second place. For it is the
> central service asked by God of human souls; and its
> neglect is responsible for much lack of spiritual depth
> and power.
>
> Perhaps we may find here the reason why we so
> often run dry. We do not give time enough to what
> makes the depth, and so we are shallow; a wind, quite
> a little wind, can ruffle our surface; a little hot sun,
> and all the moisture in us evaporates. It should not be
> so . . .
>
> Today if we will hear His voice, today, this morn-
> ing, if we will draw near to Him, He will draw near to
> us. In the hush of that nearness . . . we shall forget our-
> selves, lost in the wonder, love and praise to Him . . .
> The morning never disappoints us by not coming,
> neither does our loving God.

You may be hurting emotionally and find the
thought of praise awkward. But if you will begin to
praise Him, regardless of your circumstance, He will
lift you up and give you strength to carry on.

Seeking the Lord

I will bless You while I live;
I will lift up my hands in Your name (Ps. 63:4).

❧ When you are faced with a problem, it is deceptively easy to forget God. You may pray briefly or ask for prayers of others, but seeking God must be more than a casual pursuit. You become serious about seeking God and His purposes as you realize these crucial truths:

God cares for you. As the Good Shepherd, Jesus cares passionately and personally for you, your decisions, actions, and thoughts. He has a plan for you that He is willing to make known as you seek Him and His kingdom first.

God is involved in everything. Because He cares and because He is sovereignly at work in your life, His involvement is unlimited. Your work, family, relationships, play, and other facets of daily living are His delight. The house you need, the job you desire, the spouse you are seeking—all involve the love and care of God. He watches over your life and desires for you to seek His counsel at every turn.

Are you seeking God and His face? Turn your attention to Him, and He will order your steps and strengthen your heart.

Building Blocks for Seeking God

Oh, bless our God, you peoples!
And make the voice of His praise to be heard (Ps. 66:8).

❧ Some basic building blocks can help you keep a reliable, scriptural perspective on the necessity of seeking the Lord.

1. *Develop consistent habits of seeking God in the ordinary rounds of life.* Bringing your ordinary, seemingly mundane needs and problems to Him helps you to understand His sufficiency in times of true crises. He wants you to seek Him for who He is, cultivating a personal relationship with a God who loves you and cares for you as no other.

2. *Continue in the Word and in prayer.* God speaks to you through the living words of the Scriptures. You do not have to wait on some "experience" when you have God's sure and clear Word. You must also talk to Him in prayer, pouring out your heart to Him, hiding nothing.

3. *Do all these exercises of the soul humbly and honestly.* Those who are secure in their own strength, capable in their own energies, have little reason to seek the Lord. However, because you realize your inadequacies and weaknesses, you come to God with an open, receptive heart in need of His supernatural help.

Seeking God ultimately gives you His adequacy for your inadequacy.

The Benefits of Meditation

Trust in Him at all times, you people;
Pour out your heart before Him;
God is a refuge for us. Selah (Ps. 62:8).

Not only is meditation on God's Word important for receiving His counsel and comfort, but it is essential for worship and fellowship with the Father. In *Knowing God*, Dr. J. I. Packer wrote about the benefits of meditation:

> Meditation is the activity of calling to mind, and thinking over, and dwelling on, and applying to oneself, the various things that one knows about the works and ways and purposes and promises of God.
>
> It is an activity of holy thought, consciously performed in the presence of God, under the eye of God, by the help of God, as a means of communion with God. Its purpose is to clear one's mental and spiritual vision of God, and to let His truth make its full and proper impact on one's mind and heart.
>
> Its effect is to ever humble us, as we contemplate God's greatness and glory, and our littleness and sinfulness and to encourage and reassure us . . . as we contemplate the unsearchable riches of divine mercy displayed in the Lord Jesus Christ.

Loving Jesus

Not that I have already attained, or am already perfected; but I press on, that I may lay hold of that for which Christ Jesus has also laid hold of me (Phil. 3:12).

❧ Is your relationship with the heavenly Father one of duty or delight? God, who is love, desires your fellowship with Him to be motivated by personal, growing, demonstrated love.

God is a person. Although He could have existed without creating humankind, He made us for Himself. As His child, you are free to love Him for all He is and for what He has done and will do for you. Each day is an opportunity to express your love for Jesus.

There is no such thing as true love in a marriage without verbal encouragement and praise. Likewise, God wants to hear the words of your lips that proclaim His excellence. You can also tell Him you love Him by cheerful obedience. Work heartily at your task, knowing Christ is your Master. Carry out principles of Scripture He has laid on your heart. Serve others with compassion and understanding as Christ's ambassador on earth.

The more you know Christ, the more you love Him. The more you love Him, the more passionately you want to honor and praise Him. It is a divine circle of love filled with blessings.

Rekindling Your Wick

O Lord, open my lips,
And my mouth shall show forth Your praise (Ps. 51:15).

❧ Most Christians sincerely desire to love God and please Him. Although if we are honest, we feel distant and detached from God at times.

Perhaps you have become entrapped in the hectic pace of work, school, family, or other meaningful obligations. Your times of communion with Christ have diminished.

Perhaps you have been ensnared by a sinful habit that you will not abandon, and your guilt is so overwhelming that you are ashamed to approach Christ. Whatever the reason for your broken intimacy with God, there is good news. Jesus waits to embrace you now in the arms of unconditional, divine love.

Stop today, take a deep breath, admit your misplaced priorities, and begin again to seek the kingdom of God. It may take time for feelings of intimacy to return, but fellowship can again be sweet.

If you have sinned, your guilt is washed away by the blood of the Cross. Confess your sin, receive His infinite forgiveness, and ask Christ to restore your soul. Once you are saved, no sin can keep you outside the love of God. He never condemns you.

Corporate Worship

Give unto the LORD the glory due to His name;
Worship the LORD in the beauty of holiness (Ps. 29:2).

❧ Personal worship of God is a vital part of knowing Him. Likewise, corporate worship is an instrumental facet of healthy Christianity. Corporate worship, the body of believers worshiping together, was common in the Old Testament. It does not vanish in the New Testament but is the prominent feature of the body of Christ following pentecost (Acts 2:46–47).

The Holy Spirit, who indwells each believer, desires to honor Christ through public expressions of reverence. Corporate worship fosters unity and harmony, supernaturally removing barriers of division and discord. It is a powerful weapon against Satan's disruptive schemes.

Corporate worship underscores our uniqueness as God's people, placed in Christ and adopted in His family. We are not alone in this world. We have other brothers and sisters who share similar experiences. Worshiping together is a catalyst for the exercising of spiritual gifts that build up one another for fruitful Christian service.

If you are not worshiping with a body of believers, ask God to direct you to a church. You will be encouraged, strengthened, and renewed for the daily battles awaiting you.

Seeing God as He Is

The Mighty One, God the LORD,
Has spoken and called the earth
From the rising of the sun to its going down (Ps. 50:1).

❧ In Mathew 17:1–9, Peter, James, and John saw their Friend and Teacher as they had never seen Him before. Just a moment earlier, Jesus stood beside them in the plain clothes of a humble workman. Then suddenly He shone forth in brilliant, dazzling light like the sun, and His clothing glowed like fire.

What was the disciples' reaction? Immediate worship: "A bright cloud overshadowed them; and . . . a voice out of the cloud, saying, 'This is My beloved Son . . .' And when the disciples heard this, they fell on their faces and were much afraid" (Matt. 17:5–6 NASB).

As God's glory engulfed them, they were stricken with a sense of His absolute holiness and prostrated themselves before Him, the almighty Lord of all. At first, Peter was focused on human effort, what they could do in their own strength to show their love. But Jesus had a bigger plan. The moment that Peter saw Him "unveiled" as sovereign God, his worship was transformed and centered on God alone.

How do you worship God? Do you recognize Him as the holy, all-powerful Lord of your life and submit to Him without reservation? You worship God properly when you see Him as He is.

Learning to Praise

Let everything that has breath praise the LORD
Praise the LORD! (Ps. 150:6).

❧ God created you to praise Him, to recognize Him as eternal, sovereign Lord and King of all creation. There are no other gods before Him, and none besides the Almighty deserve your adoration and love.

When you pray, do you praise God before you bring Him your petitions? Is worship your primary concern? Learning to praise God is key to spiritual growth, to understanding who He is and how He works in your life.

It is difficult to pull your mind off personal problems and place it on God, especially when your heart is troubled. But by focusing on Him, you can see your life the way God does. You are aware of His grace and daily care, and your spirit is revitalized. Pride and self-reliance vanish in the face of an all-sufficient Lord.

Read and heed Psalm 147:1: "It is good to sing praises to our God." As you give God glory and honor, you experience His joy and peace in a fresh, transforming way.

The Names of God

Sing to the LORD, bless His name;
Proclaim the good news of His salvation from day to day (Ps.
96:2).

❧ Sir Winston Churchill. Albert Einstein. Bill Cosby. President George W. Bush. Already your mind has formulated thoughts and opinions concerning these individuals. That is because a person's name reflects far more than mere identity. It suggests character and personality, the sum of each person's being.

Your worship experience can likewise be elevated through a new appreciation for the names by which God is called in Scripture. God's name is indicative of His personal essence.

Listed here are just a few of the names ascribed to God in the Bible along with the particular aspect of His character they reveal:

El Olam—Everlasting or Eternal God. Refers to God's eternal existence (Gen. 21:33).

El Shaddai—God almighty. Refers to the all-sufficient power and might of God (Gen. 17:1).

El Elyon—God the Most High. Refers to the sovereignty of God (Gen. 14:18).

Jehovah—the Self-Existent One. Refers particularly to God's covenant relationship with His people and His redemptive work (Ex. 3:14; 34:6).

The Attributes of God

Who is like You, O LORD, among the gods?
Who is like You, glorious in holiness,
Fearful in praises, doing wonders? (Ex. 15:11).

❧ Another aid to the worship of God is meditation on His divine attributes. God's attributes are the inherent features that express His distinct personality.

God is immutable. God never changes in His character or in His dealings with humankind. He can always be counted on to act consistently with His unchanging personhood, giving you great stability (Mal. 3:6; James 1:17).

God is sovereign. God is in complete control of both good and evil. Nothing can come into your life that can thwart His plan for you. This gives you incredible confidence for the present and future. God uses even your mistakes and the mistakes of others for His purposes (Rom. 8:28).

God is faithful. God always acts for your good and His glory. He can always be counted on to be true to His revealed character. This gives you security as you face uncertain problems (Ps. 89:2).

God is loving. God always moves in history and toward humankind according to His benevolence and grace. Even His wrath and judgment can be used for His loving purposes. This gives you great comfort as you face rejection and frustration (Ps. 86:5).

The Secret of Nevertheless

His anger is but for a moment,
His favor is for life;
Weeping may endure for a night,
But joy comes in the morning (Ps. 30:5).

❧ A heart of true praise never uses the word *if*.

"If God heals my son, I will thank Him." "If God takes care of my financial need, I will praise Him."

Rather, the fountain of genuine worship flows through all the peaks and valleys of *nevertheless*.

"If my son is not healed, nevertheless I will praise Him." "If my bills are not paid, nevertheless I will extol Him."

Pure praise for our great and awesome God is never diminished by circumstance. Unfettered worship comes from the hearts of ones who understand that God owes us nothing, but has given us everything. We could not earn physical life—God gave it. We cannot merit our salvation—God bestows it through His Son, Jesus Christ, as we believe. True praise focuses on the astounding attributes and character of God. It rejoices in His goodness.

Are you delighting yourself in knowing God? Learn the secret of nevertheless. Praise God for who He is, and your song of celebration will light your path and gladden all about you.

A Man Worthy of Our Praise

Make a joyful shout to God, all the earth! (Ps. 66:1).

❧ There have been many courageous warriors through the ages—Charlemagne, Napoleon, Grant, Lee, Patton. Many brilliant minds have made significant contributions—Galileo, Pasteur, Bell, Einstein, Salk. Dozens of inspiring leaders have influenced world events—Washington, Lincoln, Churchill.

Yet all the brightest minds through the ages, all the mighty men of the centuries, and all the notable accomplishments of good men everywhere can never invoke the praise and admiration of the God-man, Jesus Christ. Think on His names.

He is the God of the whole earth; Immanuel, God with us; the Creator of all things; the Upholder of all things; the everlasting Father; the Beginning and the Ending; the Rock of my strength; the Chief Cornerstone; the Redeemer; the Great High Priest; the Amen; the Holy One of God; the Firstborn from the dead; the Lord of lords; the King of kings; the Righteous Judge.

These titles represent only a few of the attributes of our Savior. Meditate on the wonder of His person; you cannot help ascribing to Him supreme, unsurpassed, consummate worth.

Jesus is worthy of all your praise. No one can compare with Him.

The Priority of Worship

You are great, and do wondrous things;
You alone are God (Ps. 86:10).

❧ The book of Revelation reveals the priority of worship. Both angels and people, prostrate before the brilliant throne of grace, unceasingly praise the Lamb and the Father. Yet the clear teaching of the Bible is that resounding, reverberant praise should be the priority of the believer during the earthly pilgrimage also.

How much time do you engage in worship? Perhaps more tellingly, what does worship mean to you? Do you have a strong reverence for God that is obvious in your lifestyle and witness?

The role of worship in your life can be dramatically elevated when you think correct thoughts about God. Martin Luther once said to his contemporary Erasmus, who had adopted a humanistic theology, "Your thoughts of God are too human."

You may unintentionally reduce the divine splendor of God. You may lose sight of the majesty of God, reducing Him to your very finite definitions. The less highly you think of God, the less you will worship Him. The more exalted your thoughts of God, the more you will bow humbly before Him, acknowledging His supernatural attributes.

Worshiping with Confidence

You are a chosen generation, a royal priesthood, a holy nation, His own special people, that you may proclaim the praises of Him who called you out of darkness into His marvelous light; who once were not a people but are now the people of God, who had not obtained mercy but now have obtained mercy (1 Peter 2:9–10).

❧ Thinking great thoughts about God is the impetus for cultivating a life of meaningful worship. But the spiritual momentum that worship engenders will sputter if you do not understand your worth in God's eyes. Thus, worship is not only thinking correctly about God but also thinking correctly about yourself.

Too many people fail to enjoy the delight of worship because they feel guilty about their past or present sins. Once they are saved, they live in the constant light of God's unconditional love, their guilt completely atoned for through Christ's sacrificial death. They are not under condemnation any longer, even when they sin.

God declares you are of inestimable worth to Him. His Son's blood was shed for you; His heaven waits for you; His Spirit indwells you. You are precious, beloved, and honored in His sight, for you are made in His image and are His child through faith in Christ.

Turn away from unnecessary anxieties. God is for you, and you can worship Him with unfettered simplicity and confidence.

The Ability to Worship

Make a joyful shout to God, all the earth! (Psalm 66:1).

❧ In his book *Worship: The Missing Jewel of the Evangelical Church*, A. W. Tozer wrote of the urgency for God's people to grasp the importance of devoted, passionate praise of our Savior:

> We have almost everything, but there's one thing that the churches do not have: that is the ability to worship. It's the one, shining gem that is lost to the modern church . . .
>
> Now what are the factors that you will find present in worship? First there is boundless confidence. You cannot worship a being you cannot trust . . . Worship rises or falls in any church altogether depending upon the attitude we take toward God, whether we see God big or whether we see Him little. Most of us see God too small; our God is too little.
>
> David said: "O magnify the Lord with me," and *magnify* doesn't mean to make God big. You can't make God big. But you can see Him big.
>
> Then there is admiration, that is appreciation of the excellency of God . . . This admiration for God grows and grows. The God of the modern evangelical rarely astonishes anybody . . . But when the Holy Ghost shows us God as He is, we admire Him to the point of wonder and delight.

The Power of Praise

Oh, give thanks to the LORD, for He is good!
For His mercy endures forever (Ps. 107:1).

❧ Many of us do not engage in worship when diffi-culty arises because we work hard at being self-reliant. We want to work it out in our wisdom, our strength, and our way. Involving ourselves in worship is tantamount to admitting defeat.

But we will all face some things that cannot be humanly resolved. There will be times when we come to the end of ourselves. Praising God in times of trouble sharpens our humility. We realize our help-lessness, admitting His matchless superiority and supremacy.

As you humble yourself before God, He will exalt you at the right time. There are many promises in the Bible for you to claim, and humility is the one condi-tion for receiving them.

Admitting your inadequacy strips away human pride, preparing your heart for the display of God's awesome power. Pride stunts worship; worship repels pride. In your trouble, readily confess your inade-quacy. You can do some things, but you cannot do what God can.

Praising Him in trouble releases His power to work on your behalf. Rely on Him, not yourself.

Communion with God

Oh come, let us sing to the LORD!
Let us shout joyfully to the Rock of our salvation.
Let us come before His presence with thanksgiving;
Let us shout joyfully to Him with psalms (Ps. 95:1–2).

❧ The Word of God gives you the basis for knowing and worshiping God, clearing away the obstacles of ignorance, apathy, and error. But when you take what you have learned about God in the Scriptures and pour your heart out through prayer, worship is fully realized on this terrestrial ball.

When you pray with your lips and your heart, you magnify God. Worship is not a subject for a textbook but the outpouring of your dependence on and love for Jesus Christ. Do not let prayer become a list. Do not let prayer drift into repetition. Do not let prayer be just a discipline.

Allow your prayer life to be a living channel of worship, telling God how much you think of Him. He wants the glory that is due His name, and your prayerful worship ascribes His worth. Prayer intimately enters the throne room of God, allowing you to exalt and glorify your Savior. Prayer links heaven and earth. When you pray, always begin with "Hallowed be Your name," and all else will fit into place.

Overtaken by Love

I will praise You with my whole heart;
Before the gods I will sing praises to You (Ps. 138:1).

❧ A. W. Tozer once stated:

For millions of Christians . . . God is no more real than
He is to the non-Christian. They go through life trying
to love an ideal and be loyal to a mere principle. Over
against all this cloudy vagueness stands the clear
scriptural doctrine that God can be known in personal
experience. A loving Personality dominates the Bible,
walking among the trees of the garden and breathing
fragrance over every scene.

God enjoys your fellowship. He knows your needs
and longs to fulfill each one as you bring them to Him
in prayer. When you grow in your desire to know
Him, you become concerned about His desires and
seek to please Him out of love.

Intimacy doesn't just happen. Jesus didn't just
choose Peter, James, and John and immediately take
them to the Mount of Transfiguration. Time weathered their relationship. Their view of Christ deep-
ened, and their desire for His fellowship expanded.
They were no longer satisfied with a casual knowledge of the Savior. Intimacy had overtaken them and
changed the way they would live forever.

Has love for God overtaken you yet?

The Quest for Intimacy

Jesus said to him, "'You shall love the Lord your God with all your heart, with all your soul, and with all your mind.' This is the first and great commandment" (Matt. 22:37–38).

❧ To experience genuine intimacy with Christ, you must be willing to lay down your love for the things of this world. This doesn't mean giving up peanut butter and jelly sandwiches. But it does mean your desire for God and His fellowship exceeds your friendship with the world. God wants to bless you, yet blessings must never become what you seek above the Blesser.

A. W. Tozer commented on the quest for intimacy:

> There can be no doubt that this possessive clinging to things is one of the most harmful habits in the Christian life. Because it is so natural, it is rarely recognized for the evil that it is. But its outworkings are tragic.
>
> We are often hindered from giving up our treasures to the Lord out of fear for their safety. This is especially true when those treasures are loved relatives and friends. But we need to have no such fears. Our Lord came not to destroy but to save. Everything is safe which is so committed.

Step Forward in Worship

When my spirit was overwhelmed within me,
Then You knew my path.
In the way in which I walk
They have secretly set a snare for me (Ps. 142:3).

❧ Consider this scene depicted in Matthew 8: "And when He had come down from the mountain, great multitudes followed Him. And behold, a leper came to Him, and bowed down to Him, saying, 'Lord, if You are willing, You can make me clean.' And He stretched out His hand and touched him, saying, 'I am willing; be cleansed.' And immediately his leprosy was cleansed" (vv. 1–3 NASB).

The man dared to venture into the city in hopes of talking to Jesus. When Christ came near, the man immediately knelt before Him, demonstrating his adoration. Next he told Jesus: "If You are willing, You can make me clean." Those words of tremendous faith were spoken by a man who did not doubt God's ability but feared that somehow he might be overlooked.

Perhaps you have suffered a long time. Jesus can heal your infirmity. He may choose to do so completely, or He may change the circumstances so that you can find peace and rest in your suffering. Don't let the Savior pass by. Step forward in worship, and allow Him to work in your life.

The Praise of His Glory

The heavens declare the glory of God;

the skies proclaim the work of his hands.
Day after day they pour forth speech;

night after night they display knowledge.
There is no speech or language

where their voice is not heard.
Their voice goes out into all the earth,

their words to the ends of the world (Ps. 19:1–4 NIV).

Our Maker designed all creation to be to the praise of His glory. The tiniest pebble and the tallest mountain bear testimony to God's power and love. Warbling birds, chirping crickets, and croaking frogs lend their special voices to the chorus.

Have you ever been outdoors on a clear night in an open space, where there are no artificial lights to get in the way? You cannot count the thousands of stars in the sky. In that moment outside, your feelings of awe may well up so strongly inside that you are unable to speak.

"O LORD, our LORD, / How excellent is Your name in all the earth" (Ps. 8:1).

The Cure for a Heavy Heart

And now my head shall be lifted up above my enemies all around me;
Therefore I will offer sacrifices of joy in His tabernacle;
I will sing, yes, I will sing praises to the Lord (Ps. 27:6).

God understands how your emotions are built; He made them. He also knows the cure for a heart weighed down by concerns and irritations—praise.

Praise focuses your attention on God. When you take a long and deliberate look at the character and ways of the Lord who loved you enough to die for you, your eyes are naturally shifted away from the difficulty and onto His ability to care for you.

Praise increases your faith. Telling God what you love about Him always involves reciting His past actions of might and power on your behalf. You can look back at the times He sent special provision at just the right moment and thank Him for them. This process results in a heart that expands with joy and security in Him.

Praise gives you a sense of identity. When you praise God, you are acting as one who belongs to Him. First Peter 2:9 says that you are a member of "a people for God's own possession, that you may proclaim the excellencies of Him who has called you out of darkness into His marvelous light" (NASB). That is reason enough to praise Him forever.

Keys to a Glad Heart

One cried to another and said:
"Holy, holy, holy is the LORD of hosts;
The whole earth is full of His glory!" (Isa. 6:3).

❧ Carole Mayball in her book *When God Whispers* takes a look at how awe of our holy, righteous, loving God translates into everyday living:

> What makes a person old at twenty and keeps another young at eighty? I think it is that sense of wonder—the insatiable curiosity and delight concerning God, the world, and people. Solomon, for all his wisdom, was jaded. When I read the book of Ecclesiastes, I see that he had too much of everything . . .
>
> For the wisest man on earth, Solomon was kind of dumb! He knew great truth . . . But apparently knowing that and experiencing it were two different things for Solomon . . . We Christ-ones know the keys to having a glad heart. They are spelled out for us clearly . . .
>
> Enjoy what we have (enabled by God) as we accept our "lot"—which means accepting whatever "portion and cup" (Psalm 16:5) God has given. If we do that we won't feel guilty if we "have" or cheated if we "have not."
>
> . . . Live in the present with each moment being lived "to the hilt" and let God keep us occupied with gladness of heart.

A Heart of True Praise

Sing aloud to God our strength;
Make a joyful shout to the God of Jacob (Ps. 81:1).

❧ The scene of John 12:1–8 was familiar. Jesus was at Lazarus's house in Bethany, reclining at the table with His friends. How He loved spending time there! However, the dynamics of their relationship had changed dramatically. Only six days before, Jesus had raised Lazarus from the dead in a miracle that drew many to faith.

Mary's relationship with the Lord had changed as well. She knew His death was at hand.

Quietly she knelt next to Jesus at the table, and without a word, she delicately poured out every ounce of perfume onto His feet. Then she wiped the costly rivulets away with her hair until the entire house was filled with the aroma of the spikenard and with the even sweeter fragrance of her sacrifice.

Praise doesn't have a single, narrow definition. Praise can be Mary's gentle, silent gift that expressed the longing of her heart to worship. Praising is singing songs and saying private prayers. As you grow in the Lord, your praise will assume many forms, and all are worthy when given out of love for God.

Giving Thanks in Everything

Giving thanks always for all things to God the Father in the name of our Lord Jesus Christ (Eph. 5:20).

❧ Cultivating and maintaining a grateful heart that continues to pulsate with thanksgiving, even in trials, present a challenge.

Your circumstances today may be bright. If so, remember that God is your Source, and give Him the praise that He deserves. However, if your situation is bleak, God still desires your sincere thanksgiving because He knows the alternatives are passivity, self-pity, depression, and possibly withdrawal from intimate fellowship with the Savior.

Giving thanks in everything (that does not leave you with many exceptions, does it?) is possible when you understand that every situation, good or evil, is used by your loving Father to further your dependence on Him and make you more like Him.

We all like control; we dislike anything or anyone that disturbs our sense of security. But God is not interested in your ease or comfort. He is determined to conform you to the image of Christ through the inevitable afflictions that accompany life.

Thanking God in the trials may be difficult, but when you do, His purposes and presence will illuminate your path and carry you through.

Praise in Troubled Times

In everything give thanks; for this is the will of God in Christ Jesus for you (1 Thess. 5:18).

❧ Like a flashlight, praise is the most illuminating in your hour of darkness. The problem is that when trouble strikes, the last thing you feel like doing is giving thanks to God. But if you can regain your worship composure for a moment, you can become the turning point for deliverance, renewed trust, and confident hope.

Praising God in times of trouble focuses your attention on God, not the problem. When you worship, His presence, although always near, becomes even closer. Just as what happens when you wipe away the morning mist from the windshield, worship clears your vision and helps you see God in the midst of your affliction.

When you praise God in times of trouble, your sense of anticipation is intensified. God is all-powerful, all-loving, all-wise; and He is able to work in your circumstances for your good and His glory.

When you praise Him, you realize that you are not at the mercy of whim or fate, but your times are in His capable hands. Are you praising God in your trouble? Do so; and although your problem may not dissolve, God's ability to handle your problem will pervade your heart and mind.

The Pursuit of Happiness

Meditate on these things; give yourself entirely to them, that your progress may be evident to all (1 Tim. 4:15).

❧ We often complain because of the violence and impurity that plague our world. Timothy was in an even narrower place of service In Ephesus. Just as we do, he probably felt at times like putting his desk in order and walking away.

In a letter to his young prodigy, Paul encouraged him to hold on and not give up. One of Satan's greatest temptations is to get us to take our eyes off God's work or plan and put them onto our circumstances. He tells us there are greener pastures someplace far from where we are right now. This is when we become frustrated and begin looking for a way out.

Nothing can beat being in the will of God. Happiness is a feeling; joy is a fact. You can be happy for a season, but joy comes from obeying God over the long haul. There is nothing wrong with feeling happy as long as you realize it can come and go. However, joy is eternal. Seek God above everything else, and He will bless your life with an overflowing sense of joy.

A Glimpse of Heavenly Praise

The heavens will praise Your wonders, O Lord;
Your faithfulness also in the assembly of the saints (Ps. 89:5).

❧ It is wonderful to read of the tidal waves of worship that unceasingly sweep over heaven's celestial shores. But what good does that do you as you wake up to a rainy morning, a car with a dead battery, an angry boss, or a sick child? How can you worship with such sheer, constant joy in the face of a world that has only tribulations?

Well, you know this: God wants you to experience the pleasure of worship now as well as in heaven, so He must have a way.

And He does. Each time you open the Word of God, you encounter God, revealed accurately and divinely to you during your earthly journey. As you sink your mind and heart into studying and meditating on His Word, you will learn more and more about God and His ways.

As you do, a sense of growing reverence and awe should spring up within. Worship of God should adorn your days. He has given you His Word so that you might know and praise Him as often as you like.

Are you taking advantage of the opportunity now? If so, heaven will simply be a continuum of adoration.

December

THEME: The Miphkad Gate (*Miphkad* means "to review")

REPRESENTING: Self-examination, judgment, and finishing well

Examine yourselves as to whether you are in the faith. Test yourselves. Do you not know yourselves, that Jesus Christ is in you?—unless indeed you are disqualified (2 Cor. 13:5).

A Tragic End to a Promising Beginning

The Strength of Israel will not lie nor relent. For He is not a man,
that He should relent (1 Sam. 15:29).

❧ The race of life that God has placed us in requires
daily, deliberate exercise as well as a good start if we
are to finish well and strong. Initially Saul loved God
and did His will. However, this great man's life
became one of bitterness, hatred, and depression.

We see in 1 Samuel 15:13–23 that Saul offered a
sacrifice when he became impatient for Samuel to
arrive. It didn't seem that much at the time, but it
grew into increased rationalization. He began to
blame others—"the people took some of the spoil" (1
Sam. 15:21 NASB)—until Saul no longer took responsibility for his sin, and his self-will loomed larger than
God's will for him.

The process hasn't changed. We flirt with a particular sin, we rationalize it—and before long we are
captive to it. Our hearts are hardened to God's loving
conviction, and we pursue our own destruction.

Are you rationalizing a sin today? Is there a known
area of disobedience in your life? If so, go to God and
confess and repent of it. God will restore you.

Losing Your Spiritual Bearings

Your word is a lamp to my feet
And a light to my path (Ps. 119:105).

🕊 You may lose your spiritual bearings when circumstances seemingly navigate you farther into the blackness of despair, deepening your sense of helplessness and heightening your fears and anxieties.

You gradually may become disoriented, losing your sense of God's care and love, even wondering if He exists. God understands your frailty in these times and provides you with sure and certain guides to uphold you.

You can cling to God's Word. David, who knew soul-darkness as well as any writer of Scripture, said, "Your word is a lamp to my feet / And a light to my path" (Ps. 119:105). Each word of Scripture is a light and life giver. Elisabeth Elliot wrote in *Discipline: The Glad Surrender* that "the Bible does not explain everything necessary for our intellectual satisfaction, but it explains everything necessary for our obedience."

You can count on God's character and presence. God is ineffably kind, good, merciful, and just, despite appearances to the contrary. He is never against you, but is heartily for you and ever with you.

What He began in your life, He will complete, using even times of darkness to strengthen your trust and love for Him.

Finish the Course

I am already being poured out as a drink offering, and the time of my departure is at hand (2 Tim. 4:6).

❧ If anyone had occasion to quit the course God had planned for him, it was Paul. Persecutions, trials, misunderstanding, and emotional and physical distress plagued the apostle for most of his adult life. How did he arrive at the terminus of his life with such a winning spirit? How can you?

Paul didn't focus on the past. His actions before he was saved were atrocious. They would have been an albatross had he fixated on them. Christ forgives your foolish acts of the past. Don't carry around a mental ballast of guilt that will only weigh you down and steal your joy. Receive God's forgiveness and forgive yourself.

Paul didn't nurse grudges. Perhaps you have an emotional greenhouse to nourish past hurts. It's pain you can live without. Paul was betrayed and reviled at almost every stop, but his spirit remained free of bitterness or self-pity.

Paul majored on grace and embraced weakness. He was the apostle of grace, ever cognizant that his sense of worth and value was entwined in his relationship with Christ, not his performance or behavior.

Don't give up when your spirit is faint. Count on the sufficiency of God's grace, and the adequacy of His help.

Sacrificing Your Future

There is a way that seems right to a man,
But its end is the way of death (Prov. 14:12).

❧ The turning point came on one dark night when, after too many drinks, he slammed his speeding car into a group of teenagers, killing several and injuring others. For a moment of alcohol-induced pleasure, he is now reaping a bitter harvest of tears and regrets.

He is not alone. Countless others, lured by the appeal of the moment, have sacrificed future success and happiness. It might have been the sexual enticement to immorality or the unethical pursuit of an "attractive" business deal. Now, years later, the price is still being paid.

That is the essence of temptation. The tempter, Satan, deceives us by playing with our instincts, emotions, and attitudes. He disguises the poison hidden within the temptation, knowing that we will seldom succumb to an obviously devilish proposition.

Is there anything you are considering at the moment that you know will bring pain and distress if you yield? Stop now before it is too late. Today's pleasure may look and taste sweet, but if it is outside the love and will of God, it will leave you with a bitter aftertaste.

Facing Failure

Being confident of this very thing, that He who has begun a good work in you will complete it until the day of Jesus Christ (Phil. 1:6).

❧ "If at first you don't succeed, try again." That Puritan work ethic is solidly ingrained in the minds of many Americans. When you become a Christian, you naturally tend to integrate this attitude into your walk with Christ. If you fail to conquer certain habits, you keep trying. If you fall short in obeying key Scripture verses, you buckle down and try again.

Although perseverance is necessary, mere grit and determination alone will not cure your problems. Without a proper understanding of spiritual growth, pursuit of this work ethic can lead you into the proverbial brick wall.

Admission of failure in the spiritual realm is a step toward a truly abundant life. Repeated failure from your efforts is often the prerequisite for coming to the end of yourself, acknowledging that you can do nothing apart from Christ.

Failure can be the catalyst that leads you from mere trying to trusting. The difference is startling, and understanding the spiritual dynamic can be the key to a consistently satisfying Christian walk.

The One Who Never Fails

Are you so foolish? Having begun in the Spirit, are you now being made perfect by the flesh? (Gal. 3:3).

❧ If you had taken a poll of Christ's apostles before His arrest and crucifixion, no doubt Peter would have been voted "most loyal." Of all Jesus' followers, Peter seemingly possessed all of the right qualities for unquestioned leadership. He was honest, unafraid of challenge, and eager to learn. When Jesus took His inner circle along on special occasions, Peter was always included.

But as we see in Luke 22:31–34, when the darkness of Gethsemane and Calvary drew near, Peter failed, denying his Lord and retreating into the sorrow of regret. Peter, as most of us would have done, had relied on his superior talents and commanding personality during his apprenticeship with Christ. When the crisis of Calvary appeared, however, the fault line of human frailty appeared and Peter's confidence fell to pieces.

It is still so with all of us who draw near to the Cross. We must end reliance on our own resources—education, appearance, personality, and abilities. Then we can move into the life and power that our indwelling Christ longs to impart.

Shipwrecked Saints

Having faith and a good conscience, which some having rejected, concerning the faith have suffered shipwreck (1 Tim. 1:19).

❧ There are Christians who demonstrate little of the vibrant faith they once possessed, having gone aground on the shoals of lukewarmness and compromise. Joy is passing; growth is stagnant; peace is transient. Worst of all, they seldom express love for the person of the Lord Jesus Christ, and they rarely experience His love. What happened?

The apostle Paul wrote that a shipwrecked faith can occur when people reject a solid faith and a good conscience. The teachings of God's Word are slowly and subtly replaced with counterfeit philosophies, such as humanism, materialism, and/or secularism. The authority of the Scriptures is rejected regarding personal behavior. Obedience is subjective and conditional. The quiet voice of the Holy Spirit is ignored repeatedly as they allow their conduct to be guided by reason or instinct, not God.

Is your personal faith in Christ at a low ebb? Has the adventure of faith turned sour? If you are willing, restoration is but a heartbeat away.

Restoration

Nevertheless My lovingkindness I will not utterly take from him,
Nor allow My faithfulness to fail (Ps. 89:33).

❧ Some of the great battleships of World War II were retired to mothballs following the end of the conflict. However, in the 1990s some were retooled, refitted, and refurbished for new duty on the high seas.

Similarly God delights in restoring to full service those whose faith has been idle for years. Restoration begins with genuine repentance.

Whatever the reason for your spiritual decline—a bad church experience, a negative encounter with another believer, a serious moral mistake—God is waiting for you to assume personal responsibility and repent. You cannot blame others. Repentance realizes you have grieved God with your behavior and missed out on God's best through your rebellion and negligence.

When your repentance is genuine and complete, the next step is a rekindling of your love for Christ. The rekindling occurs when you return your focus to what Christ has done for you and who He is within you. You rediscover the greatness, love, mercy, and goodness of God. The love affair begins again.

Cultivating Spiritual Endurance

Take heart, men, for I believe God that it will be just as it was told me (Acts 27:25).

ﾋ For runners, the most discouraging moments are about halfway through the race. They are tired and drained, and the prospect of growing even wearier is sometimes enough to cause them to quit.

All of us face those times in our Christian experience. We start joyfully at salvation and run with eagerness as we learn new biblical principles. Then we come to a point where the feelings fade, the blessings seem to dwindle, and our commitment level fluctuates.

It is at this point that determination and endurance are developed. We read the Scriptures because we know the value of their priority, not because we always gain obvious, immediate benefits.

The determination to continue comes from the knowledge that God has set the course for you. Yesterday's troubles, today's problems, and tomorrow's circumstances are all a part of the pilgrimage. Together, they form the course God has chosen. In addition, you run because God will reward you in the end. There is a finish line. Your exhaustion and perplexity will be over. You will be in the Lord's presence forever.

Before giving up, remember that the Lord Jesus Christ is cultivating your spiritual endurance.

Are You Growing?

Grow in the grace and knowledge of our Lord and Savior Jesus Christ. To Him be the glory both now and forever. Amen (2 Peter 3:18).

❧ Are you a growing Christian?

That can be a difficult question to answer, for we all experience seasons of stagnation. But the essence of Christian growth is this: Are you experiencing and exhibiting the reality of Christ in a progressive manner?

The Bible says that God wants you to mature as a believer. As your walk with Christ matures, the fruit of your relationship with Him should be increasingly evident. Your knowledge of God, not intellectual but hearty devotion to Him and His ways, should be on the upswing (Col. 1:10). That entails clearer understanding of His will and ways.

Your awareness of the reality of the spiritual world should also be developing; you realize that the root cause of many problems lies in the spiritual arena. For example, people may spend too much money because they are not content. The issue is not money but personal fulfillment and peace, which ultimately are satisfied by Christ alone.

You grow not through mere self-effort, but through the abiding life, drinking in the fullness of Christ through the indwelling work of the Holy Spirit. It is growing in grace.

Measuring Your Spiritual Growth

Search me, O God, and know my heart;
Try me, and know my anxieties;
And see if there is any wicked way in me,
And lead me in the way everlasting (Ps. 139:23–24).

❧ All growth is measured by some means—profit or stature—but defining spiritual growth is not as standardized. However, there are some questions that you can ask yourself, allowing the Holy Spirit to reveal both your progress and your need:

- Do I want to spend more or less time in God's Word?
- Is my prayer life more meaningful and honest, or less?
- Do I exhibit the same Christlikeness in the privacy of my home as I do in public settings?
- Is regular church attendance a consistent part of my life?
- Do I persevere or give up when spiritual droughts hit?
- Am I concerned about the spiritual plight of my unsaved coworkers or friends?
- Do I seek the Holy Spirit's help on a daily basis or lean solely on my personal strengths and talents?

Where you fall short, ask for God's help. Where you respond positively, thank Jesus for His grace, and continue to obey.

A Winning Lifestyle

Consider Him who endured such hostility from sinners against Himself, lest you become weary and discouraged in your souls (Heb. 12:3).

❧ The writer of Hebrews noted that because we have "so great a cloud of witnesses surrounding us" (12:1 NASB), we should not grow weary in the race of life, but have hope and not lose heart. Never forget that Jesus endured the pain and embarrassment of the Cross so that you might gain the victor's crown. You don't have to be supernatural to be a winner, but you must contain a supernatural faith in Christ to wear the crown of life.

Hebrews 12:1–3 provides three insights into gaining a winning lifestyle:

1. *Lay aside every encumbrance.* That includes sin and anything else that holds you back from being all God wants you to be.

2. *Run with endurance.* Don't give up. At times you may wonder whether you will ever see the finish line, but God has promised you will.

3. *Fix your eyes on Jesus.* Many, like Peter, take their eyes off Christ and focus on the shifting winds and swelling waves of life. But if you will keep your eyes firmly locked on Jesus, you will receive the conqueror's garland.

The Danger of Drifting

For the wages of sin is death, but the gift of God is eternal life in Christ Jesus our Lord (Rom. 6:23).

❧ Taking the small, inflatable raft, he went out just beyond the wave break where he could relax and enjoy the coolness of the ocean water. He had left his glasses with his wife on the beach. Though his vision was blurry, he kept telling himself, "I can still see the shore." Soon, the sound of the lifeguard's horn and shouts of onlookers signaled that he had drifted out into dangerous water, never feeling the silent pull of the ocean's undertow.

Sin often operates this way in the lives of believers. Satan begins by tempting us to deviate only slightly from God's principles. Then he watches for our reaction. Do we find sin palatable or nauseating?

Spiritual drifting begins with the words, "I know I probably shouldn't do this, but I don't see any harm in doing it just once." Before you drift into harm's way and away from the fellowship of God, ask Him to surface any area of sin you may be harboring. Make the wise choice to obey, and avoid the danger of drifting.

Stopping Short of God's Plan

And you He made alive, who were dead in trespasses and sins (Eph. 2:1).

❧ In his biographical sketch of Abraham Lincoln, Willard Davis presents this information:

> Lincoln had been elected president though not even appearing on the ballot in ten states!
>
> Even before arriving in Washington, every mail delivery brought more death threats and ominous warnings. Close friends advised that he resign before taking the oath of office! A plot to assassinate the president-elect had been uncovered forcing the last leg of his trip to Washington to be in the dead of night, without family, under heavy guard, and incognito!

Lincoln refused to stop short of God's plan. He wrote, "When I went to Gettysburg, and saw the graves of thousands of our soldiers, I then and there consecrated myself to Christ."

Don't stop short of God's plan for your life. When temptation to quit comes, run to Him in prayer. Ask Him to encourage you as only He can. Then trust Him to lead you victoriously through the difficult times.

A Perfect Design

As we have borne the image of the man of dust, we shall also bear the image of the heavenly Man (1 Cor. 15:49).

❧ Working diligently with a small cross-stitch design, the woman leaned over to her friend and proudly displayed her finished product. Her friend reached out to touch it. But the woman pulled back and said, "Please don't look at the back."

Turning the needlework over revealed an abundance of knots and strings. It was the sure sign of a beginner's work. But a smile brightened on her friend's face as she said, "Don't be silly. The only thing that truly matters is the front, and it looks perfect!"

God has a design for your life. There are times when you fail to follow His plan, and several knots are sewn into your life. From the back side, your life may look disastrous. However, turn your life design over, and see it from God's perspective. Yes, there were times of failure; but there also were times of yieldedness and victory. From God's viewpoint, the knots represent times of instruction. He knew from the beginning that you would face times of discouragement and defeat. Yet He also knew there would be times when you would refuse to yield to Satan's deception.

You are God's workmanship. From His viewpoint, your life is being woven into a design that bears a remarkable resemblance to the life of His Son.

Your Kinsman-Redeemer

You were bought at a price; therefore glorify God in your body and in your spirit, which are God's (1 Cor. 6:20).

❧ Throughout the Old Testament, there were constant foreshadowings of a divine Redeemer who would deliver people from bondage and captivity. Perhaps the most interesting facet of Old Testament redemption was the kinsman-redeemer, which allowed a close family member to rescue a relative through payment of his or her debts.

The New Testament carryover is clear. Jesus is our Kinsman. He became flesh and blood so that He might share in our humanity, becoming the Son of man as well as the Son of God. By becoming human, He identified with humankind, being tempted in all things as we are, yet remaining without sin.

However, the deity of Christ provided the only acceptable price for deliverance from sin—the shedding of Christ's blood at Calvary. No one except Christ could pay the enormous, adequate price. No one except Christ could deliver us from sin's grip. He alone could purchase you from the marketplace of sin and bring you into the kingdom of God. Your Redeemer came. Your Redeemer lives.

God with You

The people who walked in darkness
Have seen a great light;
Those who dwelt in the land of the shadow of death,
Upon them a light has shined (Isa. 9:2).

❧ The Christmas story is not just the story of
Bethlehem—Christ in the cradle. It is the story of the
Incarnation, God in the flesh, revealing the Father to
us: "'Behold, the virgin shall be with child, and shall
bear a Son, and they shall call His name Immanuel,'
which translated means, 'God with us'" (Matt. 1:23
NASB).

When you look at the Lord Jesus Christ's life on
earth, you have an exact portrait of the character and
ways of the heavenly Father. Jesus said, "I and the
Father are one" (John 10:30 NASB). The Lord's kindness,
love, and holiness help you grasp the nature of the
Father in heaven.

Christ also came in the flesh that He might give you
a godly example. Jesus is your pattern for Christian living: "I have been crucified with Christ; and it is no
longer I who live, but Christ lives in me; and the life
which I now live in the flesh I live by faith in the Son
of God, who loved me, and delivered Himself up for
me" (Gal. 2:20 NASB). You can resist temptation; you
can endure suffering. You "can do all things through
[Christ] who strengthens [you]" (Phil. 4:13 NASB).

The Son of Man

He knows our frame;
He remembers that we are dust (Ps. 103:14).

❧ The Son of God became the Son of man, Immanuel—"God with us" (Matt. 1:23)—for very crucial reasons. Until Christ became the Son of man, He could not die in our place for our sins. God does not die; flesh and blood die. Christ became flesh and blood and maintained His perfect divinity so that He could pay the penalty of sin, which is death:

> God demonstrates His own love toward us, in that while we were still sinners, Christ died for us. (Rom. 5:8)

> This is My blood of the covenant, which is poured out for many for forgiveness of sins. (Matt. 26:28 NASB)

Until Christ became the Son of man, He could not represent us as our sympathetic and faithful High Priest. Christ understands how we feel in our frail humanity. He was weary, hungry, rejected, and abused.

His earthly ministry means that Christ can identify with your hurts, pains, and heartaches. He is touched by them:

> When the Lord saw her, He felt compassion for her, and said to her, "Do not weep." (Luke 7:13 NASB)

The Prince of Peace

For unto us a Child is born,
Unto us a Son is given;
And the government will be upon His shoulder.
And His name will be called
Wonderful, Counselor, Mighty God,
Everlasting Father, Prince of Peace (Isa. 9:6).

❧ Christ's incarnation was the inaugural step for establishing reconciliation between a holy God and sinful humanity. Humankind, though loved by God, was an enemy of God due to a rebellious nature. People also engaged in unending conflict with other people. Self continually sought preeminence. But at the coming of Christ, God's offer of peace through the sacrifice of His Son transformed the hopeless fight.

By faith in Christ, you and God can be reconciled; you can become a friend of God: "He has now reconciled you in His fleshly body through death, in order to present you before Him holy and blameless and beyond reproach" (Col. 1:21–22 NASB).

The Prince of Peace also can revolutionize your dealings with others. True peace can come through Christ's indwelling reign in your heart: "For He Himself is our peace" (Eph. 2:14 NASB).

The Twofold Peace of God

Peace I leave with you, My peace I give to you; not as the world gives do I give to you. Let not your heart be troubled, neither let it be afraid (John 14:27).

❧ The peace of God is twofold—positional and experiential.

When you trust Christ for salvation, you enter into peace with God. The Lord justifies you, declares you no longer guilty of your sin, and gives you a righteous standing. This is positional peace. The Judge of all people has rendered a favorable verdict for those who place their faith in Christ's work on the cross. You can now have access to the presence of God, for you are His child, born again by His Spirit and known intimately by Him.

But there is more. You also receive the peace of God as you face life's battles and uncertainties. Through His indwelling Holy Spirit, God's indescribable peace settles your fears, calms your anxieties, and anchors your mind. "Be anxious for nothing, but in everything by prayer and supplication with thanksgiving let your requests be made known to God. And the peace of God, which surpasses all comprehension, shall guard your hearts and your minds in Christ Jesus" (Phil. 4:6–7 NASB).

You are not alone anymore. God is with you. "I will never desert you, nor will I ever forsake you" (Heb. 13:5 NASB).

The Secret to Sustained Peace

Peace I leave with you, My peace I give to you; not as the world gives do I give to you. Let not your heart be troubled, neither let it be afraid (John 14:27).

❧ Peace initiatives by various parties and factions capture the attention of the news media almost daily. The terminology of these endeavors has so occupied our front pages, TV screens, and political agendas that we have defined *peace* as "the absence of conflict."

Even those of us who toil in the office, farm, or home tend to describe peace in the same manner. Peace is the removal of tension between husband and wife, parents and children, employers and employees.

We know, however, that peace can be elusive, even when such ideal conditions exist. This kind of harmony does not remove the ache, anger, and turmoil that boil within because of frustrated dreams, unreached potential, and disillusioning circumstances.

True peace is not external, not dependent upon the environment. It is internal, springing from your innermost being. This peace comes only through the inner presence of the Prince of Peace, Jesus Christ. He can settle your spirit and mind, regardless of external disarray.

If you have been restless and anxious, look to Christ for stability. His initiative at Calvary has brought you peace with God and the peace of God. This peace can never be disturbed.

The Reigning Lord

There is born to you this day in the city of David a Savior, who is Christ the Lord (Luke 2:11).

❧ Some people just cannot seem to get excited about Jesus Christ. Perhaps they have lost sight of who He was and what He did for us. Perhaps they have never known.

Jesus is the Son of God—our reigning Lord. He was that before time began, and He will be that at time's ending. He was in the Garden with Adam. His heart received sin's first blow.

Throughout time He watched His people struggle. He led them through the desert and longed for them to worship only Him. When Israel was blocked in on every side, He made a way through the wilderness. Still, they forgot Him and worshiped other gods.

Year after year, Jesus watched and prayed from heaven's doorway. When the longing to save and redeem His people grew to an overwhelming portion, He came to us.

However, the people of His day wanted a military leader—someone who would exalt the Jewish nation. They could not accept that Jesus was the Messiah. They plotted His death. His life was purchased for the price of a slave. He died a criminal's death, but God raised Him up as Lord.

May you know the power of His reigning love today.

The Returning King

The Lord Himself will descend from heaven with a shout, with the voice of an archangel, and with the trumpet of God. And the dead in Christ will rise first (1 Thess. 4:16).

❧ Jesus came as a man, a person, much like any one of us. He willingly chose to lay aside His royal robe of glory to take on the tattered robe of humanity. Though sinless, He knew what it felt like to cry, to laugh, and to suffer disappointment. He felt the encroachment of rejection and the sting of loneliness.

He could have chosen any number of avenues, but He chose to come as a baby. All power was His to command. Angels stood waiting to meet His every request. Yet He became a servant so that we might grasp the hope of God. And except for a chorus of angels singing to a band of misfit shepherds, His first coming almost went unnoticed. It was not much of a birth announcement for the King of kings and the Lord of lords.

However, when He returns, He will come as the returning Lord and ruling King. His first coming opened the way to salvation. His second coming will be to establish His kingdom.

Do you know Him as Savior and Lord? If not, take this moment to ask Him to come into your heart. Ask as a child. He will not refuse you.

Christmas: An Eternal Perspective

When the fullness of the time had come, God sent forth His Son, born of a woman, born under the law (Gal. 4:4).

❧ It was no cosmic accident that Jesus came when He did. God's timing is never random. He was born in the "fulness of the time," the exact, perfect moment in history for the accomplishment of God's purposes. The Lord had the Incarnation in mind since the beginning of time, and even before creation, when in His sovereignty only God existed.

If all of these overwhelming facts seem a bit lofty, that's because the truths of His mighty plan are wrapped in an infinite mystery that we in our finite condition cannot fully comprehend. Yet it is also true that the great wonder of salvation is as simple as a tiny, gurgling baby in a manger, for all to come and worship.

Isn't it marvelous that God does not require you to understand every detail to come to Him? The redemptive process will continue to unfold, and the cries of the baby Jesus on that still and holy night echo through eternity.

Jesus Christ Is Lord

My eyes have seen Your salvation
Which You have prepared before the face of all peoples
(Luke 2:30–31).

❧ Usually when you think of a lord or a great ruler, you envision a person of formidable power, with commanding presence and dignified bearing. He lives in magnificent wealth, and everyone gives him glory and reveres the very ground he walks on.

That wasn't the case with the Lord Jesus. In fact, the very opposite was true. Jesus gave up the grandeur of heaven, veiling His glory in the flesh of a human being, in order to live with us for a time on earth. Born in a lowly cattle stall, Jesus did not live the soft life. He learned carpentry and earned a working man's wage, never knowing the comforts of the contemporary Roman rulers. And though many acknowledged Him as Savior, Jesus certainly never enjoyed the popularity and honor that were His due.

Finally He hung naked and bleeding on a crude cross like a common criminal. Was that a picture of a reigning, sovereign Lord?

Absolutely. Appearances were certainly deceiving. Three days later, He rose again. Someday everyone will see the true picture and worship Him as almighty God. Every knee will bow, and every tongue will pronounce Him the King of kings.

Don't Give Up!

You must continue in the things which you have learned and been assured of, knowing from whom you have learned them (2 Tim. 3:14).

❧ During the last few months of Paul's life, he wrote some of his most stirring exhortations to two of his fellow workers: Timothy, who was in Ephesus, a city at the heart of paganism; and Titus, who was on the island of Crete, which had plenty of problems of its own. Both men struggled with discouragement. Timothy fought feelings of insecurity, and Titus became frustrated with the opposition from church members.

Paul gave his last words to Timothy as encouragement with the hope that when times got rough, he would not give up. When you feel like giving in, don't. Within every problem and trial is an opportunity for God to teach you more about His faithfulness.

Timothy and Titus learned a great deal from Paul, but it was through their trust in Jesus Christ that they were successful for the kingdom of God. Before you go to bed tonight, tell Him how much you need Him and ask Him to warm your heart with His love.

Holidays are especially difficult times for those who have recently lost a friend or loved one. If this is your situation, know that God is aware of your sorrow. He knows your loneliness and isolation. Let His presence strengthen you through the Holy Spirit and the power of His Word.

Caution—A Godless Age

The kingdom of God is not in word but in power (1 Cor. 4:20).

❧ Paul's description of the society that is hostile toward God is chillingly current. People without Christ, he said, become increasingly belligerent, greedy, arrogant, and demanding.

You don't need a Gallup Poll to inform you that these conditions have bulged into the cultural mainstream. But social opposition should never dissuade you from practicing your faith. Christianity has been against the moral grain of every age. Instead of focusing on the spiritual bog of godlessness (a debilitating tactic), your concentration should be on God's power and His Word.

Christ is a mighty warrior in your midst, able to accomplish awesome deeds on your behalf. Have you embraced the kingdom of God that comes in power and not word only?

You can experience Christ's strength primarily through the truth of His Word. Paul exhorted Timothy—and you—to "continue in the things you have learned and become convinced of" (2 Tim. 3:14 NASB), alluding to the body of Scripture. Knowing what God says in the Bible distills truth from error.

Perspective to face trials, wisdom to make decisions, and faith to endure—all you need to face the new year—are rooted in familiarity with God's Word.

Preparation for God's Purposes

This is he who was spoken of by the prophet Isaiah, saying:
"The voice of one crying in the wilderness:
'Prepare the way of the LORD;
Make His paths straight'" (Matt. 3:3).

❧ When the Son of God came in the flesh in a rustic Bethlehem stable around 4 B.C., His birth took place only after faithful, deliberate preparation by God: "This Man, delivered up by the predetermined plan and foreknowledge of God, you nailed to a cross by the hands of godless men and put Him to death. And God raised Him up again, putting an end to the agony of death, since it was impossible for Him to be held in its power" (Acts 2:23–24 NASB).

God had dealt with nations, preserving His people, the Israelites, through the centuries, despite persecution and captivity. He had dealt with kings and empires, allowing the advanced Roman civilization to standardize transportation and communication throughout most of Europe and Asia. God came to earth at exactly the point in time, like a ripe field of wheat ready for harvest, that His sovereign, perfect mind had planned since the foundation of the earth (Eph. 3:8–12).

Christ's timing in your life is just as precise. He is preparing you today for His purposes tomorrow.

Your Time of Preparation

I know that You can do everything,
And that no purpose of Yours can be withheld from You (Job 42:2).

❧ Before a house is repainted, long, tedious hours of scraping and sanding are required. Before the seed is sown, dusty days of tilling and plowing are necessary. But if the paint is to adhere and last and the seed is to sprout and mature, preparation is essential.

So it was as God prepared to send Christ the Savior to earth. The Lord endured the rebellion and idolatry of people and nations. He saw His prophets ridiculed, His priests despised, and His laws rejected.

Your time of preparation for usefulness in the kingdom will not be instantaneous. But it is a requirement in order for Christ's fullness to lodge deep in your life, readying you for fruitfulness that you otherwise may never experience.

Paul noted in Galatians 1:11–24 how the Lord taught him and prepared him for three years after he was saved. Then Christ accomplished through Paul what He wanted: "Every branch in Me that does not bear fruit, He takes away; and every branch that bears fruit, He prunes it, that it may bear more fruit . . . Abide in Me, and I in you. As the branch cannot bear fruit of itself, unless it abides in the vine, so neither can you, unless you abide in Me" (John 15:2, 4 NASB).

Goal Setting

The plans of the diligent lead surely to plenty,
But those of everyone who is hasty, surely to poverty (Prov.
21:5).

❧ Many people will look back over the past year with a sense of accomplishment and hope. Others may have regrets and wish they had tackled life differently. Learning to set goals for your life is an excellent way to build encouragement into your daily routine, especially when you set reasonable goals that you can achieve without fear of failure.

Always begin the goal-setting process with prayer. Ask the Lord to show you specific areas in your life that will benefit from this type of organization. Making a list of potential growth spots will help you see the overall context of your life.

Make a promise to yourself that you will be open to the will of God. Allow Him to alter your goals when necessary. Remember, He is perfectly in tune with your life and knows your strengths and weaknesses. Set goals that stretch your faith but are also attainable in nature.

God is a natural goal setter. Throughout Scripture, He encouraged men and women to achieve the goals He placed before them. God wants you to achieve His best in life; allow Him to guide you as you set goals for the future.

God Isn't Finished Yet

I have fought the good fight, I have finished the race, I have kept the faith (2 Tim. 4:7).

❧ You have probably heard someone say, "Please be patient—God isn't finished with me yet." That light-hearted saying is absolutely true. When you trust Jesus as your Savior, you begin a growing process that lasts a lifetime.

In his book *Lifetime Guarantee,* Bill Gillham explains it this way: "Once a person is born from above, his nature is already Christlike, but it's infantile in maturity . . . By faith and obedience, as he begins to act consistently with his new nature, he will look more and more like Jesus."

The Lord engineers all the circumstances of your life to conform you to Christ's image (Rom. 8:28). God works in everything that He sends and allows in your life.

Yes, God may discipline you and let you experience some painful consequences of wrong actions, but His plan hasn't changed. Someday you will stand in the presence of almighty God, radiant and complete, fully transformed. It's a goal worth the wait.

About the Author

DR. CHARLES STANLEY is pastor of the 15,000-member First Baptist Church in Atlanta, Georgia. He is well-known through his *In Touch* radio and television ministry to thousands internationally and is the author of many books, including *The Source of My Strength, The Reason for My Hope, The Glorious Journey,* and the In Touch® Study Series.

Dr. Stanley received his bachelor of arts degree from the University of Richmond, his bachelor of divinity degree from Southwestern Theological Seminary, and his master's and doctor's degrees from Luther Rice Seminary. He has twice been elected president of the Southern Baptist Convention.

You may contact In Touch Ministries at:

P.O. Box 7900
Atlanta, GA 30357
1-800-789-1473
www.intouch.org

OTHER BOOKS BY CHARLES STANLEY
FROM THOMAS NELSON PUBLISHERS

OTHER BESTSELLING BOOKS BY CHARLES STANLEY

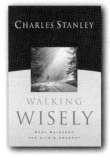

Walking Wisely

Choosing to live according to biblical precepts is a lifestyle foreign to the worldly patterns among which we live. Inevitably, there will be clashes between the wisdom of God and that of the world. Dr. Stanley teaches how to apply God's wisdom as we handle finances, relate to others, care for our physical health, and carry out day-to-day duties. This significant volume presents a way of living that embodies wisdom from above.

0-7852-7298-4 • Hardcover • 256 pages • Christian Living
Audio 0-7852-6594-5

Success God's Way

The world has its own definition of success, and Christians are often drawn into it. This book will help you understand "success" from a godly perspective and achieve the goals God helps you set.

0-7852-6590-2 • Softcover • 256 pages
• Christian Living

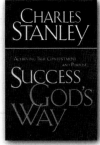

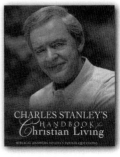
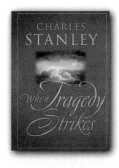